TEPS

서울대
텝스 관리위원회
최신기출
1200
문제집

서울대 텝스 관리위원회 최신기출 1200 문제집

문제제공 서울대학교 TEPS관리위원회
펴낸이 안용백
펴낸곳 (주)넥서스

초판 1쇄 발행 2011년 3월 25일
초판 31쇄 발행 2014년 9월 15일

출판신고 1992년 4월 3일 제311-2002-2호
121-893 서울시 마포구 양화로 8길 24
Tel (02)330-5500 Fax (02)330-5555
ISBN 978-89-5797-534-3 18740

www.nexusbook.com

서울대
텝스 관리위원회
최신기출
1200

How to TEPS

서울대학교 TEPS관리위원회 기출문제 제공

문제집

넥서스

서문

2006년 넥서스에서 최초로 TEPS 기출문제집 〈유형별로 분석한 NEXUS 기출 800〉을 출간한 후 〈서울대 텝스 관리위원회 최신 기출 1000〉 〈서울대 텝스 관리위원회 제공 최신기출 시크릿〉에 이르기까지 대표적인 TEPS 기출문제집 출간으로 TEPS 시장에 자리매김할 수 있도록 많은 사랑과 관심을 보여준 TEPS 수험생들과 학교 및 학원에서 강의를 담당하시는 선생님들께 다시 한번 감사의 마음을 전한다. 다른 영어 능력 검정시험과 달리 많은 기출문제가 세상에 공개된 TEPS 시험은 그만큼 과학적인 측정 도구 와 신뢰할 수 있는 콘텐츠, 정밀한 변별력 등 테스트로서의 투명성을 이미 인정받았다. 1999년 1월 첫 TEPS 시험 시행 이후 이러 한 공인된 시험에 대한 신뢰도를 바탕으로 이제는 입시·입사·승진 등 여러 분야에서 이 TEPS 시험 성적이 두루 활용되고 있는 것 이 현실이다.

TEPS를 어떻게 공부해야 하느냐는 질문을 종종 받는다. TEPS 시험이 아직 한국인들에게는 만만한 시험이 아니라는 것을 너무 잘 알고 있기 때문에 제대로 된 교재와 학습법으로 TEPS 체질로 영어 공부 환경을 세팅하라고밖에 조언해 줄 수 없다. 우리가 건 강한 체력을 위해 몸에 좋은 음식, 심지어는 유기농을 섭취하려고 하듯, 건강한 TEPS 체질을 갖고 싶다면 엉뚱한 TEPS 유사 문 제들이 아닌 시험에 출제된 기출문제들을 많이 경험해 볼 것을 권면한다. 시중에 이미 출간된 소위 베스트셀러라는 수험서에 수록 된 TEPS 문제들을 분석해 보니, TEPS 시험이 아닌 다른 영어 시험 유형 문제를 수록해 혼동을 주는 경우도 많았다. TEPS 시험 에 어떤 문제가 실제로 출제되었는지만 제대로 이해해도 시험 유형을 반 이상 경험한 거라고 볼 수 있다.

이번에 출간하는 〈서울대 텝스 관리위원회 최신기출 1200〉은 기출문제 6회분, 1,200문항이라는 방대한 양을 수록했기 때문에 학 습자 편의를 위해 문제집과 해설집을 별도로 각각 제작했다. 가장 최신 기출문제들만 선별해서 수록했고, 실제 TEPS 시험장에서 만났던 문제 그대로의 디자인, 청해 방송에서 듣던 MP3 음원을 모두 고스란히 그대로 가져왔다. 또한 군더더기 없이 핵심만 짚어 주는 문제 해설을 위해 끝없이 원고를 수정 보완해서 질 좋은 TEPS 기출문제를 더 잘 이해할 수 있도록 해설집을 따로 만들었다. 방대한 TEPS 문제들을 편하게 각자의 도서관이나 강의실, 집, 카페에서 경험하고 TEPS 고사장으로 향한다면 별로 긴장하지 않 고 좋은 결과를 기대할 수 있을 것이다.

TEPS 기출문제집 출간을 위해 넥서스 TEPS연구소의 성가시게 많은 질문과 요구사항에도 적극적으로 도움을 주신 서울대학교 TEPS관리위원회 관계자분들께 이 자리를 통해 다시 한번 감사의 마음을 전한다. TEPS 시험이 수험생 모두의 꿈을 실현하는 데 잘 쓰임받기를 기원한다.

넥서스 TEPS연구소 연구원 일동

Contents

이 책에 대하여

1 / TEPS 최신기출 1,200문항

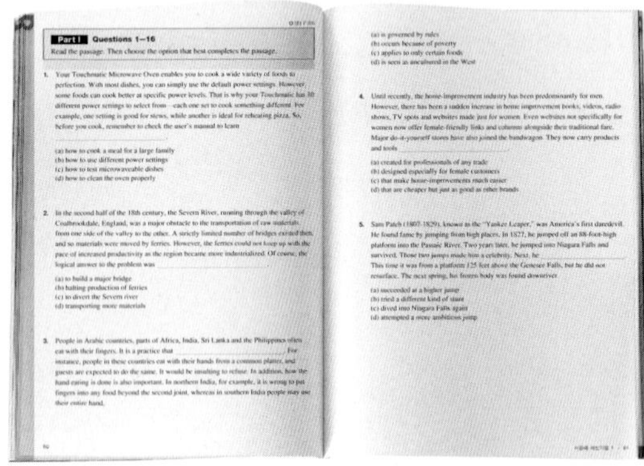

서울대학교 TEPS관리위원회가 공개한 현존 가장 최신 기출문제

1,200문항을 실제 TEPS 시험지와 동일한 디자인 환경으로 제공

2 / 수험생들에 꼭 필요한 TEPS 핵심전략

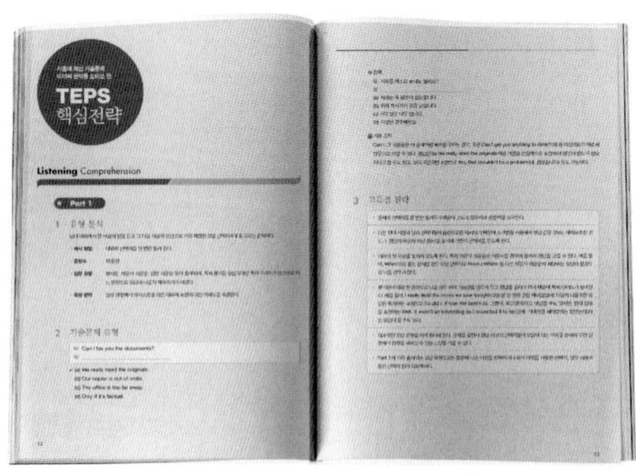

청해–문법–어휘–독해 4영역 13파트에 대한 TEPS 출제 경향 및 고득

점 대비 전략을 통합적으로 분석한 출제 비밀 노트 공개

3 / 군더더기 없는 완전 해설

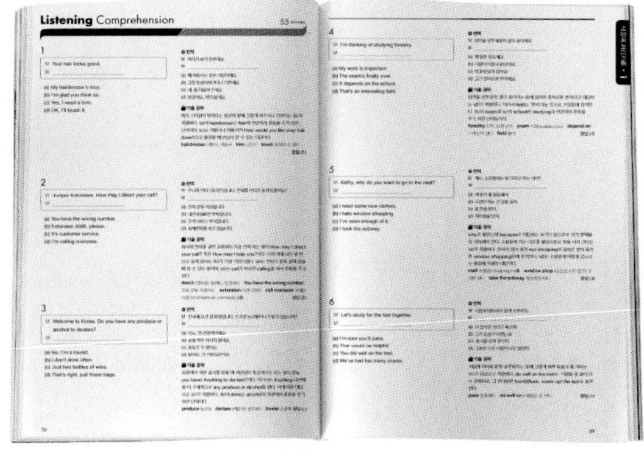

넥서스 TEPS연구소의 오랜 노하우가 녹아 있는 콤팩트한 알짜배기
해설로 오답에 대한 속시원한 해결책 제시

4 / 문제집과 해설집 별도 제작

학습자 편의를 위해 방대한 분량을 문제집과 해설집으로 별도 제작,
휴대하기 편할 뿐 아니라 학습 목적에 맞게 구매 가능

5 / 실제 고사장에서 듣던 청해 음성

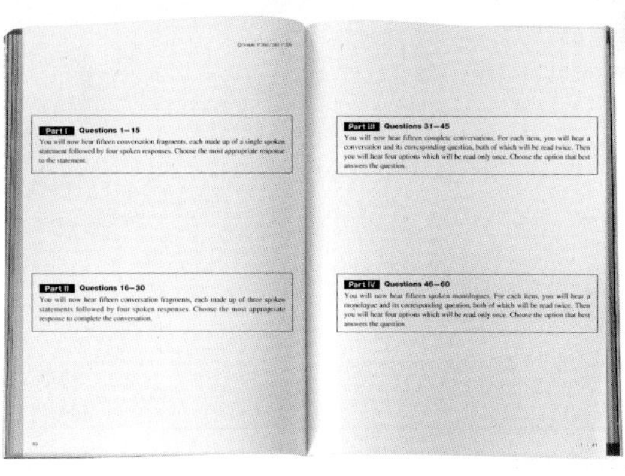

TEPS 고사장에서 청해 시험 시간에 사용했던 MP3 음원을 그대로 수
록, 생생한 청해 환경 경험

TEPS에 대하여

1 / TEPS란?

❶ Test of English Proficiency developed by Seoul National University의 약자로 서울대학교 언어교육원에서 개발하고, TEPS관리위원회에서 주관하는 국가공인 영어시험

❷ 1999년 1월 처음 시행 이후 연 12~16회 실시

❸ 정부기관 및 기업의 직원 채용, 인사고과, 해외 파견 근무자 선발과 더불어 대학과 특목고 입학 및 졸업 자격 요건, 국가고시 및 자격 시험의 영어 대체 시험으로 활용

❹ 100여 명의 국내외 유수 대학의 최고 수준 영어 전문가들이 출제하고, 언어 테스팅 분야의 세계적인 권위자인 Bachman 교수(미국 UCLA)와 Oller 교수(미국 뉴멕시코대)로부터 타당성을 검증받음

❺ 말하기 – 쓰기 시험인 TEPS Speaking & Writing도 별도로 실시 중이며, 2009년 10월부터 이를 통합한 *i*-TEPS 실시

2 / TEPS 시험 구성

영역	Part별 내용	문항수	시간/배점
청해 Listening Comprehension	Part I : 문장 하나를 듣고 이어질 대화 고르기	15	55분 400점
	Part II : 3문장의 대화를 듣고 이어질 대화 고르기	15	
	Part III : 6~8 문장의 대화를 듣고 질문에 해당하는 답 고르기	15	
	Part IV : 담화문의 내용을 듣고 질문에 해당하는 답 고르기	15	
문법 Grammar	Part I : 대화문의 빈칸에 적절한 표현 고르기	20	25분 100점
	Part II : 문장의 빈칸에 적절한 표현 고르기	20	
	Part III : 대화에서 어법상 틀리거나 어색한 부분 고르기	5	
	Part IV : 단문에서 문법상 틀리거나 어색한 부분 고르기	5	
어휘 Vocabulary	Part I : 대화문의 빈칸에 적절한 단어 고르기	25	15분 100점
	Part II : 단문의 빈칸에 적절한 단어 고르기	25	
독해 Reading Comprehension	Part I : 지문을 읽고 빈칸에 들어갈 내용 고르기	16	45분 400점
	Part II : 지문을 읽고 질문에 가장 적절한 내용 고르기	21	
	Part III : 지문을 읽고 문맥상 어색한 내용 고르기	3	
총계	13개 Parts	200	140분 990점

☆ **IRT** (Item Response Theory)에 의하여 최고점이 990점, 최저점이 10점으로 조정됨.

3 / TEPS 시험 응시 정보

현장 접수
❶ www.teps.or.kr에서 인근 접수처 및 준비물(응시료, 사진) 확인
❷ 접수처 방문: 해당 접수기간 평일 오전 10시 ~ 오후 5시

인터넷 접수
❶ TEPS관리위원회 홈페이지 접속 www.teps.or.kr
❷ 준비물: 스캔한 사진 파일, 응시료 결제를 위한 신용 카드 및 은행 계좌

4 / TEPS 시험 당일 정보

❶ 고사장 입실 완료: 9시 30분(일요일) / 3시(토요일)
❷ 준비물: 신분증, 컴퓨터용 사인펜, 수정테이프, 수험표, 시계
❸ 유효한 신분증
　성인: 주민등록증, 운전면허증, 여권, 공무원증, 현역간부 신분증, 군무원증, 주민등록증 발급 신청 확인서, 외국인 등록증
　초·중고생: 학생증, 여권, 청소년증, 주민등록증, 주민등록증 발급 신청 확인서, TEPS 신분확인 증명서
❹ 시험 시간: 2시간 20분 (중간에 쉬는 시간 없음, 각 영역별 제한시간 엄수)
❺ 성적 확인: 약 2주 후 인터넷에서 조회 가능

Listening Comprehension

● Part 1

1   유형 분석

남녀 대화에서 한 사람의 말을 듣고 그 다음 사람의 응답으로 가장 적절한 것을 선택지 4개 중 고르는 문제이다.

- **제시 방법**　　대화와 선택지를 한 번만 들려 준다.

- **문항수**　　15문항

- **질문 유형**　　평서문, 의문사 의문문, 일반 의문문 등이 출제되며, 특히 평서문 응답 유형은 특히 무리수가 많으므로 어느 방향으로 응답이 나올지 예측하기가 어렵다.

- **측정 영역**　　일상 생활에서 의사소통을 위한 대화체 표현에 대한 이해도를 측정한다.

2   기출문제 유형

> M　Can I fax you the documents?
> W　________________________

✔ (a) We really need the originals.

　 (b) Our copier is out of order.

　 (c) The office is too far away.

　 (d) Only if it's factual.

M 서류를 팩스로 보내도 될까요?

W ________________________

(a) 저희는 꼭 원본이 필요합니다.
(b) 저희 복사기가 고장 났습니다.
(c) 사무실은 너무 멉니다.
(d) 사실인 경우에만요.

기출 공략

Can I...? 의문문은 이 문제처럼 허락을 구하는 경우, 혹은 Can I get you anything to drink? (뭐 좀 마실래요?)처럼 제안문으로 쓰일 수 있다. 정답인 (a) We really need the originals처럼 거절을 간접적으로 표현하여 원본이 반드시 필요하다고 할 수도 있고, 보다 직접적인 표현으로 Yes, that shouldn't be a problem (네, 괜찮습니다) 등도 가능하다.

3 고득점 전략

- 문제와 선택지를 한 번만 들려주기 때문에 고도의 집중력과 순발력을 요구한다.

- 다른 영어 시험과 달리 선택지들이 음성으로만 제시되기 때문에 소거법을 사용해서 정답 같은 것(o), 애매모호한 것(△), 정답이 확실히 아닌 것(x)을 표시해 가면서 선택지를 듣도록 한다.

- 대화의 첫 부분을 놓치지 않도록 한다. 특히 의문사 의문문은 의문사를 정확히 들어야 정답을 고를 수 있다. 예를 들어, When으로 묻는 문제일 경우 오답 선택지로 How나 Where 등 다른 의문사 의문문에 해당하는 응답이 함정으로 나올 경우가 많다.

- 평서문이 대화 첫 문장으로 나올 경우 여러 가능성을 염두에 두고 정답을 골라야 하기 때문에 특히 난이도가 높아진다. 예를 들어, I really liked the movie we saw tonight (오늘 밤 본 영화 정말 재미있었어) 다음에 나올직한 응답은 동의하는 표현으로 So did I. It was the best (나도 그랬어. 최고였어)라고 대답할 수도 있지만, 반대 입장을 표현하는 Well, it wasn't so interesting as I expected it to be (글쎄, 기대만큼 재미있지는 않았는데)라는 응답이 올 수도 있다.

- 대표적인 오답 유형을 미리 정리해 둔다. 문제를 풀면서 정답 이외의 선택지들이 오답이 되는 이유를 분석해 두면 실전에서 함정을 피해갈 수 있는 스킬을 키울 수 있다.

- Part 1에 자주 출제되는 오답 유형으로는 질문에 나온 어휘를 반복하거나 유사 어휘를 사용한 선택지, 일부 내용이 틀린 선택지 등이 대표적이다.

Part 2

1 유형 분석

남녀 대화에서 세 번째 대화까지 듣고 그 다음 이어질 응답으로 가장 자연스러운 것을 4개의 선택지 중에서 고르는 문제이다.

- **제시 방법** 대화와 선택지를 한 번만 들려 준다.

- **문항수** 15문항

- **질문 유형** 평서문, 의문사 의문문, 일반 의문문 등이 출제되며, 이 중 특히 평서문인 경우 어느 방향으로 응답이 나올지 예측하기 어렵다.

- **측정 영역** 일상 대화 속 표현에 대한 이해도 측정이라는 점에서 Part 1과 동일한데 이와 더불어 전반적인 대화 흐름의 이해도를 측정하기도 한다.

2 기출문제 유형

> M We've been invited to Amy's for dinner.
> W What for?
> M I'm not sure, but we shouldn't go empty-handed.
> W ___________________________________

(a) Why don't we invite her?

(b) She's going to cook for us.

(c) I'd love to go with you.

✔ (d) Let's bring a bottle of wine.

❋ 번역

M 에이미네 저녁식사 초대를 받았어.

W 무슨 일인데?

M 무슨 일인지는 모르겠지만 빈손으론 가면 안 될 것 같아.

W ___________________________________

(a) 그녀를 초대하는 게 어때?

(b) 그녀가 우릴 위해 요리할 거야.

(c) 나도 같이 가고 싶어.

(d) 와인 한 병 사가자.

기출 공략

We shouldn't.../ We must.../ We have to... 등은 상대방을 강하게 설득하는 문장이다. 파티에 갈 때 빈손으로 가면 안 된다는 말에 (d) Let's bring a bottle of wine과 같이 적극적인 동의 방법을 답으로 선택해야 한다. 이렇듯 서구 문화에서는 집으로 초대받은 경우 와인이나 케이크 혹은 꽃 등 간단한 선물을 준비해 가는 것이 예의라는 것도 기억해 두자.

3 고득점 전략

- 한 번만 들려주는 세 줄의 대화를 정확하게 잘 듣도록 한다. 첫 문장을 잘 들어야 그 다음에 이어지는 두 줄의 대화를 잘 이해할 수 있기 때문에 Part 2 역시 고도의 집중력을 요한다.

- 만일 첫 줄을 놓쳤다면 당황하지 말고 그 다음 이어지는 두 줄의 대화를 잘 듣도록 한다. 가장 이상적인 청취는 세 줄을 다 알아듣는 것이지만, 혹시 그렇지 못하더라도 선택지가 나오기 직전의 말을 잘 들으면 자연스럽게 이어지는 응답을 고르는 데 도움이 된다.

- 소거법을 활용해서 정답을 고르는 것도 들려 주기만 하는 선택지에 대처할 수 있는 한 방법이다.

- 남녀 각각 어떤 말을 했는지 구분해서 들어야 오답을 피해갈 수 있다.

- 풀어본 문제의 오답을 매번 분석해서 실전에서 신속하고 정확하게 오답을 피하도록 한다.

- Part 2의 대표적인 오답 유형으로는 대화의 앞부분을 일부 놓치고 착각해서 선택할 만한 선택지, 대화에 언급된 어휘로 만든 선택지, 대화에 등장한 어휘의 또 다른 의미를 가지고 만든 선택지, 질문한 사람이 이어서 할 만한 말로 만든 선택지 등이 있다.

Part 3

1 유형 분석

남녀가 세 번씩 주고받는 대화를 듣고 4개의 선택지 중 질문에 가장 적절한 답을 고르는 문제이다.

- **제시 방법**   대화→질문→대화→질문→선택지 순으로 들려 준다.

- **문항수**   15문항

- **질문 유형**   대의 파악(7문항) → 세부 내용 파악(6문항) → 추론(3문항) 순으로 나온다.

- **측정 영역**   일상 대화에 등장하는 다양한 표현에 대한 이해도를 바탕으로 전체 대의 파악, 세부 내용 파악, 추론 능력
  을 측정한다.

2 기출문제 유형

> M Any special plans for your three-week vacation?
> W I think I'll visit my family and relax somewhere.
> M Where do you plan on relaxing?
> W Oh, I don't know, maybe go somewhere warm.
> M What about Thailand?
> W Actually, that sounds good. I'll put it on my list.

Q What is the main topic of the conversation?

(a) The best way to spend a vacation.

✔ (b) The woman's vacation plans.

(c) Popular holiday destinations.

(d) Setting aside time to visit family.

✿ 번역

M 3주 휴가 동안 특별한 계획이 있나요?

W 집에 들렀다가 어디 가서 좀 쉴 생각이에요.

M 어디서 쉬려고 하는데요?

W 글쎄요. 모르겠어요. 아마 따뜻한 곳으로 가겠죠.

M 태국은 어때요?

W 좋은 생각이네요. 그곳도 고려해 봐야겠어요.

Q 대화의 주제는?

(a) 휴가를 보낼 가장 좋은 방법.

(b) 여자의 휴가 계획.

(c) 인기 있는 휴양지.

(d) 가족을 방문하기 위한 시간을 남겨 놓기.

휴가 계획은 상당히 빈출도가 높은 주제이다. 어디로 휴가를 갈 것인지, 혹은 휴가가 어땠는지에 대해 물어보는 두 가지 내용 중 하나로 예상할 수 있다. 여자가 따뜻한 곳에서 쉬려고 하고 남자는 태국을 권하고 있으므로, 이를 간단하고 함축적으로 표현한 (b) The woman's vacation plans가 정답이다. (d)는 visiting family를 응용한 오답이다.

3 고득점 전략

- 처음 대화를 들을 때 전체 대화 내용을 파악한 뒤, 질문에 따라 집중할 부분에 더 집중하는 두 번째 듣기를 한다. 대화의 흐름을 파악해야 대의 파악 문제뿐 아니라 세부 내용 파악이나 추론 문제도 더 쉽게 풀 수 있다.

- 질문에 따라서 메모를 해야 하는 경우도 있다. 특히 세부 내용 파악 문제의 경우 숫자, 연도, 물건의 종류 등을 명확하게 기억하는 것이 유리하고, 남녀 각각 어떤 말을 했는지 구분해서 알아 두는 것이 오답을 피하는 데 많은 도움이 된다. 추론 능력은 대의 또는 세부 내용을 바탕으로 하기 때문에 세부 내용도 간과할 수 없다.

- 선택지를 한 번밖에 들려주지 않기 때문에 대화 내용을 다 이해하고도 선택지를 놓쳐서 정답을 고르지 못하는 경우가 있다. 이를 방지하기 위해 소거법을 적용해서 선택지를 차례대로 표시하면서 최종 정답을 고르도록 한다.

- 질문 종류별로 오답 확률이 높은 유형을 알아 두는 것도 도움이 된다.
  - 대의 파악 오답 유형: 대화 중 일부 세부 사항만 포함한 선택지, 너무 일반적인 내용의 선택지, 대화 중 특정 키워드를 조합한 전혀 엉뚱한 내용의 선택지 등이다.
  - 세부 내용 파악 오답 유형: 대화에서 언급된 어휘를 반복한 선택지, 대화와 전혀 무관한 선택지, 일부 내용만 사실인 선택지, 남녀의 역할이 뒤바뀐 선택지, 시제가 대화 내용과 일치하지 않는 선택지 등이 있다.
  - 추론 오답 유형: 상식적으로는 맞는 진술이지만 대화 내용과는 무관한 선택지, 대화에서 언급된 어휘로 만들었지만 대화 내용과 무관한 선택지, 추론 가능한 내용과 정반대인 선택지 등이 있다.

- 대의 파악이나 세부 내용 파악 유형에 대비해 패러프레이징(paraphrasing) 연습을 하는 것이 좋다. 대화에서 언급된 어휘가 그대로 사용된 경우는 오답일 확률이 높은 반면, 언급된 어휘를 비슷한 말로 바꾸어 만든 선택지는 정답일 확률이 높으므로 paraphrasing 연습이 많은 도움이 된다.

Part 4

1 유형 분석

담화문을 듣고 4개의 선택지 중 질문에 가장 적절한 정답을 고르는 문제이다.

- **제시 방법**   담화문 → 질문 → 담화문 → 질문 → 선택지 순으로 들려 준다.
- **문항수**   15문항
- **질문 유형**   대의 파악(7문항) → 세부 내용 파악(5문항) → 추론(3문항) 순으로 나온다.
- **측정 영역**   영어 연설, 강의, 라디오 방송 등에 나오는 다양한 표현에 대한 이해도 측정을 바탕으로 전체 대의 파악, 세부 내용 파악, 추론 능력을 측정한다.

2 기출문제 유형

> Earlier this week, animal control officials killed a bear responsible for wounding a camper. The 21-year-old camper was sleeping when the 280-pound male black bear ripped through the side of his tent. The camper sustained bite wound and scratches but was able to scare the bear off. Earlier this month, two other bears were killed in the same area after attacking several Boy Scout members at a camp.

Q What happened to the camper who was attacked by the bear?
(a) He died from wounds.
(b) He got lost in the woods.
✔ (c) He was bitten and scratched.
(d) He was rescued by Boy Scouts.

❖ 번역

이번 주 초에 동물 관리국 직원들은 야영하던 사람을 다치게 한 이유로 곰 한 마리를 사살했다. 280파운드의 검은 수컷 곰이 텐트 한 쪽을 찢었을 때 야영을 하던 21세의 피해자는 자고 있었다. 그는 물리고 긁혔지만 곰을 놀라게 해서 쫓아 낼 수 있었다. 이달 초에는 막사에 있던 보이스카우트 회원 여러 명을 공격한 다른 두 마리의 곰이 같은 곳에서 사살됐다.

Q 곰에게 공격당한 야영객에게 무슨 일이 일어났는가?
(a) 상처 때문에 죽었다.
(b) 숲 속에서 길을 잃었다.
(c) 물리고 긁혔다.
(d) 보이스카우트에 의해 구조되었다.

📕 기출 공략

이 문제는 질문 What happened to…? (~에게 무슨 일이 일어났는가?)에 초점을 맞춰 두 번째 들을 때 답을 골라 낼 수 있으며, The camper sustained bite wound and scratches를 바꿔 쓴 (c) He was bitten and scratched를 정답으로 선택해야 한다. 이 문제처럼 특정 사실을 묻는 문제도 출제된다.

3 고득점 전략

- 먼저 담화문의 전체 흐름을 파악한 뒤, 두 번째 듣기에서 질문과 연계된 부분에 집중하여 정확하게 듣는다.

- 질문 유형에 따라 맞춤식 메모를 한다. 특히 세부 사항 파악 유형 문제에 대비해서는 숫자, 연도, 물품 종류 등을 세세하게 메모해야 하고, 추론 능력은 대의 또는 세부 내용을 바탕으로 하기 때문에 세부 내용도 간과할 수 없다는 것을 기억한다.

- 질문 종류별로 오답일 확률이 높은 경우를 알아 두는 것이 도움이 된다.
  - 대의 파악 오답 유형: 담화문 내용의 일부에 해당하는 세부 사항으로 만든 선택지, 주제와 관련은 있으나 너무 범위가 넓은 일반적인 내용의 선택지, 언급된 어휘로 구성된 점 외에는 내용과 전혀 관련이 없는 선택지 등이 오답일 확률이 높다.
  - 세부 내용 파악 오답 유형: 담화문에 언급된 어휘로 만들어진 선택지나 내용과 전혀 무관한 선택지, 일부만 사실인 선택지 등이 오답으로 제시될 가능성이 크다.
  - 추론 오답 유형: 상식적으로는 맞지만 내용과는 무관한 선택지, 담화문에서 언급된 어휘로 만들었지만 내용과는 무관한 선택지, 추론 가능한 내용과 정반대의 선택지 등이 종종 사용되는 오답 유형이다.

- 대의 파악이나 세부 내용 파악 유형의 문제를 위해서는 paraphrasing 연습을 하는 것이 좋다. 언급된 어휘를 그대로 사용하면 오답일 확률이 높은 반면, 정답의 경우 언급된 어휘를 paraphrasing해서 만드는 경우가 많다.

Grammar

1 유형 분석

두 줄의 대화문을 읽고 빈칸에 문법적으로 적절한 표현을 4개의 선택지 중에서 고르는 문제이다.

- **제시 방법**　　　두 줄의 대화문이 주어진다.

- **문항수**　　　　20문항

- **측정 영역**　　　실시간과 비슷한 시간 제약 속에서 문법적으로 정확한 영어를 대화 속에서 구사할 수 있는지 측정한다.

- **빈출 토픽**　　　일상 생활 대화 중에 흔히 접할 수 있는 주제가 많이 사용되므로 청해나 어휘 영역의 대화 부분과 비슷한 내용이 사용된다.

2 기출문제 유형

> A　When is the paper due?
> B　It ＿＿＿＿＿＿＿＿＿＿ by Friday.

✔ (a) has to be done

　(b) is done

　(c) will do

　(d) has to do

✿ 번역

A　리포트 기한이 언제까지죠?

B　금요일까지입니다.

📖 기출 공략

주어가 It이므로 수동태가 돼야 한다. 하지만 (b)를 사용해 It's done이라고 하면 '그것은 끝났다'라는 뜻이 되어 by Friday와 어울리지 않는다. 따라서, 수동태이며 by Friday와의 연결도 자연스러운 (a) has to be done이 정답이다.

3 고득점 전략

- 정확한 영어를 적재적소에 사용하는 능력이 중요하므로 눈으로만 익히는 문법 지식을 배제한다. 대화체를 소리 내어 읽는 연습을 해서 문법이 내재화되어 상황에 맞게 즉각적으로 사용할 수 있는 수준까지 끌어올리도록 한다.

- 문법 네 가지 Part 중 비교적 평이한 난이도이기 때문에 시간 안배 차원에서 신속하게 풀고 다음 Part로 넘어가도록 한다. 단, 첫 줄은 빈칸에 올 적절한 답을 찾는 데 단서가 되므로 생략하고 넘어가면 함정에 빠지는 경우가 종종 있다. 신속하게 문제를 읽어나가되 읽지 않고 건너뛰는 일은 없어야 한다.

- 문법 문제의 빈칸은 주로 두 번째 줄에 오지만 일부 문제는 첫 번째 줄에 빈칸이 오기도 한다. 이런 유형에서는 두 번째 줄을 제대로 읽어야 출제자의 함정에 걸려들지 않는다. 즉, 빈칸 위치에 상관없이 문제에 나오는 대화는 모두 다 읽고 정확한 내용을 파악해야 오답 함정을 피해 정답을 찾을 수 있다.

- 문법 문제라고 해서 대화의 문법적인 요소만 신경 쓰면 안 된다. 상황에 적절한 어법을 고른다는 자세로 문제를 풀도록 한다. 예를 들어 대화 내용에 현재 시제가 여러 개 나온다고 무조건 현재 시제를 답으로 고르면 오히려 오답일 경우가 많다.

- 일상 대화 구문의 어법을 묻는 Part이므로 대화체의 정확한 표현을 익히는 것이 도움이 된다. 즉, 문법책의 모든 문법 요소를 처음부터 공부하는 것보다는 일상 대화 구문 표현 위주로 외울 수 있는 수준까지 익혀 두면 짧은 시간 내에 정확하게 구사할 수 있는 표현들이 많아질 것이다. 이렇게 되면 문법 Part 1도 쉽게 정복할 수 있다.

Part 2

1 유형 분석

한 개의 문장을 읽고 빈칸에 문법적으로 가장 적절한 표현을 4개의 선택지 중에서 고른다.

- **제시 방법**   한 개의 문어체 문장이 주어진다.
- **문항수**   20문항
- **측정 영역**   문어체 영어의 정확한 어법 구사력을 측정한다.
- **빈출 토픽**   학술문과 실용문 등 일상에서 접하는 문어체 문장에 언급되는 주제가 주로 사용된다.

2 기출문제 유형

> ____________________ David would be late was given to his boss.

✔ (a) The message that
  (b) A message is that
  (c) From the message
  (d) The message which

❋ 번역

데이빗이 늦을 거라는 메시지가 그의 상사에게 전달되었다.

🗐 기출 공략

빈칸에는 동사 was given의 주어가 필요하므로 (b)와 (c)는 제외된다. David would be late는 완전한 문장이므로 관계 대명사 which가 앞에 쓰일 수 없고, 동격절을 이끄는 that이 적절하므로 정답은 (a)가 된다.

3 고득점 전략

- 구어체 문장보다 문어체 문장은 의미 파악이 힘들 수 있으므로 평상시 문어체 문장의 직독직해 연습을 충분히 한다. 특히 관계사들로 연결된 문장, 절 안에 또 다른 절이 있는 문장 등 복잡한 문장을 평상시에 많이 접해 보도록 하자. 난해한 문장을 만났을 때 바로 의미를 파악할 수 있어야 문법 Part 2 문제를 신속하게 해결할 수 있다.

- 주어와 동사가 여러 개 나오는 긴 문장은 주절의 주어와 동사를 파악한 후, 다른 문법 사항들을 따져 보도록 한다. 특히 가장 빈출되면서도 기본이 되는 주어-동사 수 일치 문제는 주절의 주어와 동사를 파악해야만 풀 수 있는 문제이다.

- 영어를 외국어로 사용하는 한국인을 위한 TEPS 시험에서는 한국인이 특히 취약한 관사와 문장 구조 등에 대해 묻는 문제가 다수 출제된다. 이를 대비하기 위해서는 문장 내 쓰임새를 익혀 두는 것이 낱낱의 문법 지식을 알고 있는 것보다 신속하고 정확하게 문제를 푸는 데 많은 도움을 줄 것이다. 영어 활용 능력 수준 측정을 위해 TEPS가 고안된 점을 염두에 두고, 평소에 정확한 영어 구사 능력 함양에 집중하도록 한다.

- 문법 Part 1과 마찬가지로 정확한 어법을 익히려면 청해 Part 4 긴 담화문 속에 나오는 문장이나 어휘 Part 2 문장을 익혀 두는 것도 좋다. 각 분야별 어휘와 구문에 익숙해질수록 읽고 이해하는 속도가 자연히 빨라지게 되고, 아울러 문장 안에서 정확한 쓰임새도 익힐 수 있기 때문이다.

Part 3

1 유형 분석

네 줄의 대화문을 읽고 문법적으로 이상한 부분이 있는 문장을 고르는 유형의 문제이다.

- **제시 방법**　　네 줄의 대화문이 주어진다.

- **문항수**　　5문항

- **측정 영역**　　길어진 대화에서 비문법적 요소를 가려내는 능력을 측정한다.

- **빈출 토픽**　　일상 생활에서 접하는 대화에 나오는 주제가 주로 사용된다.

2 기출문제 유형

> (a) A You said you had something to discuss with me.
> (b) B Yeah, I have been debating whether to go back to work or not.
> (c) A Are you actually thinking about becoming a full-time mom?
> ✔ (d) B That's which I want to discuss with you.

❋ **번역**

(a) A　나와 의논할 게 있다고 했지.

(b) B　응, 다시 일을 시작할지 고심 중이야.

(c) A　정말 전업 주부가 될 생각이야?

(d) B　그게 바로 의논하고 싶은 점이야.

📖 **기출 공략**

관계대명사 용법을 물어보는 문제이다. (d)에서 discuss의 목적어가 없고, which는 관계대명사인데 선행사가 없으므로 선행사를 포함하는 관계대명사 what으로 고쳐야 한다.

3 고득점 전략

- 주어진 선택지가 따로 없어서 어떤 문법에 관한 문제인지 전혀 알 수 없고 주어진 대화 내용을 읽으면서 틀린 부분을 골라야 하기 때문에 보다 적극적인 태도로 문제에 임해야 한다. 즉, 각 대화에서 어느 문법 요소가 틀렸는지 모르는 상태에서 틀린 부분을 찾아야 하기 때문에 대화 내용을 파악함과 동시에 모든 품사와 구문 요소가 정확한지도 일일이 확인하는 습관을 평소에 들여야 당황하지 않고 실전에서 실력 발휘를 할 수 있다.

- 주어진 시간 내에 틀린 문법 사항을 골라야 하기 때문에 즉각적으로 비문법적인 부분을 찾아내는 훈련이 평상시에 필요하다. 이렇게 하기 위해서는 다른 문법 Part의 문제 대비와 마찬가지로 일상 대화 및 학술문과 실용문을 많이 접해서 다양한 문장에 익숙해져야 한다.

- 모든 문법 학습 요소들이 다 출제되는 것이 아니라 단골로 출제되는 문법 사항이 있음을 알자. 문장 구조, 시제, 수 일치, 관사 등에 해당하는 문법 요소들을 집중해서 훈련하는 것도 단기간에 Part 3을 정복할 수 있는 길이다. 하지만, Part 3 역시 제한된 문법 사항에만 국한해 다른 문법 요소를 무시했다가 낭패를 볼 수 있다는 것을 유의하자.

- Part 4에 비해 짧은 대화체라 약간 수월하게 보일 수 있겠지만 선택지가 주어진 Part 1과 2보다는 고난이도인 경우가 많다. 특히 재빨리 읽으면서 틀린 문법 사항도 찾아내야 하므로 평상시 대화문의 정확도를 분석하는 것도 실전에서 틀린 부분을 파악하는 데 도움이 될 것이다. 즉, 정답을 찾는 데에만 급급하지 말고 한 문제를 풀더라도 문법적으로 옳고 그른 부분들에 대한 분석을 자세히 하다 보면 실전에서 당황하지 않고 틀린 부분을 찾아낼 수 있다는 것이다.

Part 4

1 유형 분석

4개의 문어체 문장을 읽고 문법적으로 어색한 부분이 있는 문장을 고르는 유형의 문제이다.

- **제시 방법**   4개의 문어체 문장이 하나의 지문으로 주어진다.

- **문항수**   5문항

- **측정 영역**   문어체 문장으로 구성된 지문에서 비문법적인 요소를 가려내는 능력을 측정한다.

- **빈출 토픽**   신문, 잡지, 교재 등 일상 생활에서 문어체로 접하게 되는 주제가 사용된다.

2 기출문제 유형

> (a) Major League Baseball will begin mandatory testing for steroids. (b) From next March, each player will be tested and samples thoroughly analyzed. (c) The penalty for a first positive test will submit to treatment. (d) After their fifth positive test, players will receive a one-year suspension.

✿ 번역

(a) 메이저리그 야구에서 의무적으로 스테로이드 검사를 시작할 것이다. (b) 내년 3월부터, 모든 선수들이 검사를 받을 것이며, 혈액 샘플들은 철저히 분석될 것이다. (c) 첫 양성 반응에 대한 처벌은 치료를 받는 것이다. (d) 양성 반응을 다섯 차례 보인 선수들은 1년 동안 출전 정지된다.

■ 기출 공략

(c)에서 서수(first) 앞에는 정관사 the가 오는 것이 원칙이다. 물론 이 원칙이 깨지는 경우도 있지만, the first positive test가 올바른 형태이다.

3 고득점 전략

- Part 3의 대화체에 비해 Part 4는 지문 길이도 더 길고 문어체라서 내용 파악이 훨씬 더 어렵고 시간도 가장 많이 걸린다. 그렇기 때문에 비문법적인 요소를 찾기가 특히 더 어려울 수 있으므로 신속하게 문어체 문장들을 읽고 직독 직해를 통해 내용을 즉시 파악할 수 있는 능력을 평상시에 훈련하도록 한다.

- 지문 내용은 물론 문제에서 요구하는 문법 사항 예측이 어렵기 때문에 더욱 적극적인 문제 풀이 전략이 필요하다. 4개의 문장을 읽으면서 내용 파악을 하는 동시에 모든 가능성을 열어 두고 비문법적으로 보이는 부분을 찾아 나가야 하는데 이때 가능성이 있는 부분을 일단 밑줄 그어 놓은 뒤 신속하게 다시 그 부분들을 재확인하는 것도 정확도를 높이는 한 방법이 될 수 있다.

- 주어진 시간 내에 틀린 문법 사항을 골라야 하기 때문에 즉각적으로 비문법적인 부분을 찾아내는 훈련이 필요하다. 이를 위해서는 정확한 표현을 즉각적으로 사용할 수 있을 정도로 알고 있어야 한다. 즉, Part 3 대비를 위해서 대화체를 많이 익혀 둠으로써 신속하게 비문법적인 대화 부분을 알아차리는 훈련을 하듯이, Part 4 대비책으로 학술문과 실용문을 접하면서 거의 암기할 정도로 정독하는 것도 문법 내재화를 도울 것이며, 이런 훈련 과정을 거치고 나면 자연스럽게 틀린 부분이 눈에 잘 띌 것이다.

- Part 2에 나오는 문장 네 개가 한꺼번에 출제된다고 생각하면 좀 부담이 덜어질 것이다. Part 2 문장들에서 문법적 오류를 찾는다고 생각하면 이제 마음 편해질 것이다.
  - 시제 문제: 각 문장마다 여러 시제가 혼합되어 있는 경우가 대부분이기 때문에 시제의 형태만 참고해서 틀린 시제를 찾는 것은 거의 불가능하다고 봐야 한다. 내용 파악이 선행되어야만 시제가 잘못 쓰인 곳을 찾을 수 있다.
  - 관사 문제: a와 the의 쓰임 여부는 4개 문장에서 어떤 명사가 이미 앞서 언급된 것이고 아닌지를 이해한 후에 결정되므로 내용 파악이 우선되어야 한다.

Vocabulary

1 유형 분석

두 줄의 대화문을 읽고 빈칸에 가장 잘 어울리는 어휘를 고르는 문제이다.

- **제시 방법**　　두 줄의 대화문이 주어진다.
- **문항수**　　25문항
- **측정 영역**　　대화에서 사용하는 구어체 표현을 적소에 활용할 수 있는지 측정한다.
- **빈출 토픽**　　일상 생활과 관련 있는 주제가 많이 출제된다.

2 기출문제 유형

> A　How did Beth hurt her leg so bad?
> B　I heard she ___________________ coming down the mountain yesterday.

(a) faltered

(b) limped

(c) lingered

✔ (d) tripped

✿ 번역

A　베스는 어쩌다 그렇게 다리를 심하게 다쳤니?

B　어제 산을 내려오다가 걸려 넘어졌대.

(a) 흔들리다

(b) 절뚝거리다

(c) 버티다

(d) 발을 헛디디다

📦 기출 공략

다리를 다친(hurt her leg) 이유로는 산을 내려오다(coming down the mountain) '넘어졌을' 가능성이 가장 크다. '넘어지다'는 표현에는 (d)에 사용된 trip 외에 fall, tumble down 등이 있다.

3 고득점 전략

- 짧은 시간 내에 문맥에 어울리는 어휘를 골라야 하기 때문에 많은 어휘를 알고 있는 것뿐만 아니라 문맥(context)에 적절한 어휘를 사용할 수 있는 능력을 키우는 것도 중요하다. 따라서 어휘를 처음 접할 때엔 참고 자료를 동원해서 문장 내에서 쓰이는 다양한 예문을 동시에 익혀 두어야 한다. 시간 내에 모든 어휘 문제를 잘 풀기 위해서는 특히 문맥 속에서 각 어휘의 쓰임을 거의 외우다시피 알고 있어야 시간 낭비 없이 즉각적으로 빈칸에 올 정답을 고를 수 있을 것이다.

- 해당 어휘의 우리말을 단순하게 암기하는 것은 별 도움이 안 된다. 우리말로는 그럴싸해도 쓰임이 어색한 어휘의 뉘앙스 차이를 구분할 줄 알아야 하므로 문장 전체로 어휘를 이해하는 것이 장기적으로 유리하다.

- 청해의 대화 Part뿐만 아니라 문법 Part 1과 3에 언급된 대화들도 어휘 실력 향상을 위해 활용될 수 있음을 기억하고 어휘 영역 이외의 빈출 표현도 문맥 속에서 익혀 두도록 한다.

- 대화를 신속히 읽고 즉각적으로 빈칸을 채워 넣어야 하기 때문에 실제 대화를 하면서 적절한 어휘를 사용할 수 있을 정도의 실력이 되도록 많은 표현을 통째로 익혀 두어야 한다.

- 일상적인 대화 속에서 자주 등장하는 어휘뿐만 아니라 이어동사, 이디엄 등도 출제되므로 숙지해 두도록 한다.

- 형태상 · 의미상 혼동되는 어휘, 의미 덩어리로 사용되는 연어 등의 정확한 활용법도 아울러 알아 둔다.

● Part 2

1 유형 분석

한 개의 문어체 문장을 읽고 빈칸에 가장 잘 어울리는 어휘를 고르는 문제이다.

- **제시 방법**　　한 개의 문어체 문장이 주어진다.
- **문항수**　　25문항
- **측정 영역**　　일상 생활에서 접할 수 있는 문어체 표현을 즉각적으로 사용할 수 있는지 측정한다.
- **빈출 토픽**　　학술문뿐만 아니라 실용문에 이르기까지 매우 다양한 주제를 다룬다.

2 기출문제 유형

> The management has decided to _________________ a complex strategy to resolve the crisis.

(a) breach

(b) withdraw

(c) alternate

✔ (d) implement

✿ 번역

경영진은 위기를 해결하기 위해 복합적인 전략을 이행하기로 결정했다.

(a) 위반하다

(b) 철수하다

(c) 번갈아 나오게 만들다

(d) 시행하다

🗐 기출 공략

'전략을 수행하다'에 해당하는 동사를 골라야 한다. 위기 해결을 위해선(to resolve the crisis) 다양한 전략을 세우거나 (establish)나 수행(implement)해야 한다. 선택지 중 이와 가장 어울리는 동사는 (d) implement이다.

3 고득점 전략

- 학술문과 실용문의 주제별 빈출 어휘를 익혀 둔다. 빈출 어휘는 정답 선택지뿐만 아니라 오답 선택지에 나오는 어휘도 포함한다. 주제별로 자주 출제되는 어휘는 한정되어 있기 때문에 기출 어휘가 다시 출제될 확률은 높다.

- Part1과 마찬가지로 각 어휘의 쓰임새를 알아야 하기 때문에 전체 문장을 익히도록 한다. 그래야만 문법적으로도 정확한 어휘 활용 능력을 키울 수 있기 때문이다.

- 미묘한 뉘앙스 차이가 있는 쉬운 어휘의 용례 예문을 적극적으로 활용해야 한다. 의미가 비슷해 보이는 어휘들끼리 묶어서 따로 정리하면 도움이 될 것이다.

- 신문 기사, 잡지, 광고, 학술지, 비평 등의 실용문과 전문적인 학술문에서 다양하게 출제되므로 평상시 이런 종류의 글을 많이 접하는 것이 도움이 된다. 15분이라는 짧은 시간 내에 50문항이나 되는 문제를 무리 없이 풀기 위한 대비법 중 하나가 주제별로 다양한 문장을 평소에 자주 읽는 것이다. 이렇게 함으로써 필수 어휘를 자주 접할 수 있을 뿐만 아니라 문장 이해 속도도 향상될 수 있다.

- 대화체 문제와 마찬가지로 주제별 어휘뿐만 아니라 연어 및 형태상 · 의미상 혼동되는 어휘를 잘 알아 두도록 한다.

Reading Comprehension

1 유형 분석

100단어 내외의 단일 지문을 읽고 빈칸에 들어갈 적절한 선택지를 고르는 문제이다. 14문항은 구나 절을 고르는 문제이고, 나머지 2문항은 문장과 문장 사이를 이어주는 연결어를 찾는 문제이다.

- **제시 방법**　지문의 처음 문장이나 마지막 문장, 드물게 중간 문장에 빈칸이 있는 한 개의 글이 주어진다.
- **문항수**　16문항
- **측정 영역**　글의 전반적인 이해 능력 및 논리적인 흐름 파악 능력을 평가한다.
- **빈출 토픽**　학술문과 실용문에서 골고루 출제된다.

2 기출문제 유형

> The idea that people live according to how others will perceive them has been established as the rule, not the exception. The real question now lies in the reasons for this way of life. It was hypothesized by C. S. Lewis that this desire to belong and to fit in is a natural human characteristic. He believed that people have ＿＿＿＿＿＿＿＿＿＿.

- (a) a tendency to regard themselves as normal
- (b) no idea how to deal with human nature
- (c) a need to distinguish themselves as unique
- ✔ (d) an instinctive drive to belong to a group

✽ 번역

다른 사람이 자신을 어떻게 인식하느냐에 따라 인간의 행동이 결정된다는 개념은 예외가 아닌 법칙으로 굳어졌다. 이런 상황에서의 현실적인 물음은 왜 그렇게 사느냐이다. C. S. 루이스는 어딘가에 소속되고 맞춰지고 싶은 욕망은 인간의 본능적인 특성이라고 가정했다. 그는 사람들은 특정 그룹에 소속되고자 하는 본능적 욕구를 갖고 있다고 믿었다.

- (a) 자신을 평범하다고 여기는 성향을
- (b) 인간의 본성을 어떻게 다룰지에 대해 아무런 생각도 없는
- (c) 자신을 특별한 존재로 여기고자 하는 욕구를
- (d) 특정 그룹에 소속되고자 하는 본능적 욕구를

▤ 기출 공략

첫 문장에서 people live according to how others will perceive them이라는 내용과 세 번째 문장의 desire to belong and to fit in이라는 표현에서, 사람들에게는 집단에 소속되고자 하는 욕구가 있다는 (d)를 추론할 수 있다.

- 모든 지문을 자세히 읽겠다는 생각을 접는다. 1분에 한 문제씩 풀어야 하기 때문에 정독을 하기에는 절대적으로 시간이 부족하므로 주요 어휘 위주로 대의 파악 및 흐름 파악에 주력해야 시간 내에 문제를 다 풀 수 있다.

- 주제별 어휘를 평소 많이 알아 둔다. 청해, 문법, 어휘 등 TEPS의 다른 영역과 마찬가지로 방대한 어휘 지식을 갖추고 있어야 독해 속도도 빨라지고 정확한 이해가 가능하다.

- 빈칸의 위치에 따라 독해의 목적이 달라져야 한다. 빈칸이 첫 문장에 있는 경우 대의 파악만 해도 되지만 마지막 문장에 올 때에는 대의 파악뿐만 아니라 논리적 흐름도 염두에 두면서 독해를 해야 한다.

- 오답 함정 선택지 유형을 연습해 둔다.
  - 지문에 나오는 어휘로 만들었지만 문맥과 전혀 상관없는 선택지
  - 너무 일반적인 내용으로 만든 선택지
  - 상식적으로는 괜찮아 보이지만 내용과는 무관한 선택지
  - 지문 내용의 일부처럼 보이기는 하지만 논리적인 흐름 면에서는 어울리지 않는 선택지

Part 2

1 유형 분석

100단어 내외의 단일 지문을 읽고 주어진 질문에 적절한 답을 4개의 선택지에서 고르는 유형이다.

- **제시 방법** 한 개의 지문에 한 개의 질문이 주어진다.

- **문항수** 21문항

- **측정 영역** 단일 지문에 대한 전체 및 세부 내용 이해 및 추론 능력을 측정한다.

  대의 파악(6문항) → 세부 내용 파악(10문항) → 추론(5문항) 순으로 나온다.

- **빈출 토픽** 학술문과 실용문에서 모두 골고루 출제된다.

2 기출문제 유형

After years of negotiations, an agreement on ownership of five islands off of Queensland, Australia, has been finalized. The state government has finally agreed that the islands should become private property. For the past two years, it had argued that the islands belonged to the government rather than the natives of the islands. The agreement ends years of anguish. Native Don Banu, who has been following the debate for many years, said, "It's a great relief for all of us. Now we can start to move forward." The government is currently consulting islanders and expects to hand over the deeds of ownership in December.

Q What can be inferred about the decision made by the government?

(a) It was about who can own the island businesses.

✔ (b) It favored the local inhabitants of the islands.

(c) It could result in widespread disagreements.

(d) It was made sooner than expected.

✱ **번역**

수년간의 협상 끝에, 호주 퀸즐랜드 근해의 다섯 개 섬에 대한 소유권 협정이 체결되었다. 주 정부는 결국 섬을 개인 소유로 하는 데 동의했다. 정부는 지난 2년 동안 섬이 원주민 소유가 아닌 정부 소유라고 주장해 왔다. 이번 협정으로 인해 수년 간 지속된 고통도 끝이 났다. 많은 세월 동안 논쟁을 지켜본 원주민 돈 바누는 "이번 일은 우리 모두에게 커다란 안심이 됩니다. 이제 우리는 새로운 일을 시작할 수 있게 되었습니다"라고 말했다. 정부는 현재 섬 주민들과 논의 중이며, 12월 소유권 이양을 할 작정이다.

Q 정부가 내린 결정에 대해 추론할 수 있는 것은?

(a) 누가 섬 사업을 소유할 수 있는가에 관한 것이었다.

(b) 섬 지역 주민들을 지지했다.

(c) 광범위한 반대를 야기할 수 있었다.

(d) 예상보다 일찍 이루어졌다.

🗐 **기출 공략**

두 번째 문장에서 섬이 개인 소유(private property)가 되었다는 것은 결국 섬이 원주민의 소유임을 의미하며, 세 번째 문장의 natives가 local inhabitants of the islands와 같은 의미임을 파악할 수 있으면 쉽게 정답이 (b)임을 찾을 수 있다.

3 고득점 전략

- 직독직해하는 습관을 들인다. 우리말로 번역하려 하지 말고 신속하게 영어 지문을 읽으면서 내용을 이해하는 습관을 들여야 한다.

- 지문을 다 읽겠다는 생각을 버려라. 대의 파악 문제의 경우 주요 내용어 중심으로 읽고, 세부 내용 파악 문제는 질문에 따라 선택지의 진위 여부를 한 개씩 확인해 가며 읽거나 육하원칙 문제는 질문 내용을 제대로 파악하고 해당 부분을 신속히 찾아서 그 부분을 자세히 읽는다. 추론 문제는 대의 파악 및 세부 내용 파악이 선행되어야 하기 때문에 좀 더 시간을 할애해야 될 것이다.

- 오답 함정을 각 문제 유형마다 미리 알아 두고 잘 피하도록 한다.
  - 대의 파악 오답 유형 : 세부 사실을 대의로 혼동하게 하는 오답이 자주 출제된다.
  - 세부 내용 파악 오답 유형 : 일부 내용만 사실인 경우, 지문에서 언급된 어휘로 만들었지만 내용과는 상관없는 선택지를 주의하자.
  - 추론 오답 유형 : 그럴듯해 보이지만 지문 내용과는 상관없는 오답, 정답과 정반대 진술이 선택지로 제시되기도 한다.

Part 3

1 유형 분석

5개의 문장으로 구성된 100단어 내외의 단일 지문을 읽고 글의 흐름상 어색한 문장을 찾는 유형의 문제이다.

- **제시 방법**　　　　주제문에 이어 4개의 문장이 제시된다.
- **문항수**　　　　　3문항
- **측정 영역**　　　　지문의 응집력 파악 능력을 측정한다.
- **빈출 지문 토픽**　　학술문과 실용문 모두 골고루 출제된다.

2 기출문제 유형

In 1871, American Indians were placed on federal land reservations. (a) Today, American Indian tribes must be understood as nations within the nation of the United States. (b) The Indians had no control of their communities and no power to affect federal polices over them. (c) They were under the jurisdiction of the Bureau of Indian affairs, which decided what they would eat, where they would live, and ultimately how they would live. (d) Thus, they were stripped of their political rights and even their cultural heritage.

✢ 번역

1871년 미국의 인디언들은 연방정부가 정한 거주지로 옮겨졌다. (a) 오늘날 인디언 부족은 미국이라는 나라 안에 존재하는 별개의 나라로 이해되어야 한다. (b) 인디언들은 공동체에 대한 지배권도, 그들에 대한 연방정부의 정책에 영향을 미칠 힘도 없었다. (c) 무엇을 먹을지와 어디서 살지, 그리고 궁극적으로 어떻게 살 것인지를 결정하는 것도 인디언 사무국의 관할이었다. (d) 이런 식으로 그들은 정치적 권리와 심지어 문화적 유산마저 빼앗겼다.

📖 기출 공략

첫 문장(주제문)과 (b), (c), (d)는 1871년 이래 인디언들이 미국에서 겪어온 박해와 수탈에 대해 언급하고 있다. 그러나 (a)는 인디언 부족을 미국 안에 존재하는 별개의 국가로 인정해야 한다는 내용으로, 미국과 인디언 부족을 동등한 위치에서 언급하고 있으므로 개연성이 없다.

3 고득점 전략

- 처음 제시되는 주제문에서 벗어난 문장을 찾는 것이므로 4개의 선택지 문장을 읽을 때에 항상 주제문과의 연관성을 염두에 두고 읽도록 한다. 문법 Part 4의 경우 각 문장 간의 연관성까지 염두에 두고 내용을 파악할 필요는 없으나 독해 Part 3에서는 주제문과의 연관성이 문제 풀이의 핵심이다.

- 주제문과 연관성은 있으나 문장의 위치가 잘못되어 흐름을 깨는 유형도 있으니 흐름상 잘 어울리는지도 살피도록 한다.

- 글의 어조가 갑자기 바뀌는 경우도 어색한 문장에 해당하므로 어조의 변화도 주의하도록 한다.

- 주어진 주제문에 대한 문장이 3개 나온 뒤 새로운 주제문이 4번째 문장으로 나오게 되면 어색한 문장이 된다는 것도 기억한다.

Listening Comprehension

Grammar

Vocabulary

Reading Comprehension

LISTENING COMPREHENSION

DIRECTIONS

1. In the Listening Comprehension section, all content will be presented orally rather than in written form.

2. This section contains 4 parts. In parts I and II, each passage will be read only once. In parts III and IV, each passage and its corresponding question will be read twice. But in all sections, the options will be read only once. After listening to the passage and question, listen to the options and choose the best answer.

Part I **Questions 1—15**

You will now hear fifteen conversation fragments, each made up of a single spoken statement followed by four spoken responses. Choose the most appropriate response to the statement.

Part II **Questions 16—30**

You will now hear fifteen conversation fragments, each made up of three spoken statements followed by four spoken responses. Choose the most appropriate response to complete the conversation.

Part III ## Questions 31—45

You will now hear fifteen complete conversations. For each item, you will hear a conversation and its corresponding question, both of which will be read twice. Then you will hear four options which will be read only once. Choose the option that best answers the question.

Part IV ## Questions 46—60

You will now hear fifteen spoken monologues. For each item, you will hear a monologue and its corresponding question, both of which will be read twice. Then you will hear four options which will be read only once. Choose the option that best answers the question.

GRAMMAR

Part I   Questions 1—20

Choose the best answer for the blank.

1. A: Is this work urgent?

B: Yes, it needs to be done ___________ .

(a) possibly as quick
(b) it is possible quick
(c) as possible quickly
(d) as quickly as possible

2. A: How do you stay in such great shape?

B: Well, I jog ___________ and lift weights in the evening.

(a) every morning
(b) any morning
(c) a morning
(d) morning

3. A: Why is John working long hours?

B: He ___________ a project by the end of this month.

(a) has to finish
(b) had to finish
(c) will have to finish
(d) will have to be finishing

4. A: I'm worried that I'm going to fail my exam.

B: Well, hopefully ___________ .

(a) the case won't be it
(b) that won't be the case
(c) it won't be of that case
(d) that the case won't be it

5. A: Let's make a snowman!

B: Sorry. ___________ outside in the cold is not my idea of fun.

(a) Playing
(b) Played
(c) Plays
(d) Play

6. A: Please ask Jim to call me right away.

B: Sure. I'll have him call you when he ___________ .

(a) will have arrived
(b) is arriving
(c) will arrive
(d) arrives

7. A: You really need to improve your grade point average.

B: That's exactly what ___________ .

(a) have I tried to do
(b) I've been trying to do
(c) I've been trying doing
(d) have I been trying doing

8. A: Is that estimate you gave me fixed?

B: Yes, you'll get it ___________ in writing.

(a) confirming
(b) to confirm
(c) confirmed
(d) confirm

9. A: I just read an article about a plan to
   study kimchi in space.

   B: Yeah. I think some researchers with
   the government __________ to do it.

   (a) have been hoped
   (b) has been hoped
   (c) hopes
   (d) hope

10. A: Can I take three bags on my flight?

    B: No, __________ on this flight is
    restricted to one item.

    (a) baggage
    (b) baggages
    (c) a baggage
    (d) the baggages

11. A: Why are you eating again? We just
    had lunch.

    B: Yes, but it's never __________.

    (a) long again I am hungry
    (b) hungry I am before long
    (c) long until I'm hungry again
    (d) long until hungry again I am

12. A: Grab your jacket, Janet. We should
    get going.

    B: Oh, yeah—it's __________ we left.

    (a) time
    (b) a time
    (c) the time
    (d) one time

13. A: Hey, let's eat out today.

    B: I'd really prefer __________.

    (a) a home meal cooked
    (b) a cooked at home meal
    (c) a meal at home cooked
    (d) a meal cooked at home

14. A: Do you support the council's
    proposal?

    B: Yes, I'm __________ in favor of it.

    (a) all
    (b) far
    (c) that
    (d) ever

15. A: Did you check whether the door was
    locked before you came to bed?

    B: Could you __________? I'm too
    tired.

    (a) for me check it
    (b) check it for me
    (c) checking it for me
    (d) for me checking it

16. A: Tom and Sue are going on a date.

    B: I know, __________.

    (a) liking each other a lot they seem
    (b) they seem to like each other a lot
    (c) seem as they each other like a lot
    (d) each other they seem are liking a lot

17. A: Which of the skirts are you buying?

    B: Well, it seems that neither of them
    __________ well with my tweed
    jacket.

    (a) are to go
    (b) is to go
    (c) goes
    (d) go

18. A: What was the favorite part of your trip?

    B: ___________ was the ethnic food.

    (a) The most of what I liked
    (b) My liking the most
    (c) Most of my liking
    (d) What I liked most

19. A: What did you say to Andrew about his essay?

    B: I just suggested that he ___________ a little more logic next time.

    (a) would employ
    (b) be employed
    (c) employs
    (d) employ

20. A: Was I right in declaring bankruptcy?

    B: Well, ___________, I might have tried some other options.

    (a) I had been in your position
    (b) had I been in your position
    (c) your position I had been in
    (d) in your position had I been

Part II   **Questions 21–40**

Choose the best answer for the blank.

---

21. It is possible to extend the dining table ___________ ten people.

    (a) seats
    (b) to seat
    (c) seating
    (d) to be seating

22. Transit strikers ___________ go back to work by next Monday, or they will lose their jobs.

    (a) would
    (b) must
    (c) may
    (d) can

23. As of next week, two Ryanair flights will connect Oujda to Marseille, ___________ several others will connect Fez to Nice.

    (a) until
    (b) when
    (c) while
    (d) unless

24. Even though many feel that email is impersonal, it is faster, ___________, than writing by hand.

    (a) and also cheaper to mention
    (b) not mentioning as cheap as
    (c) and mentioning as cheaper
    (d) not to mention cheaper

25. The Juilliard School ___________
scores of singers since opening its opera
department in 1930.

(a) trains
(b) has trained
(c) was training
(d) will be training

26. The boy had to stay up late to finish
his homework even though he did not
___________.

(a) want
(b) want it
(c) want to
(d) want to do

27. ___________ hope of finding the lost
hikers, the police plan to continue their
search.

(a) Not given up
(b) Not giving up
(c) Not to give up
(d) Not being given up

28. Andersen Consulting is truly global,
with offices ___________ the world.

(a) over
(b) amid
(c) around
(d) through

29. A clean environment ___________
people are proud is important for public
health reasons.

(a) what
(b) which
(c) for what
(d) of which

30. The US population, now 300 million,
___________ to grow by almost 30
percent to 387 million by 2050.

(a) expects
(b) is expected
(c) will be expecting
(d) will have been expected

31. There was no security guard at the
building's entrance, ___________ the
intruder to enter easily.

(a) allowed
(b) allowing
(c) and allows
(d) they allowed

32. It has not been confirmed ___________
Anson Chan will be promoted to the
post of chief executive.

(a) yet
(b) still
(c) instead
(d) whether

33. The country's industrial sector is
growing ___________ 15 percent each
year.

(a) with
(b) for
(c) by
(d) in

34. Senator Susan Rockwell's tough
exterior and brash manner of speaking
___________ her sensitive side.

(a) obscure
(b) obscures
(c) is obscured
(d) are obscured

35. Outback Adventure Camps are designed to be __________ any teacher would want in a student field trip.

(a) that
(b) who
(c) what
(d) which

36. Since the twins were together all the time, the neighbors never saw one without __________.

(a) other
(b) another
(c) the other
(d) one another

37. After the controversial verdict, the news team rushed to cover the violence that __________ in the streets.

(a) breaks out
(b) had broken out
(c) will have broken out
(d) has been breaking out

38. __________ laid off, Fred was devastated and uncertain as to what to do next.

(a) Had been
(b) He had been
(c) Having been
(d) To have been

39. Not to spend more on a mass defense system would __________ nuclear attack.

(a) leave it vulnerable for the nation
(b) the nation be left vulnerable to
(c) be left vulnerable the nation a
(d) leave the nation vulnerable to

40. The new law prohibits __________ intentionally.

(a) employing aliens unauthorized
(b) employing unauthorized aliens
(c) unauthorized aliens employed
(d) aliens unauthorized employed

Identify the option that contains an awkward expression or an error in grammar.

41. (a) A: I think Janice is still angrily with me.
(b) B: Have you apologized for what you said?
(c) A: Yes, but she didn't really accept it.
(d) B: Well, maybe she'll forgive you in time.

42. (a) A: Hi there. What seems to be the problem today?
(b) B: Well, I have a really sharp pain in my chest.
(c) A: How long you have been feeling this way?
(d) B: It started about two days ago.

43. (a) A: Hello, I'm calling about your tennis camp in June.
(b) B: Sure. What would you like to know about it?
(c) A: My son is seven years old. Is that too young?
(d) B: No, our camp is for the children aged seven and up.

44. (a) A: You know, I really don't want to go to your class reunion.
(b) B: But you said you would. Just come along for a little while.
(c) A: OK, but I'm not staying any longer than that is necessary.
(d) B: Fine. Just give me some time to catch up with everyone.

45. (a) A: I think the incumbent President is going to lose this election.
(b) B: I'm not so sure. He hasn't done such a terrible job.
(c) A: Seriously? I think you must be hard-pressed to find anyone who agrees with you.
(d) B: Don't count on it. The latest polls suggest I'm not alone.

Part IV Questions 46—50

Identify the option that contains an awkward expression or an error in grammar.

46. (a) A tornado is a violently rotating column of air that descends to the earth from a thunderstorm. (b) Few other weather phenomena can match the fury and destructive power of tornadoes. (c) They are able to destroy large buildings and even lift 20-ton railroad cars from their tracks. (d) Tornadoes occur main in the southern areas of the US, and the peak season is March through May.

47. (a) In the 18th century, Europeans sailed west to look for a short trade route to Asia. (b) They were convinced that North America will have a waterway through it to the Pacific Ocean. (c) Several countries spent vast fortunes sending explorers to cross North America by water, only to be bitterly disappointed each time. (d) Part of the reason was that explorers were fooled by the immense size of the continent's lakes and rivers.

48. (a) Martha Salinger, the well-known actress, seems to think that celebrity status exempts her from paying bills. (b) Yesterday she tried to leave a posh Los Angeles bistro without paying for an expensive meal. (c) After a confrontation with the bistro's owner, Salinger ended up paying her bill like everyone else. (d) But the bistro owner told reporters that if Salinger were to visit again, she will not find a table for her.

49. (a) Two months after being laid, sea turtle hatchlings emerge from their nests on the beach at night. (b) They orient themselves to the brightest light, which is usually the moon and stars reflecting off the ocean. (c) They struggle towards this light, with their lives depending on getting into the ocean. (d) If hatchlings get lost, they die of dehydration when the sun comes up or caught by predators like birds and crabs.

50. (a) Comets have long inspired fear and awe because they suddenly appear for no apparent reason. (b) Ancient people believed that they were warnings that something unusual or terrible would happen. (c) But the word comet is unrelated to these fears and derives from the ancient Greek word kometes, meaning "long-haired." (d) The name originated because people thought comets looked like heads with hair stream out behind them.

This is the end of the Grammar section. Do NOT move on to the next section until instructed to do so. You are NOT allowed to turn to any other section of the test.

VOCABULARY

DIRECTIONS

This part of the exam tests your vocabulary skills. You will have 15 minutes to complete the 50 questions. Be sure to follow the directions given by the proctor.

Part I Questions 1—25

Choose the best answer for the blank.

1. A: Would you like to join me for lunch?
B: Yes, ___________! That'd be great.

(a) absolutely
(b) truthfully
(c) specially
(d) nicely

2. A: Excuse me. Would you mind filling out a customer survey?
B: Sure. I'd be ___________ to.

(a) glad
(b) satisfied
(c) accepted
(d) agreeable

3. A: Can Kevin keep everything in this report a secret?
B: Yes, you can definitely ___________ him.

(a) trust
(b) count
(c) suspect
(d) identify

4. A: Excuse me, is there a public phone near here?
B: Yes, it's just around the ___________.

(a) road
(b) corner
(c) crosswalk
(d) pavement

5. A: John is fortunate to be able to speak both Korean and English.
B: Yeah, it gives him a(n) ___________ in some situations.

(a) ease
(b) pride
(c) reward
(d) advantage

6. A: Is the experiment going well?
B: Yes, everything seems to be ___________ all right.

(a) falling in
(b) bringing up
(c) working out
(d) turning over

7. A: Thanks for coming over tonight.
B: No. Thank you! I'm happy you ___________ us.

(a) held
(b) invited
(c) noticed
(d) promised

8. A: Just two minutes ago Alice looked happy, but now she's crying.
B: Well, teenagers can be ___________ sometimes.

(a) untidy
(b) moody
(c) critical
(d) unreliable

9. A: Are these electronic check-ins faster than counter check-ins?

B: Yes, they ___________ the check-in process.

(a) force
(b) drive
(c) quicken
(d) proceed

10. A: How about a short break?

B: Good idea. I need to ___________ my legs.

(a) kick
(b) push
(c) jump
(d) stretch

11. A: Let's open the window. This room needs some air.

B: Yes, it's pretty ___________ in here.

(a) cozy
(b) stuffy
(c) drafty
(d) breezy

12. A: Hi Jack, I'm calling about the party.

B: Oh, good. I've been meaning to ___________ you.

(a) chat
(b) attend
(c) contact
(d) acquire

13. A: A lot of teens are buying those minibikes.

B: Yeah. They are extremely ___________ these days.

(a) popular
(b) general
(c) special
(d) bright

14. A: Why don't you like Professor Jones?

B: He's so ___________ with his remarks.

(a) rude
(b) stable
(c) caring
(d) broken

15. A: Jane, I'm so sorry about your mom's passing.

B: Oh, thank you for your ___________.

(a) exultation
(b) grievances
(c) condolences
(d) appreciation

16. A: Hey Becky, this is Sam. You two haven't met yet, have you?

B: No, but we have mutual ___________.

(a) exposures
(b) individuals
(c) relationships
(d) acquaintances

17. A: Did you pass on my message to Ted?

B: Oh no, I'm really sorry. It totally ___________ my mind.

(a) missed
(b) passed
(c) slipped
(d) evaded

18. A: Did the storm hit your town hard?

B: Yeah, falling trees downed power lines and ___________ the electricity.

(a) put down
(b) gave out
(c) sent up
(d) cut off

19. A: What will the weather be like today?

B: Mostly cloudy with sunny ___________.

(a) holes
(b) briefs
(c) periods
(d) options

20. A: Will my pacemaker set off the airport metal detector?

B: It might, but it's something our staff is ___________ to.

(a) indebted
(b) restrained
(c) committed
(d) accustomed

21. A: Ouch! I cut my finger!

B: Lift up your hand. ___________ it stops the bleeding.

(a) Placating
(b) Elevating
(c) Alleviating
(d) Withdrawing

22. A: How do you like the soup, ma'am?

B: Actually, it tastes a bit ___________.

(a) rare
(b) raw
(c) dim
(d) bland

23. A: Is the new director qualified?

B: I think so. His credentials are certainly ___________.

(a) tumultuous
(b) impeccable
(c) inexorable
(d) inglorious

24. A: I can't really make up my mind about the agreement.

B: Well, you can't just ___________.

(a) sit on the fence
(b) play your cards
(c) steal my thunder
(d) bend over backwards

25. A: The candidates for mayor this year have all been involved in major scandals.

B: Yes, it's a shame anyone with a(n) ___________ past can still run.

(a) sordid
(b) elliptical
(c) scrupulous
(d) conscientious

Part II **Questions 26—50**

Choose the best answer for the blank.

26. When the students heard they would have to do homework during the holidays, they were __________.

(a) trustworthy
(b) annoyed
(c) clueless
(d) fluent

27. If your current __________ is not satisfying, then you should look for a job that is more enjoyable and has a better future.

(a) position
(b) trend
(c) order
(d) state

28. Canada's only transcontinental railroad __________ the eastern and western parts of the country was completed in 1885.

(a) bracing
(b) matching
(c) including
(d) connecting

29. "Energetic" and "evolving" are two words that could be used to __________ the famous fashion brand Armani.

(a) describe
(b) contract
(c) employ
(d) apply

30. The candidate's opponent in the debate made several good __________ that were difficult to argue against.

(a) plots
(b) notes
(c) goals
(d) points

31. For a refund, bring the item and the credit card used to __________ it to any one of our stores.

(a) take
(b) cover
(c) purchase
(d) accomplish

32. Fossils can __________ insights into life forms that lived tens of millions of years ago.

(a) provide
(b) consult
(c) enclose
(d) install

33. With no __________ evidence, the judge could not convict the accused man.

(a) moral
(b) concrete
(c) dreadful
(d) indefinite

34. Research __________ the impact of work on family life often assumes that work is perceived differently by men and women.

(a) locating
(b) examining
(c) preventing
(d) transporting

35. The abundance of "spinster-finds-love" novels has critics of romance fiction __________ what the next trend will be.

(a) obtaining
(b) generating
(c) wondering
(d) moderating

36. Our website __________ news headlines and summaries from other sources, and it allows you to scan them all in one place.

(a) delegates
(b) compiles
(c) markets
(d) remits

37. On New Year's Eve, people often sing the first __________ of the song "Auld Lang Syne" but do not know the rest.

(a) verse
(b) chord
(c) frame
(d) melody

38. Some poets are best at dealing with upbeat themes, while others seem to prefer more __________ subjects.

(a) jovial
(b) elated
(c) belittled
(d) melancholy

39. Entrepreneurs must __________ strong leadership skills and determination if they want to succeed in business.

(a) imply
(b) direct
(c) possess
(d) transfer

40. One goal of discipline is to help children understand that their actions have

__________.

(a) consequences
(b) attributions
(c) demands
(d) misuses

41. This year, record numbers of Chinese tourists are __________ to destinations such as London and Cairo.

(a) idling
(b) relating
(c) flocking
(d) mingling

42. Historically, a great leap in agricultural productivity __________ through new sources of power.

(a) met
(b) occurred
(c) improved
(d) transmitted

43. Bird lovers search for Great Gray Owls in the Bridger Mountains region, but these birds are rarely __________.

(a) spotted
(b) glanced
(c) checked
(d) watched

44. Experts believe that the global increase in gambling addiction is in part __________ by a new generation of gambling machines.

(a) fueled
(b) endured
(c) conveyed
(d) dispatched

45. The __________ of the lilac tree was covered in blossoms.

(a) lash
(b) stalk
(c) prong
(d) bough

46. Despite assurances from police, everyone attending the economic conference should take __________ to avoid conflict with protesters.

(a) assertions
(b) exceptions
(c) precautions
(d) contraventions

47. Smallpox has been __________, so there is no longer any need for immunization.

(a) denuded
(b) procured
(c) eradicated
(d) scrutinized

48. Find out how popular our products are by reading these __________ reviews from satisfied customers.

(a) high
(b) rave
(c) gruff
(d) brash

49. Writing is a system for translating language sounds into visual symbols that can be produced on a physical __________.

(a) medium
(b) terrain
(c) arena
(d) slate

50. Strict federal sentencing guidelines have been adopted that __________ harsh penalties for weapons offenses.

(a) mandate
(b) hamper
(c) solicit
(d) avow

This is the end of the Vocabulary section. Do NOT move on to the Reading Comprehension section until instructed to do so. You are NOT allowed to turn to any other section of the test.

READING COMPREHENSION

DIRECTIONS

This part of the exam tests your ability to comprehend reading passages. You will have 45 minutes to complete the 40 questions. Be sure to follow the directions given by the proctor.

Part I   **Questions 1—16**

Read the passage. Then choose the option that best completes the passage.

1.   Your Touchmatic Microwave Oven enables you to cook a wide variety of foods to perfection. With most dishes, you can simply use the default power settings. However, some foods can cook better at specific power levels. That is why your Touchmatic has 10 different power settings to select from—each one set to cook something different. For example, one setting is good for stews, while another is ideal for reheating pizza. So, before you cook, remember to check the user's manual to learn ________________________.

(a) how to cook a meal for a large family
(b) how to use different power settings
(c) how to test microwaveable dishes
(d) how to clean the oven properly

2.   In the second half of the 18th century, the Severn River, running through the valley of Coalbrookdale, England, was a major obstacle to the transportation of raw materials from one side of the valley to the other. A strictly limited number of bridges existed then, and so materials were moved by ferries. However, the ferries could not keep up with the pace of increased productivity as the region became more industrialized. Of course, the logical answer to the problem was ________________________.

(a) to build a major bridge
(b) halting production of ferries
(c) to divert the Severn river
(d) transporting more materials

3.   People in Arabic countries, parts of Africa, India, Sri Lanka and the Philippines often eat with their fingers. It is a practice that ________________________. For instance, people in these countries eat with their hands from a common platter, and guests are expected to do the same. It would be insulting to refuse. In addition, how the hand eating is done is also important. In northern India, for example, it is wrong to put fingers into any food beyond the second joint, whereas in southern India people may use their entire hand.

(a) is governed by rules
(b) occurs because of poverty
(c) applies to only certain foods
(d) is seen as uncultured in the West

4. Until recently, the home-improvement industry has been predominantly for men.
    However, there has been a sudden increase in home improvement books, videos, radio
    shows, TV spots and websites made just for women. Even websites not specifically for
    women now offer female-friendly links and columns alongside their traditional fare.
    Major do-it-yourself stores have also joined the bandwagon. They now carry products
    and tools ______________________________.

    (a) created for professionals of any trade
    (b) designed especially for female customers
    (c) that make home-improvements much easier
    (d) that are cheaper but just as good as other brands

5. Sam Patch (1807-1829), known as the "Yankee Leaper," was America's first daredevil.
    He found fame by jumping from high places. In 1827, he jumped off an 88-foot-high
    platform into the Passaic River. Two years later, he jumped into Niagara Falls and
    survived. Those two jumps made him a celebrity. Next, he ______________________.
    This time it was from a platform 125 feet above the Genesee Falls, but he did not
    resurface. The next spring, his frozen body was found downriver.

    (a) succeeded at a higher jump
    (b) tried a different kind of stunt
    (c) dived into Niagara Falls again
    (d) attempted a more ambitious jump

6.

Dear Mr. Meadows,

The purpose of this letter is to inform you that I will be leaving my position with New Planet Entertainment effective March 1. I plan to relocate to the New York City area to start my own consulting business. I appreciate both having been a part of the NPE team and having had the opportunities that I was given over the past several years. Please let me know ________________________________. You can reach me at my desk at 867-5309 if you have any questions.

Sincerely,
Douglas Brown

(a) why you have terminated my contract
(b) how things are going at your company
(c) whom I should thank for this opportunity
(d) how I can be of help until my departure

7. Before processed foods became common, humans consumed omega-3 and omega-6 fatty acids in almost equal amounts. Now there is a considerable imbalance. People seem to be consuming far too much omega-6 and not enough omega-3. This dietary imbalance may account for the increase in such diseases as asthma, coronary heart disease and various types of cancer. The imbalance of fatty acids may also lead to obesity, depression, dyslexia, hyperactivity and even tendencies toward violence. It is therefore essential that people ________________________________.

(a) stop eating too many fatty foods
(b) take dietary supplements once a day
(c) eat a variety of vegetables and fruits
(d) consume balanced portions of fatty acids

8. According to a new study by researchers in Sweden, placebos, or plain sugar pills presented as medicine, can trick the mind into feeling not only less physical pain but less emotional pain as well. In a two-day experiment, 15 volunteers were asked to rate their reactions to disturbing pictures. They were given an anti-anxiety drug to reduce distress. When the exercise was repeated the following day, however, the anti-anxiety drug was secretly replaced with a placebo. Tests showed that it was also effective in reducing the subjects' stress levels. Researchers concluded from this that ________________________________ some psychological stress.

(a) severe physical stress can lead to
(b) the mere expectation of relief can reduce
(c) graphic images in photos and movies cause
(d) simple anti-anxiety medication can alleviate

9. At his favorite neighborhood "costume café," Shunsuke Yamagata, a college student
    who proudly calls himself a nerd, smiles shyly at waitresses hurrying about wearing
    cat's ears and mini-dresses inspired by Japanese comics. The café is a dream come
    true for Yamagata, whose passion is collecting comics and cartoons. He giggles when
    addressed in the squeaky character voices that waitresses use to delight their fantasy-
    loving customers. Such businesses are springing up all over Japan to cater to thousands
    like Yamagata who _______________________________.

    (a) work in Japan's competitive animation industry
    (b) visit Japan to experience its unique culture
    (c) are obsessed with the world of animation
    (d) love dressing up as cartoon characters

10. The forefathers of Australia's Aborigines came from southeast Asia approximately
    50,000 years ago. They developed in isolation, coming up with their unique cultures and
    hundreds of languages. That isolation is confirmed in the fact that no relationship can be
    found between these Aborigine languages and any other Asian languages. Indeed, their
    languages are unlike any others on earth. Thus, as is commonly acknowledged, the
    Aborigines _______________________________.

    (a) show as much diversity as Asian languages
    (b) have undergone many linguistic changes
    (c) were truly Australia's first inhabitants
    (d) spread their culture across the region

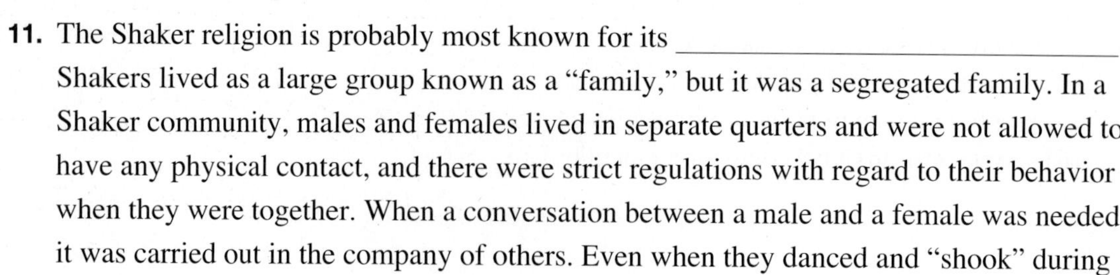

11. The Shaker religion is probably most known for its __________________________.
Shakers lived as a large group known as a "family," but it was a segregated family. In a Shaker community, males and females lived in separate quarters and were not allowed to have any physical contact, and there were strict regulations with regard to their behavior when they were together. When a conversation between a male and a female was needed, it was carried out in the company of others. Even when they danced and "shook" during worship, the two genders always kept their distance.

(a) promotion of large families
(b) strong views on Christian worship
(c) avoidance of modern conveniences
(d) rigid separation of men and women

12. By the 1930s, the big Hollywood movie studios had all become well-established. Each studio had set up its own business philosophy and a creative "personality" to go along with it. MGM produced lavish, star-oriented films, whereas Columbia Pictures was famous for relatively leaner productions. The clean family films created by Paramount were in stark contrast to Warner Brothers' more sensationalized, tough character movies. It was obvious to those who knew the studios that __________________________.

(a) their aim was to make money rather than art
(b) their films reflected their business approaches
(c) they made films according to common guidelines
(d) they were treating their actors and actresses poorly

13. Stable trade prices are vital to a national economy. Even if a certain product represents a minor share of the gross domestic commodity, fluctuations in its trade price can impact the entire economy. Cheaply imported grain, for example, results in cheap bread, and cheap bread frees up wages that can be spent on other goods. Of course, the reverse applies if prices increase. In this way, __________________________.

(a) local markets are hurt by free trade
(b) national economies can ensure prosperity
(c) trade can greatly affect a nation's economy
(d) grain prices become ever more unpredictable

14. Maxine Hong's autobiographical work, *The Lost Immigrant*, has earned her the enmity of some critics. They object to its ___________________________________. It would seem, however, that these critics are approaching her work from the point of view of the dominant American culture. They perceive her book as they do perhaps because they have not truly experienced the obstacles she encountered as a newcomer to the US. Hong's traumatic experience is representative, she proclaims, and only those who have been in her shoes can judge that authoritatively.

(a) overt criticisms of early immigrants
(b) excessive use of secondary sources
(c) unfair condemnations of Chinese-Americans
(d) alleged exaggeration of immigrants' hardships

15. New studies from California show that attending a community college is highly beneficial for students interested in eventually transferring to a university. The studies, conducted by the University of California (UC) and California State University (CSU), have found that community college transfer students consistently do well in junior and senior year courses, and they graduate at an equivalent rate to those who begin their studies at the universities. _______________________________, almost two-thirds of all CSU graduates and one-third of all UC graduates began their academic careers at a California community college.

(a) In fact
(b) Instead
(c) And yet
(d) Likewise

16. At Cars4U, we've eliminated the negotiation and haggling process, so your shopping experience is pleasant and hassle-free. Cars4U provides actual Porsche 911 prices. These are fixed transactional market values, not theoretical prices. ___________________, Cars4U lists out any rebates and incentives offered by the manufacturer for a particular automobile. Those discounts are then incorporated into the Porsche 911 prices. We also offer a great deal of research information, such as specs, photos and reviews to help you with your car selection. Visit Cars4U today.

(a) Instead
(b) What's more
(c) On the contrary
(d) In the meantime

Part II **Questions 17—37**

Read the passage and the question. Then choose the option that best answers the question.

17. A penguin's feet are particularly vulnerable to heat loss, so it has two vital bodily functions that help it maintain its body temperature. First, the rate of blood flow to the penguin's feet is controlled by a varying of the diameter of arterial vessels, thereby allowing less blood to flow to its feet as conditions grow colder. Second, blood vessels arranged at the top of the penguin's legs create a heat exchange, where heat from blood going to the feet passes cold blood coming back from the feet. In this way, the penguin's body is able to cyclically warm its own blood.

Q: What is the passage mainly about?
(a) Why penguins expand their blood vessels
(b) Why penguins need to keep their feet warm
(c) How penguins preserve their body temperature
(d) How penguins exchange body heat with one another

18. When he published his first novel *Things Fall Apart* 60 years ago, Nigerian writer Chinua Achebe had only modest hopes for its success. Yet the novel has since sold over 11 million copies in some 50 countries and has been translated into many languages. It is arguably the most influential work of fiction by an African writer, and it still appears on college and high-school reading lists around the world.

Q: What is the passage mainly about?
(a) Achebe's impressive literary career
(b) Renewed interest in *Things Fall Apart*
(c) Achebe's influence on African writers
(d) The unexpected success of *Things Fall Apart*

19. In the University of North Carolina's early days, servants kindled fires in students' rooms and chopped wood for their stoves. But this public state university, proud of being the nation's oldest, is not proud to disclose that those servants were slaves. The fact was recently unveiled when archivists were researching the university's first 100 years. Written documentation and pictures confirmed that slaves helped build campus buildings and labored on campus grounds. "This university was built by slaves and free blacks," the university's Chancellor, James Moeser, has admitted. Other documents demonstrate that many faculty members were also slave owners.

Q: What is the best title for the passage?
(a) University Uncovers Past Links to Slavery
(b) Archivists Discuss Corruption at University
(c) Chancellor Critical of Discrimination Incident
(d) Slaves Who Built Schools are Finally Honored

20. The ancestors of today's Inuit devised a number of games for recreation during the harsh
arctic winters. Winter was a time when the Inuit were confined to their ice huts for
extended periods of time to escape the winter darkness, excruciatingly cold temperatures
and icy winds. Playing games helped stave off boredom, and offered them entertainment.
The games also taught valuable skills, promoted physical exercise and provided a means
of communicating Inuit culture, values and attitudes.

Q: What is the passage mainly about?
(a) The impact of winter on Inuit customs
(b) The adept cultures of the Arctic region
(c) The origins and purpose of Inuit games
(d) The way the Inuit learned through games

21. In the past, historical studies of the United Kingdom largely focused on Anglo-Saxon
and Norman history. However, British historians have come to realize that this led not
simply to a neglect of the history of the greater British Isles, but also created a
fundamental misunderstanding of the nature of the United Kingdom itself, as a culture
and a polity. Accordingly, historians now strive to take a more holistic view of the
British Isles as made up of peoples and cultures that have all mutually shaped the history
of the United Kingdom.

Q: What is the writer's main point about the United Kingdom?
(a) Its beginnings were more ancient than historians once thought.
(b) It has recently been receiving renewed attention from historians.
(c) Its historians have realized that past studies of it were too narrow.
(d) It has influenced world history more than any other nation.

22. Critics often look down on the prolificacy of young up-and-coming artists, labeling their works as pop fiction or pop art with a dismissive tone. This mindset is not conducive to encouraging a new generation of artists, nor does it come from a valid critical apprehension or an innocent aspiration to categorize—rather, it stems from a desire of those in power within the artistic community, both critics and canonized artists alike, to preserve the status quo and protect their positions. It is a stance that does a great disservice to the cause of cutting-edge art.

Q: What is the passage mainly about?
(a) Criticisms of pop fiction and pop art by powerful critics
(b) Young artists and their struggles with experimental art
(c) Elitism against rising artists in the artistic community
(d) Poor judgments by critics of today's youth culture

23. Looking for an ideal summer holiday rental home near Barcelona? We have a fully refurbished 18th-century stone farmhouse that is now ready for lease in the beautiful foothills of Monserrat, a 45-minute drive from Barcelona. The house has a 15-meter three-lane swimming pool, three bedrooms, two bathrooms, a kitchen and a living room. Good restaurants are only a five-minute walk away. Both short and long leases are available, starting from $350 US per week. For more information, contact philipa.b@ yahoo.com.

Q: Which of the following is correct about the advertised property?
(a) It dates back to the 18th century.
(b) It is located 45 minutes from Monserrat.
(c) It features a large circular swimming pool.
(d) It is a short walk from Barcelona's city center.

24. Marvel at the underground wonderland of Crystal Cave! See a breathtaking exhibit of crystals that have been gradually and exquisitely etched by Mother Nature's hands through the ages. Witness centuries-old, milky white stalactites, stalagmites and dripstone formations that stand like the columns of a grand palace. Prepare to be dazzled by such marvels as the Cathedral Chamber, the Giant's Tooth and the Crystal Ballroom. Crystal Cave is a unique experience the whole family can share. Our one-hour tour is along concrete walkways and is supervised by a certified guide.

Q: Which of the following is correct about Crystal Cave according to the advertisement?
(a) Visitors are taken on a guided half hour tour.
(b) The cave is home to dark colored stalactites.
(c) One feature of the cave is the Cathedral Chamber.
(d) The underground tour is recommended for adults only.

25.

Dear Mr. Black,

I would like to apply for the position of chief accountant at Sanders Enterprises, as posted in the August 20th issue of the *New York Times*. I believe that I am an ideal candidate for the position with my extensive experience as an accountant at Matheson Business Associates. In my current position, I perform the exact same tasks required for the advertised position. Please find enclosed my CV and three letters of reference. I look forward to hearing from you regarding an interview. I appreciate your time and consideration.

Sincerely,
Ken Jacobs

Q: Which of the following is correct according to the passage?
(a) Sanders Enterprises needs a new salesperson.
(b) Sanders Enterprises was mentioned in a news article.
(c) Ken Jacobs is presently employed as an accountant.
(d) Mr. Black has already been offered an interview.

26. New Zealand's South Island Tours offers you phenomenal value for your money, with a 21-day tour for only $2,300. Explore New Zealand's South Island in a 49-seat, air-conditioned tour bus. Hotel accommodations with breakfast are included in the price. This tour takes a leisurely pace but has a comprehensive itinerary. Contact New Zealand's South Island Tours for more information and a detailed schedule. Please note that the tour is usually fully booked months in advance. Our next available tour departs in December.

Q: Which of the following is correct according to the advertisement?
(a) The tour lasts about two weeks.
(b) Hotel accommodation and all meals are included.
(c) The tour schedule is available at the travel agency.
(d) All the tours are already fully booked for the year.

27. Each foot of a fly has two plump sticky footpads that give it the ability to adhere to a surface even when upside down. The footpads, called pulvilli, come equipped with tiny hairs that include spatula-like tips. Scientists once believed that the curved form of the hairs were what helped flies stick to ceilings and walls, but in fact, the hairs produce a glue-like matter composed of sugar and oil, which is what gives a fly its sticky walk.

Q: Which of the following is correct about a fly's footpads according to the passage?
(a) A fly has a total of four, all of which are adhesive.
(b) Each one of them is shaped like a spatula.
(c) Their curved hairs make clinging to the walls possible.
(d) The glue-like substance from their hairs help flies stick.

28. To install your ceiling fan successfully, be sure to read the instructions and review the diagrams thoroughly before beginning. Since a typical fan draws about the same power as a light fixture, the electrical circuit should not become overloaded. But if your fan includes lights, be sure the circuit it uses has enough extra capacity to handle the load. If not, you must run a new circuit with a new circuit breaker from your home's main service panel or sub panel to the fan. If you are unfamiliar with how to do this, secure the services of a qualified licensed electrician to carry out the installation.

Q: Which of the following is correct according to the instructions?
(a) Fans often exceed the power requirements for lights.
(b) More electrical output is needed for fans with lights.
(c) Service panels should be set up after fan installation.
(d) An electrician should be employed for all installations.

29. The religious system of Zoroastrianism predates Christianity, Islam and Judaism, and its doctrines of one God, a dualistic universe of good and evil and a final day of judgment influenced those later religions. Zoroastrianism was once practiced across a vast area stretching from what is now Rome and Greece to India and Russia. Practitioners still exist, but their global population has dwindled to perhaps as few as 124,000. However, the precise number is difficult to know because of wildly diverging estimates in Iran, where the faith originated.

Q: Which of the following is correct about Zoroastrianism according to the passage?
(a) It was established at the same time as Christianity.
(b) Its doctrines affected Jewish and Christian faiths.
(c) It still dominates in parts of India and Russia.
(d) It continues to grow in popularity.

30. Scotch whisky is indeed a global commodity, with healthy, expanding markets around the globe. The two major Scotch whisky markets are, interestingly, America and France; indeed, the French consume four times as much Scotch whisky as brandy. Also responsible for strong sales of Scotch whisky are emerging economies, such as those in Russia and China. Countries where a dramatic increase in Scotch whisky sales has been seen are Spain, Greece, Germany and South Africa. Indeed, Scotch whisky sales have doubled in South Africa over the last five years, reflecting that nation's economic growth.

Q: Which of the following is correct according to the passage?
(a) More Scotch is drunk in China than in France.
(b) Brandy outsells Scotch by four to one in France.
(c) Russia represents a growing market for Scotch whisky.
(d) South Africa is the second largest market for Scotch whisky.

31. The traditional Roman calendar featured 12 months with 30 days each, but because it inaccurately reflected the solar year, it had to be corrected periodically by adding an extra month. Seeking an alternative, Julius Caesar had the Julian calendar created based on 6 months of 30 days and 6 months of 31 days. Later revisions set it at 7 months with 31 days and 4 months with 30 days. Despite having a leap year rule, the Julian calendar year was still slightly too long. So, in 1582, Pope Gregory XIII decreed a modified calendar based on the Julian but with a more accurate leap year calculation. This is basically the calendar we use today.

Q: Which of the following is correct according to the passage?
(a) The Julian calendar featured 12 months of 30 days each.
(b) Pope Gregory XIII introduced a revised calendar in 1582.
(c) Pope Gregory XIII was the first to propose a leap year rule.
(d) Julius Caesar's calendar was identical to today's calendar.

32. Because of their enormous size and speed, blue whales were safe from early whalers who were unable to pursue them in open boats nor kill them with hand harpoons. However, in 1864 a Norwegian, Sven Foyn, revolutionized the whaling industry by inventing the exploding harpoon gun. This, combined with motorized ships, meant that the whaling industry could hunt blue whales. By 1900, blue whales were being slaughtered by the thousands. The slaughter peaked in 1931, when over 29,000 were killed in one season. Not surprisingly, this massacre left the blue whales facing extinction, and whalers were forced to hunt other species.

Q: Which of the following is correct according to the passage?
(a) Early whalers pursued blue whales in open boats.
(b) The whaling industry was revolutionized in 1900.
(c) In 1931 the number of blue whales killed reached near 29,000.
(d) Near extinction of blue whales made the whalers stop the slaughter.

33. Do you have what it takes to motivate and lead others? Do you enjoy teaching, supervising and helping a team develop and prosper? If so, our company has a position for you. DataWorks is looking for a Telecommunication Sales Manager with extensive experience in local or long-distance phone-plan sales. The position comes with an excellent salary, a car allowance, annual bonuses and exceptional fringe benefits. Submit your résumé along with at least two reference letters to jobapp@dataworks.com.

Q: What type of person is best suited for the advertised position?
(a) A person seeking an entry-level position
(b) A person who has worked in customer support
(c) Someone who is good at negotiating with management
(d) Someone with previous experience as a sales manager

34. When it comes to accommodation, Paris offers endless possibilities. There are nearly 1,500 hotels (and more than 75,000 hotel rooms) in the city, a large proportion of them small and privately owned. Prices range widely—a single room with shared shower and toilet might start at 35 euros per night, while a grand suite at a new five-star hotel can cost up to 15,000 euros. Travelers usually rely on the universal five-star rating system, but ratings can be deceptive. You might be surprised by what's available when you venture off the beaten path.

Q: What is likely to be discussed next?
(a) Advice for finding the cheapest hotels in Paris
(b) Examples of unexpectedly pleasant lodgings
(c) Small hotels in Paris that should be avoided
(d) Possible problems with Parisian hotels

35. Japanese literature today remains strongly influenced by Japan's two oldest surviving literary works. One of these is *The Kojiki Record of Ancient Matters*, a prose work assumed to have been written in 712. It was composed at the request of the emperor with the goal of recording and justifying imperial rule. The other is the *Manyo-shu (Collection of Ten Thousand Leaves)*, a 20-volume anthology of poems compiled around the year 770. It boasts some 4,500 poems by a number of male and female writers from virtually every walk of life. Many of these poems, which touch on a wide range of subjects, are known for their moving candor and bold simplicity.

Q: What can be inferred from the passage?
(a) Japanese culture is increasingly reverting to its past.
(b) The *Kojiki* is more political in focus than the *Manyo-shu*.
(c) Prose is now more highly regarded than poetry in Japan.
(d) The *Manyo-shu* is more closely studied today than the *Kojiki*.

36. Sociologists of religion are dedicated to studying the practices and roles of religions in society. They examine how religion affects society and vice versa. They also study the nature of the many religions that have emerged throughout recorded history. However, practitioners in this field are not necessarily religious. In fact, their theories and conclusions can be antithetical to the goals and purposes of a religion, which often makes them unpopular with religious devotees.

Q: What can be inferred about sociologists of religion from the passage?
(a) Their field has less scope for research in the modern era.
(b) They tend to be biased towards some religions over others.
(c) Their research might cover the impact of religion on politics.
(d) They avoid criticizing certain religions for fear of retribution.

37.

Dear Editor,

The article by Barry Milton in your last issue, entitled "A Better Way to Fight Drug Abuse," is seriously misinformed. There is no evidence that harsher punishment deters people from using or selling drugs. It would be especially ridiculous to include "soft" drug use in such a scheme. In fact, a link has been shown between Hawaii's marijuana eradication efforts and the increase in that state of hard drug use. So, targeting soft drug dealers actually makes hard drug dealers richer. The logical solution is to be more lenient on soft drugs like marijuana and just combat the dealers of the hard, truly dangerous drugs.

Sincerely,
Spike Brady

Q: What was the likely subject of Barry Milton's article?
(a) An argument for being lenient on some drugs
(b) An insight into the causes and effects of hard drug use
(c) A proposal to raise drug abuse penalties across the board
(d) A criticism of the government's policy of legalizing marijuana

Part III **Questions 38 — 40**

Read the passage. Then identify the option that does NOT belong.

38. In 1939, in Manitoba, Canada, Alfred Hole took in four orphaned goslings and decided to look after them. (a) That eventually led to what we now know as the Alf Hill Goose Sanctuary, a nature park frequented by various species of geese. (b) Throughout North America, non-migratory Canadian Geese populations have been on the rise. (c) As well as the geese and several beautiful nature walks, there are many displays on the history of the sanctuary. (d) From spring to fall, guides at the park also provide scheduled programs, activities and park information.

39. When renting out a house, you need to decide what kind of accommodation you want to provide. (a) If you intend your rental to be a vacation house, for example, then it needs to be fully furnished. (b) Keep in mind that renting a house is not about making friends, it's about managing an investment. (c) If you do not want to provide furniture, renting to long-term family tenants is probably your best option. (d) Families wanting to stay for several years are likely to have their own furniture and appliances.

40. Though I have taken pictures of vultures on many occasions, I've never heard a sound from them, as I've never gotten close enough. (a) Yet, I've had to spend excessive amounts of time in the Everglades to get good shots of my various traveling companions. (b) Then one day there I was, crouched over my low tripod in a parking lot in the Everglades, all ears in the midst of a flock of black vultures. (c) The sound they produced is not what I would call a grunt, hiss, coo or snarl, but rather a kind of soft, back-of-the-throat woof. (d) And as I kept taking pictures, I found myself enchanted with this new, mysterious sound that was unlike anything I had ever heard.

This is the end of the Reading Comprehension section. Please remain seated until the proctor has instructed otherwise. You are NOT allowed to turn to any other section of the test.

Listening Comprehension

Grammar

Vocabulary

Reading Comprehension

LISTENING COMPREHENSION

Scripts P 276 / 정답 P 327

Part I **Questions 1—15**

You will now hear fifteen conversation fragments, each made up of a single spoken statement followed by four spoken responses. Choose the most appropriate response to the statement.

Part II **Questions 16—30**

You will now hear fifteen conversation fragments, each made up of three spoken statements followed by four spoken responses. Choose the most appropriate response to complete the conversation.

Part III **Questions 31—45**

You will now hear fifteen complete conversations. For each item, you will hear a conversation and its corresponding question, both of which will be read twice. Then you will hear four options which will be read only once. Choose the option that best answers the question.

Part IV **Questions 46—60**

You will now hear fifteen spoken monologues. For each item, you will hear a monologue and its corresponding question, both of which will be read twice. Then you will hear four options which will be read only once. Choose the option that best answers the question.

GRAMMAR

DIRECTIONS

This part of the exam tests your grammar skills. You will have 25 minutes to complete the 50 questions. Be sure to follow the directions given by the proctor.

Part I Questions 1—20

Choose the best answer for the blank.

1. A: Is anyone from the city council in favor of the proposal?

B: As a matter of fact, quite a few members ___________ shown support.

(a) has
(b) have
(c) has been
(d) have been

2. A: Are there any job openings in the department for this semester?

B: Yes, they ___________ more lab assistants.

(a) are hiring
(b) had hired
(c) hired
(d) hire

3. A: How was the visit to the dentist?

B: It didn't hurt like last time, ___________ it took a lot longer.

(a) or
(b) so
(c) once
(d) though

4. A: I lost some files when my PC crashed.

B: ___________ that from happening again, make backup copies.

(a) Prevent
(b) Prevented
(c) To prevent
(d) To be prevented

5. A: Isn't graduate school very expensive?

B: Yes, but I like to think ___________ investment in my future.

(a) it as one of
(b) of it as an
(c) it of an
(d) as it of

6. A: Sorry, but you can't take photographs in the museum.

B: Oh, I didn't see a sign saying ___________.

(a) not to take
(b) not to do
(c) not to it
(d) not to

7. A: I spent almost 5,000 dollars on my trip to Johannesburg.

B: That's almost the price of ___________!

(a) three vacations combined
(b) three combining vacations
(c) combined by three vacations
(d) vacations combining by three

8. A: Sue, what are you doing around 7 this evening?

B: I ___________ a walk with my dog.

(a) take
(b) have taken
(c) will be taking
(d) have been taking

9. A: I get so thirsty after working out.
    B: Me, too. I like to have ___________ .

    (a) something cold to drink
    (b) to drink cold something
    (c) cold something to drink of
    (d) to drink of something cold

10. A: I hear Jennifer said some insulting
       things about me to her friends.
    B: That wouldn't have happened, if you
       ___________ her names.

    (a) had not called
    (b) are not calling
    (c) have not called
    (d) were not calling

11. A: I heard the bride insists on having
       the wedding on a boat.
    B: Very strongly. She ___________
       have it any other way.

    (a) won't
    (b) mustn't
    (c) couldn't
    (d) shouldn't

12. A: Has your brother's move to the US
       worked out?
    B: Yes, except that he has the problem
       of not ___________ English well.

    (a) speaks
    (b) to speak
    (c) speaking
    (d) to be speaking

13. A: How do you sell your coffee?
    B: We sell by ___________ .

    (a) pound
    (b) a pound
    (c) its pound
    (d) the pound

14. A: Why are you in such a good mood?
    B: You won't believe ___________ .

    (a) how wonderful I met a girl
    (b) I met how wonderful a girl
    (c) I met what a wonderful girl
    (d) what a wonderful girl I met

15. A: What did the news say about the
       automobile workers?
    B: ___________ a salary cut, they went
       on strike.

    (a) They feared
    (b) It fearing
    (c) Fearing
    (d) To fear

16. A: I got accepted at two universities,
       but I don't know where to go.
    B: Just choose ___________ you think is
       better for your future.

    (a) that
    (b) which
    (c) whatever
    (d) whichever

17. A: You're out of breath! Did you run
       home?
    B: Yes, there was a school bully
       ___________ me.

    (a) chase
    (b) chased
    (c) chasing
    (d) to chase

18. A: When should we do our homework together?

    B: Let's do it right after ___________ .

    (a) school
    (b) a school
    (c) the school
    (d) our school

19. A: Is there anything exciting on TV?

    B: Not ___________ the moment.

    (a) at
    (b) in
    (c) to
    (d) on

20. A: When do you want to go out for dinner?

    B: Well, ___________ .

    (a) choose to feel free whenever you like
    (b) feel free to choose whenever you like
    (c) free to choose whenever you like to
    (d) choose free whenever you feel to

Part II Questions 21—40

Choose the best answer for the blank.

---

21. With all flights ___________ full, getting a seat seems unlikely.

    (a) far
    (b) most
    (c) much
    (d) almost

22. Whether it rains or not, ___________ .

    (a) the mail always gets delivered
    (b) always gets delivered the mail
    (c) delivered the mail always gets
    (d) gets delivered the mail always

23. After the burglary last week, the elderly couple ___________ to get a burglar alarm installed.

    (a) was decided
    (b) is decided
    (c) decided
    (d) decides

24. ___________ maturity, the adult sperm whales moved to higher latitudes where feeding was more productive.

    (a) Reach
    (b) Reached
    (c) Having reached
    (d) To have reached

25. Children ___________ run the risk of becoming unfit or overweight.

    (a) watch television too much
    (b) too much watching television
    (c) who watch too much television
    (d) who watching television too much

26. Customers may take __________ two of the free gifts that are on display.

(a) any
(b) each
(c) some
(d) every

27. No matter __________ while on exercises, he or she just has to keep going.

(a) how is a soldier tired
(b) how tired a soldier is
(c) tired how is a soldier
(d) is how tired a soldier

28. Although clearly __________, the boxer did not look discouraged.

(a) defeating
(b) defeated
(c) defeats
(d) defeat

29. The new tax reform __________ to benefit low-income workers.

(a) supposes
(b) is supposed
(c) was supposing
(d) was being supposed

30. By last Saturday, construction on the building __________.

(a) is being completed
(b) has been completed
(c) had been completed
(d) will have been completed

31. Perhaps nothing is as surprising to the observer as the __________ of the Grand Canyon.

(a) yet vast intricate landscape
(b) vast yet intricate landscape
(c) vast landscape as yet intricate
(d) landscape as vast yet as intricate

32. Each business must decide __________ potential customers it wants to reach and how it wants to reach them.

(a) whom
(b) where
(c) which
(d) who

33. __________ to stay together, they might have become very successful.

(a) Managed the band
(b) The band had managed
(c) Had the band managed
(d) It had managed the band

34. For over 200 years, the Bill of Rights of the United States Constitution __________ as a barricade in defense of personal freedoms.

(a) are standing
(b) is standing
(c) have stood
(d) has stood

35. By June, Tom __________ about 3,000 dollars and will be able to afford a trip to Europe.

(a) saves
(b) saved
(c) will be saving
(d) will have saved

36. __________ that competition in the telecommunications market has reduced costs.

(a) No indication is whatsoever there
(b) There is no indication whatsoever
(c) Indication is not whatsoever there
(d) Whatsoever is not there indication

37. The student's budget did not permit him to buy __________ an expensive computer.

(a) really
(b) such
(c) too
(d) so

38. According to the spokesman for the Dalai Lama, the Tibetan spiritual leader was discharged from the hospital where he __________ tests for abdominal pain.

(a) will undergo
(b) is undergoing
(c) will be undergoing
(d) had been undergoing

39. There are several kinds of cholesterol, but __________ people should focus on are LDL and HDL.

(a) that
(b) each
(c) them
(d) those

40. Scientists are evaluating __________ of a previously unknown species of prehistoric human ancestor.

(a) evidence
(b) evidences
(c) an evidence
(d) the evidences

Part III Questions 41—45

Identify the option that contains an awkward expression or an error in grammar.

41. (a) A: It was fun coming over to see your new apartment.

(b) B: I'm glad you enjoy it. I'm sorry that it was so messy.

(c) A: Don't worry. I'm sure you'll be settled in soon.

(d) B: Yeah, I should have everything unpacked by Sunday.

42. (a) A: Shall we meet for dinner next Saturday evening?

(b) B: Oh, no. Unfortunately, Saturday isn't good to me.

(c) A: Then, how about meeting up on Sunday?

(d) B: OK. That would be great. Let's make it 7:30.

43. (a) A: Why are you such nervous today?

(b) B: I have a job interview tomorrow.

(c) A: That explains it. Good luck.

(d) B: Thanks. I need it.

44. (a) A: You should better not spend all of your allowance at once.

(b) B: But there are so many things I want to buy.

(c) A: Just remember that you won't get your next allowance until February.

(d) B: You're right. Thanks for the reminder.

45. (a) A: Just yesterday I discovered some old oil paintings up in my mom's attic.

(b) B: You just discovered them? You had never been in her attic before?

(c) A: Yes, but hidden behind furniture, I never realized they were up there.

(d) B: They could bring you a huge windfall. I'd get them appraised if I were you.

Part IV   Questions 46—50

Identify the option that contains an awkward expression or an error in grammar.

46. (a) When was the last time you accomplished something big? (b) Most likely you were engaged in an activity that stirred your passion. (c) Passion is a powerfully motivating force what can drive you to achieve your goals. (d) When driven by passion, you are more likely to succeed than when driven by other, external forces.

47. (a) Ex-convict Tyrone White now warns teenage students against joining gangs. (b) Until being released from prison, he has been speaking at schools about his criminal past. (c) His hope is that other youths will not make the same mistakes he did. (d) In his opinion, it is unlikely that they will after they hear what happened to him.

48. (a) Because Andrew did not understand Stacey's mood swings, he avoided her, which just made matters worse. (b) He thought her bouts of emotional instability were an indication that something was wrong with her. (c) One minute she would appear to be happy, even euphoric, and the next then she was angry and depressed. (d) Stacey, meanwhile, felt she was misunderstood by Andrew and refused to see a psychiatrist.

49. (a) Today's shuttle astronauts are usually in orbit only 250 miles above Earth's surface. (b) From that distance, they can view an amazingly detailed and ever-changing global panorama. (c) They can see the varying shades of blue and turquoise that mark the intermingling of oceans and rivers. (d) Such views are a dramatic reminder that two-thirds of Earth's surface are covered by water.

50. (a) Cloning is the process of making a copy of an organism using its genetic material. (b) Scientists have so far managed to make clones of dogs, horses, sheep and cows, but not humans. (c) If scientists can clone humans, however, the clone would never be an exact copy. (d) Like identical twins, human clones would share DNA but not minds or memories.

This is the end of the Grammar section. Do NOT move on to the next section until instructed to do so. You are NOT allowed to turn to any other section of the test.

VOCABULARY

DIRECTIONS

This part of the exam tests your vocabulary skills. You will have 15 minutes to complete the 50 questions. Be sure to follow the directions given by the proctor.

Part I   Questions 1—25

Choose the best answer for the blank.

---

1. A: Hi, Brad. I didn't think I'd see you at the mall.

B: Oh, hi, Mandy. I didn't __________ you here either!

(a) greet
(b) catch
(c) expect
(d) welcome

2. A: Do you need help with that box?

B: Yes, I can't __________ it by myself.

(a) fix
(b) lift
(c) pile
(d) stick

3. A: Hello, Dr. Lupe's office. How may I help you?

B: Hi, I'd like to make a(n) __________ to see Dr. Lupe.

(a) deal
(b) notice
(c) invitation
(d) appointment

4. A: Andrew is always breaking the house rules.

B: I know. He never __________ them.

(a) tries
(b) does
(c) follows
(d) protects

5. A: I hear you passed your biology final!

B: Yes, I'm really __________ that's over.

(a) settled
(b) relieved
(c) confused
(d) established

6. A: Do you promise to be home on time?

B: Yes, you __________.

(a) drag your feet
(b) have my word
(c) cut to the chase
(d) go the extra mile

7. A: Is the Eurail pass best for exploring Europe by train?

B: Oh, yes, you'll find it cheap and __________.

(a) plain
(b) basic
(c) comforting
(d) convenient

8. A: Don't forget to cut the lawn today.

B: Yes, I'll have to get fuel for the __________.

(a) razor
(b) scissor
(c) mower
(d) clipper

9. A: It looks like we'll land only 30
        minutes behind schedule.
    B: Still, we'll have to hurry to catch our
        ___________ flight.

    (a) connecting
    (b) matching
    (c) linking
    (d) joining

10. A: You should put on a darker tie.
    B: But this is the darkest one I have in
        my ___________.

    (a) wear
    (b) clothes
    (c) fashions
    (d) wardrobe

11. A: Let's meet somewhere that's easy to
        find.
    B: How about the war memorial? It's
        the best-known ___________ in the
        city.

    (a) landmark
    (b) oversight
    (c) guidepost
    (d) foundation

12. A: Do you think I should take an
        umbrella?
    B: I would. I heard we might get a bit
        of a ___________.

    (a) flood
    (b) liquid
    (c) splash
    (d) drizzle

13. A: Pardon me. Am I headed the right
        way to get downtown?
    B: No, it's in the ___________ direction.

    (a) reverse
    (b) contrary
    (c) opposite
    (d) backward

14. A: Do you enjoy dancing?
    B: If I weren't so ___________, I might.

    (a) clumsy
    (b) sneaky
    (c) tacky
    (d) hasty

15. A: Did you ___________ the spare
        room?
    B: No, I'll go open the windows now.

    (a) clear out
    (b) wind up
    (c) free up
    (d) air out

16. A: Are you enjoying the fried potatoes?
    B: No. They're too ___________.

    (a) slippery
    (b) choosy
    (c) greasy
    (d) racy

17. A: How did your brother find your
        diary?
    B: He ___________ through my dresser.

    (a) strolled
    (b) thumbed
    (c) pondered
    (d) rummaged

18. A: Why don't we just buy a computer now and pay later?

B: Yes, it's probably best to buy it on _____________.

(a) offer
(b) credit
(c) warranty
(d) guarantee

19. A: I hate it when people spit in the street.

B: Me, too. It's _____________.

(a) brutal
(b) lavish
(c) morbid
(d) repulsive

20. A: I heard you were all set to be married abroad.

B: Yeah. I just need to get a proof of my current marital _____________.

(a) class
(b) level
(c) status
(d) position

21. A: The songs on this CD are so _____________.

B: I agree. It's quite comforting.

(a) scathing
(b) seething
(c) soothing
(d) salivating

22. A: I'm really nervous about teaching my first class.

B: Don't _____________. You'll do fine.

(a) push it
(b) ditch it
(c) blow it
(d) sweat it

23. A: I'm going to complain about having to do mandatory overtime.

B: I wouldn't do that. You'll run the risk of seeming _____________.

(a) refractory
(b) moribund
(c) tractable
(d) jocular

24. A: I regret not investing in gold earlier, when the price was low.

B: Well, if I were you, I wouldn't waste time _____________ over what's past.

(a) straining
(b) actuating
(c) ruminating
(d) exacerbating

25. A: Robert's unusual behavior puts me off sometimes.

B: Yes, he does have his _____________.

(a) fortes
(b) quirks
(c) lesions
(d) baubles

26. Fortunately, all the passengers in the car __________ the accident because they were wearing seat belts.

    (a) missed
    (b) survived
    (c) destroyed
    (d) experienced

27. In times of economic __________, the government needs to take strong steps to solve the country's financial problems.

    (a) dilemma
    (b) plague
    (c) crisis
    (d) riot

28. Police are urging Internet users not to reveal __________ information such as bank account numbers or addresses unless they are sure a site is secure.

    (a) common
    (b) personal
    (c) general
    (d) minor

29. Historian Jason Sanders recently __________ new facts about Maya origins.

    (a) directed
    (b) designed
    (c) decreased
    (d) discovered

30. An adult dog generally only requires one or two meals a day to get __________ nutrition for good health.

    (a) ordinary
    (b) sufficient
    (c) occasional
    (d) influential

31. Most __________ of the movie has centered around its lack of originality.

    (a) survey
    (b) criticism
    (c) deflation
    (d) measurement

32. Over two million __________ of the singer-songwriter's album have been sold.

    (a) hits
    (b) issues
    (c) copies
    (d) chapters

33. One trick that can be used by interior designers to make a room feel larger is __________ tiles diagonally from corner to corner.

    (a) tying
    (b) laying
    (c) holding
    (d) burying

34. Once your real estate __________ is complete, our mortgage company will offer you a vacation package as a special gift.

   (a) expenditure
   (b) transaction
   (c) commerce
   (d) brokerage

35. These plants will __________ if they are put in rich soil and have access to sunlight and water.

   (a) reside
   (b) uphold
   (c) expand
   (d) flourish

36. Not expecting such a great welcome, the singer was __________ at the applause she received upon entering the auditorium.

   (a) illuminated
   (b) promoted
   (c) shocked
   (d) spotted

37. This textbook series is guaranteed to increase your __________ in English communication.

   (a) competence
   (b) edification
   (c) usability
   (d) latitude

38. __________ gloves can be used by doctors only once, and then must be discarded.

   (a) Reachable
   (b) Disposable
   (c) Retractable
   (d) Containable

39. Some spiders __________ their prey near by displaying attractively colored stripes on their bodies.

   (a) lure
   (b) fumble
   (c) enslave
   (d) contract

40. A fan of murder mysteries, Brian could not __________ why his wife enjoyed reading romance novels so much.

   (a) unfold
   (b) fathom
   (c) acquire
   (d) beguile

41. After test digs are done to reveal the most promising areas, archaeologists will begin a full __________.

   (a) manipulation
   (b) restoration
   (c) fabrication
   (d) excavation

42. Andrea learned to be __________ from her mother, who always looked for bargains.

   (a) frugal
   (b) meager
   (c) affluent
   (d) diminutive

43. The meeting will run more smoothly if __________ interpretation of Russian and English is provided.

   (a) simultaneous
   (b) exchanging
   (c) desolate
   (d) residual

44. Some religious leaders complain that science has undermined spirituality and led to a more __________ society.

(a) secular
(b) mediocre
(c) entranced
(d) conscientious

45. Distinctive watermarks are often added to official documents such as transcripts, making them harder to __________.

(a) pursue
(b) detect
(c) shred
(d) forge

46. Although 70 percent of the population remains rural, Indians are steadily __________ paddy fields for a city lifestyle.

(a) rebuking
(b) forsaking
(c) irrigating
(d) engaging

47. The *Car Buyer's Guide* includes everything you need to know about car shopping, including invaluable tips on __________ for the best possible price.

(a) gabbing
(b) haggling
(c) jabbering
(d) swaggering

48. Couples with children should only resort to divorce when they are so __________ that reconciliation is inconceivable.

(a) gravitated
(b) evacuated
(c) estranged
(d) gestated

49. To win formal debates, you must learn to quickly distinguish valid arguments from __________ ones.

(a) specious
(b) effectual
(c) morose
(d) ardent

50. The excellent navigational ability of bats can be __________ to their sensitivity to Earth's magnetic fields.

(a) positioned
(b) attributed
(c) modified
(d) justified

This is the end of the Vocabulary section. Do NOT move on to the Reading Comprehension section until instructed to do so. You are NOT allowed to turn to any other section of the test.

READING COMPREHENSION

Part I Questions 1—16
Read the passage. Then choose the option that best completes the passage.

1. As many as 24 published studies have shown a link between abortion and breast cancer. Some studies show that women who have had abortions have a 50 percent greater chance of getting cancer than those whose pregnancies were not terminated. One study found high instances of cancer among women who, in the former Soviet Union, had commonly used abortion as a means of contraception. Between 1960 and 1987, the rate of breast cancer among such women tripled. A similar phenomenon is found in other places where ________________________.

(a) women use faulty contraceptives
(b) abortion is a common practice
(c) there are low rates of cancer
(d) the birth rate is declining

2. Illegal immigration is once again at the forefront of state policy discussions. In examining the scope of the problem, the State of Michigan has issued a report which provides an objective estimate of the cost incurred by illegal immigrants who are in violation of federal and state law. The report also addresses weaknesses in the current ID system and the way in which these can impact homeland security. This alarming report ultimately finds that the State of Michigan should ________________________.

(a) act now to better secure its borders
(b) recognize the contributions of immigrants
(c) produce an estimate of lost revenues
(d) start categorizing immigrants differently

3. A new book by Clarke Snell and Tim Callahan, *Building Green*, provides green-minded home builders with 615 full-color pages of detailed explanations and how-tos. It chronicles, for example, the process of building a home with clay, cordwood, straw and organic roof materials. The two authors approach the book's projects from different perspectives: one from an environmentalist's point of view and the other from a seasoned commercial builder's. But it is a combination that covers all ground on the subject. At less than $20, this book is a bargain for ________________________.

(a) those looking to build their own suburban dream home
(b) experienced home builders interested in saving money
(c) anyone considering environmentally-friendly housing
(d) students and professionals of architecture and design

4. The way your furniture is arranged may dictate the kind of life you lead. If your living room is full of armchairs with strategically positioned reading lights, then you are likely to read a lot. If the most comfortable places to sit all face the TV, which is prominently situated in the living room, then you will spend considerable time watching TV. So, next time you redo your house or room, __________________________________.

(a) look for indirect lighting fixtures to protect your eyes
(b) save money by visiting some local second-hand stores
(c) try to position furniture to suit the life you want to live
(d) remember it is OK to be bold and think outside the box

5.

Dear Mr. Collins,

Please accept my heartiest congratulations on your achieving initial sales of 100,000 units. This accomplishment greatly impressed me and should fill you with confidence with regard to your future. No one else has achieved such a high level of sales in their first six months with our firm, and so arrangements are being made to present you with a token of my appreciation. My secretary will contact you shortly. I

__________________________________.

Sincerely yours,
J. H. Kim, CEO.

(a) hope that you will get well soon
(b) would like to hear from you again
(c) look forward to your continued success
(d) would be glad to have you on board with us

6. This Public Announcement has been issued to ________________________.
The Department of State advises US citizens to consider carefully the risks of travel to Nicaragua due to the unresolved political situation in the country. On November 9, 2008, "municipal elections took place across Nicaragua. Physical violence between law enforcement and protesters followed and witnesses have reported numerous injuries. The situation remains fluid and risks to the personal safety of expatriates and tourists continue. Protections ordinarily afforded by the rule of law are not guaranteed.

(a) update tourists on the risks of natural disaster in Nicaragua
(b) inform travelers of the security situation in Nicaragua
(c) warn Americans to depart Nicaragua immediately
(d) notify residents of Nicaragua's municipal election

7. Death rates in the Stone Age, like those of today, were highest among infants and dropped throughout childhood. Many early fatalities in certain groups were from infanticide and may have been the result of the parents' financial troubles. Furthermore, while fictional stories of Stone Age conditions probably overstated the dangers of wild-animal attacks, lions, hyenas and poisonous snakes were ever-present menaces and took a steady toll on human life, with ________________________.

(a) infanticide being most common
(b) children being especially vulnerable
(c) few means of defense being available
(d) mortality rates often being unaffected

8. Recent research has revealed that in some communication situations, ________________________. Indeed, this very point has become the central focus of an exciting new area of study known as kinesics. Research has revealed that over 700,000 possible expressions can be communicated through gesture, facial expression, eye contact and posture. Moreover, on certain occasions, these signals deliver much of the meaning communicated by speakers. When a speaker's body language is not consistent with their speech, listeners will simply go with what they perceive from their body language.

(a) gesture is often the key to comprehension
(b) people trust their eyes less than their ears
(c) non-verbal communication is not trustworthy
(d) speech and body coordination is closely related

9. Modern British drama is said to have begun around 1890, and until the 1930s it
_______________________________. The Edwardian Age (1901-1910) had a distinctive
political character, but its dramas were not significantly different from those before or
that followed. The Great War period (1914-1918) infused British drama with new
themes, but its basic forms and techniques largely remained the same. It was not until the
Great Depression and the rise of capitalism and fascism in the 30s that any significant
developments emerged.

(a) saw little change or innovation in its form
(b) was viewed as too radical by theater-goers
(c) could be divided into three distinct periods
(d) had a tremendous impact on American drama

10. Although research shows that workers generally lose enthusiasm for their jobs after the
first couple of years of employment, employers should _______________________________.
Experts refer to this attitude shift as the "honeymoon effect," where enthusiasm remains
high for the first year of employment but then drops over the next 2-3 years. Ironically,
this is when most employees work at their optimum level, benefitting from the training
they received upon being hired. This fact coupled with the potential financial burden of
hiring and training new staff is thus a major incentive for employers to remotivate less
enthusiastic workers.

(a) terminate any employees who lack motivation
(b) find ways to reinspire unenthusiastic workers
(c) begin large-scale hiring of fresh employees
(d) cut back on overly expensive training programs

11. Sometime in the near future, the Benbo College Theatre Department will
_______________________________. The College has obtained a storage facility of
11,800 square feet, some two-tenths of a mile from the main campus. This acquisition
enables Benbo College to stage extra theatrical performances and offer more fine arts
programs. The extra facilities will feature a backstage technical center for set design,
production and rehearsal purposes. A patio theatre area will also be used for public
theatre performances outdoors.

(a) add to the number of yearly theater performances it hosts
(b) increase arts offerings on campus and in the community
(c) be relocating to a facility slightly off the main campus
(d) expand its program for majors in theater design

12. Austrian researcher Irenäus Eibl-Eibesfeldt studied the facial expressions of a group of children who had been blind from birth. Amazingly, when he compared these facial expressions with those of sighted children, nearly identical expressions were produced for sadness, happiness, fear and anger. In fact, the same patterns of muscular activity were used to express emotion by both groups. Blind children could not have learned these behaviors through imitation. Thus, the research strongly suggests that emotional expression is _________________________________.

(a) a manifestation of normal intelligence
(b) a genetic characteristic shared by all humans
(c) an acquired action in the case of blind children
(d) an example of different body languages across cultures

13. Advertising Archives holds over four million British and American press advertisements and illustrations dating from the 19th century up to today. All products and services that have been advertised over the past 150 years have been collected, classified and catalogued in our rich collection. We have also _________________________________, such as Romance, Self-Improvement, Sci-Fi, Innovations, Sports, Race and Religion, Politics, Westerns, and more.

(a) solicited ideas on topics
(b) created ads of various genres
(c) cross-referenced all ads by theme
(d) collected extensive literature in categories

14. A tiny fossil skull excavated within 195-million-year-old Chinese sediments now provides proof that essential traits of mammal anatomy developed over 45 million years earlier than previously thought. The well-preserved fossil features several components of mammals; most importantly, there is no groove in the back of the jawbone. This demonstrates that the three bones of the middle ear were parted from the ancient animal's mandible. Such a separation can be observed in modern mammals but not in reptiles. The significance of this discovery is that it _________________________________.

(a) proves that mammals lived among reptiles
(b) traces the development of hearing among reptiles
(c) changes the timeline for the evolution of mammals
(d) indicates that human ancestors did have a large brain

15. In the 16th century, superior varieties of plant species that already existed in Europe were found in the New World. For example, beans were found that were far plumper and richer. Before long, these were brought back to Europe and displaced the fibrous, chewy variety of beans grown there. _________________________________, once Europeans got sight and taste of the fat, sumptuous strawberries that grew wild in America, they gladly abandoned the mushy little button strawberries that they were used to.

(a) And yet
(b) Likewise
(c) Therefore
(d) In contrast

16. Copyright law seeks to achieve a balance between the rights of copyright owners and the interests of society. To this end, the fair use doctrine was worked out through numerous court decisions and was eventually codified in the Copyright Act of 1976. Fair use excludes the necessity to get permission or pay royalties for such purposes as news reporting, teaching and scholarships. The act does not clearly indicate, however, what is permitted and what is not. _________________________________, the user must determine on a case-by-case basis whether or not his or her use is fair.

(a) Consequently
(b) Nonetheless
(c) Additionally
(d) Meanwhile

> **Part II** **Questions 17—37**
>
> Read the passage and the question. Then choose the option that best answers the question.

17. Believing that the mentally ill were affected by the moon, the Romans coined the term "lunatic." They came up with this name because "luna" is Latin for moon. The Romans also thought that as the moon got fuller, lunatics became more and more insane. For centuries, people continued to have this belief. Today we know better, but the word "lunatic" is still sometimes used to describe a person with mental problems.

Q: What is the passage mainly about?
(a) The lunatics of ancient Rome
(b) The origins of the word "lunatic"
(c) Ways the moon affects mental health
(d) Attitudes towards mental illness in Rome

18. With the help of *Getting Into Universities* and a little luck, you can gain admission to the university of your choice. This book gives you a comprehensive overview of the entry process, from applications, financial aid and interviews to SATs, ACTs and waiting lists. It has the latest information on new admissions procedures, from revised early action plans to the way colleges are dealing with the new 2,400-point SAT. Take the mystery out of university entry—pick up a copy of *Getting Into Universities* today!

Q: What is the advertised book mainly about?
(a) Deciding on a major in college
(b) Getting top scores to get into a university
(c) Selecting a university that is easy to enter
(d) Understanding university admissions processes

19. Enjoy perfect sunsets every day at Selosa Cove, Singapore's most exclusive marina residential community. Close to world-class leisure amenities and just minutes away from Singapore's Central Business District, Selosa Cove is the ideal location for your dream home. With breathtaking ocean views, magnificent waterways and a championship golf course, Selosa Cove truly is one of the world's most desirable addresses.

Q: What is the advertisement mainly about?
(a) A coastal residential area in Singapore
(b) A Singapore-based business opportunity
(c) A first-class vacation package to Singapore
(d) A stay at Singapore's most luxurious resort

20.

Dear Ms. Burling-Ward

I am enjoying my time as a new employee at Stegner Publishing, and you in particular have been most welcoming and helpful. However, I wish to point out that the position you advertised and that I was interviewed for was Production Editor. Yet during my three weeks here, I have only done copyediting. After learning from the Director yesterday that this is not a training stage but my permanent position, I suspect there has been a misunderstanding. I hope we can meet soon to clarify this situation.

Sincerely,
Jacob Brodie

Q: What is Jacob Brodie's main purpose for writing the letter?
(a) To express gratitude for help he received
(b) To apologize for misunderstanding his task
(c) To point out a discrepancy in his work duties
(d) To inquire about a new production editor's job

21. The second half of the 19th century was the age of Realism, a time when painters sought to depict nature and contemporary life in an accurate and objective way. During this period, religious paintings tended to focus on the daily aspects of human experience to convey the presence of the divine, rather than on traditional subjects such as the cross or angels. For example, the Realist painter Jean-Francois Millet, in his painting called *The Angelus*, depicts a peasant couple in a field who have stopped work to pray in quiet devotion. Though poor laborers, they are presented as holy.

Q: What is the writer's main point about the religious paintings of Realist painters?
(a) They showed the divine in everyday life.
(b) They often depicted major religious events.
(c) They were strongly influenced by the work of Millet.
(d) They were created using traditional painting techniques.

22. New research has found that damage to a certain part of the brain can stop the urge to smoke. The research was inspired by a man who had suffered brain damage during a stroke and simply "forgot" his smoking addiction. He stopped smoking without cravings or even a conscious desire to quit. The portion of his brain that sustained damage was the insula. The finding suggests that development of future aids to help people quit smoking should target this region of the brain.

Q: What is the best title for the passage?
(a) Treatments for Stroke Damage Target the Insula
(b) Smoking Addiction Seen As a Major Cause of Strokes
(c) Certain Brain Regions More Severely Affected by Addictions
(d) Area of Brain Responsible for Smoking Addiction Discovered

23. Although a star in his native India since being awarded the 1998 Nobel Prize in Economics, Amartya Sen is otherwise little known outside of academic spheres in the West. Nevertheless, his theories have had a global impact. Sen has made major contributions to social choice theory, welfare economics, economic measurements and development economics. He has also conducted comprehensive research on the factors of famine and the fundamental mechanisms behind poverty.

Q: Which of the following is correct about Amartya Sen according to the passage?
(a) He won the 1998 Nobel Peace Prize.
(b) He is the world's most famous economist.
(c) He contributed ideas on globalization theory.
(d) He has studied causes of famine and poverty.

24. Archaeologists are hailing the discovery of well-preserved eight-million-year-old cypress trees at a mine in eastern Hungary. The discovery was made after coal miners uncovered some ancient trees that had turned to coal. Archaeologists then dug deeper and found 16 cypress trees preserved in sand. The find is exceptional, as all of the trees have kept their wooden structure and not turned into coal or become petrified. Scientists are taking steps to protect the trees, which cannot be exposed to air or sunlight.

Q: Which of the following is correct about the 16 preserved trees according to the report?
(a) Miners led to their discovery.
(b) They were found buried in mud.
(c) Some of them had turned into coal.
(d) Sunlight is needed for them to survive.

25. The brain is made up of two cerebral hemispheres, one on the right and the other on the left. Generally, the left hemisphere controls the right side of the body, whereas the right hemisphere controls the left side. Similarly, sensory information from the right side of the body is taken in by the left hemisphere of the brain, while sensory input to the left side of the body is received by the right hemisphere. The corpus callosum, which is found in the longitudinal crevice that bridges the two hemispheres, allows them to communicate with each other. Without it, the two hemispheres would function independently.

Q: Which of the following is correct according to the passage?
(a) The left hemisphere of the brain controls the left side of the body.
(b) The right hemisphere of the brain does not receive sensory input.
(c) The corpus callosum is located in between the two hemispheres.
(d) The corpus callosum enables the hemispheres to operate independently.

26. Cavities may become a thing of the past thanks to an unlikely source of medicine—tobacco. Doctors and researchers at Guy's Hospital in London have come up with what appears to be an effective cavity vaccine, derived from a genetically altered tobacco plant. The resulting vaccine is clear, odorless and tasteless, and it is not injected but applied directly to the teeth. However, the scientists believe that this vaccine will not be effective after a year.

Q: Which of the following is correct about the vaccine according to the passage?
(a) It is made from common tobacco plants.
(b) It has a taste similar to chewing tobacco.
(c) It has to be applied directly to a patient's gums.
(d) It cannot prevent cavities for longer than a year.

27. Even dietary supplements purchased at a reputable store may be unsafe. While most supplements are safe, studies have found a dozen that should not be on sale due to the dangers they pose to human health. These supplements include aristolochia, an herb associated with kidney failure and cancer, as well as chaparral, comfrey and kava, all of which could cause liver failure. Even so, these supplements said to be harmful can be purchased without difficulty over the Internet and in retail stores.

Q: Which of the following is correct according to the passage?
(a) All dietary supplements are relatively safe.
(b) Kava and aristolochia are linked to kidney failure.
(c) Some harmful supplements are still on the market.
(d) Unsafe supplements can be purchased online only.

28.

Dear Mr. Henley

I am writing to apply for the advertised position of Human Resources Director. As my enclosed résumé outlines, I have had considerable experience in the area, including extensive training of human resources managers. I have also lectured on the subject before university students and professional associations. Although I am currently living overseas, I will be in Boston for one month beginning February 27. I would be glad to meet with you then to discuss your needs and my qualifications.

Yours sincerely,
Jacqueline Landon

Q: Which of the following is correct about Jacqueline Landon according to the letter?
(a) She is looking for someone to head the Human Resources Department.
(b) She is practically a novice in training human resources managers.
(c) She has given talks to students and professionals.
(d) She will stay in Boston until late April.

29. A senior nuclear expert has exposed efforts to steal a total of 88 pounds of radioactive substances from highly secured facilities in Russia over the last 10 years, hinting that its huge stocks are in greater danger than was previously thought. Western officials already know of 70 attempts to misappropriate nuclear materials. However, Viktor Kuznetsov, a former Russian top nuclear safety inspector, now insists that the authorities have concealed another 30 instances. Kuznetsov is concerned that terrorist groups could attain these nuclear materials.

Q: What information have Russian officials hidden from the public?
(a) News of radioactive leaks from nuclear plants
(b) Lists of Russian contacts with Western nuclear experts
(c) Data on the quantity of nuclear materials still stocked
(d) Facts about attempted thefts of nuclear materials

30. Yom Kippur, the Jewish day of repentance, is regarded as the holiest and most dignified Jewish holiday. Its rituals of fasting and praying are carried out even among the majority of non-practicing Jews. The number of people attending synagogue on this day is often double or even triple the regular number. In Israel, television broadcasts and public transportation are shut down and the airports are closed. With very little traffic around, children everywhere ride their bicycles out in the streets, which has led to Yom Kippur earning the nickname "Festival of Bicycles."

Q: Which of the following is correct about Yom Kippur according to the passage?
(a) It celebrates the deliverance of the Jewish people.
(b) It is observed with rowdy banquets and songs.
(c) It draws larger crowds to worship than usual.
(d) It coincides with the "Festival of Bicycles."

31. All Smitty's Gifts Online products are shipped throughout the United States using the Super Express courier service. Orders within the US are subject to delivery charges ranging from $4 to $20, depending on weight and destination. Please be aware that the minimum order amount for delivery is $30. All orders placed on Friday and Saturday are shipped Monday, or, for an additional $8, we can expedite your order so that it is shipped Saturday. International shipping is only available for selected items.

Q: Which of the following is correct according to the passage?
(a) Delivery costs are uniform throughout the US.
(b) No shipping is available for orders under $30.
(c) Orders can be shipped Saturday for no extra charge.
(d) All items are eligible for shipping outside of the US.

32. Term papers must adhere to the following guidelines. First, plagiarism will not be tolerated. University policy states that students found guilty of plagiarism will be expelled. It is better to hand in work that is inelegantly written than to turn in something that is not authentic. Second, papers should be about 7-10 pages, but length can be negotiated. Third, the topic is to be chosen by you, but must be approved beforehand. Finally, extensions will be granted only if the request is submitted in writing at least one month in advance.

Q: Which of the following is correct according to the instructions?
(a) Students who commit plagiarism may be suspended.
(b) No term paper more than 10 pages long will be accepted.
(c) The professor will assign a research topic to each student.
(d) Students may postpone the due date by a written request.

33. In colleges and universities across the US, new faculty members begin as lecturers or assistant professors and move up to associate professorships and, eventually, full professorships. To obtain these promotions they must conduct research, teach courses and publish a substantial number of books and articles. They also have to compete for grants to finance their research. Higher education is an extremely competitive field, and so academics must work long hours with great dedication to get ahead.

Q: What can be inferred from the passage?
(a) University professors are largely underpaid.
(b) New faculty members are unlikely to have published much.
(c) Professors often find current research funding inadequate.
(d) Many faculty members prefer doing research than lecturing.

34. People worldwide are concerned about the pervasive influence of Western culture. Some see it as becoming more dominant as a result of globalization and fear that it now threatens cultural diversity. Indeed, they increasingly use the terms "cultural hegemony" and "monoculturalism" with reference to the West. A Western cultural presence can be found across the globe in such things as movies, music, clothing and television. However, does the presence of Western pop culture products mean that a cultural takeover is in progress, or that it is occurring against the will of a local population?

Q: What will most likely be discussed next?
(a) Cases which prove that people adopt Western culture voluntarily
(b) Influences of the American entertainment industry worldwide
(c) A way to promote domestic culture over imported culture
(d) A clarification of the expression "cultural hegemony"

35. The *Voynich manuscript*, a 16th-century book written in an unknown language, may be nothing more than a hoax, according to linguist Gordon Rugg, head of the Knowledge Modeling Group at England's Keele University. Rugg used 16th-century techniques to generate random text that was as linguistically complex as that of the manuscript. By producing the same amount of text per page, he found that most pages of the manuscript could be replicated in one to two hours by one person. Rugg concluded that the manuscript's text is probably a hoax rather than some form of elaborate code.

Q: What can be inferred about the *Voynich manuscript* from the passage?
(a) It was most likely not written in the 16th century.
(b) Rugg does not believe that it contains valuable information.
(c) It was written in a complex language that has now been lost.
(d) Rugg used computer analysis for his work on the manuscript.

36. We live in a time when people famous for being good at one thing decide they must be multitalented. And whether they are or not, they still get attention. Take Sir Paul McCartney, singer and songwriter, who, now also seeing himself as a poet, has just published a book of poetry. There is no denying McCartney's legacy, but it is unlikely this little collection will take the literary world by storm. It does not seem fair that a work no better or worse than those of thousands of "wannabes" should receive the spotlight just because its author is famous.

Q: What can be inferred about the writer?
(a) He enjoys reading the latest in poetry.
(b) He believes in judging art on merit alone.
(c) He is a huge fan of Paul McCartney's poetry.
(d) He admires artists that try other professions.

37. According to UNESCO, over 50 percent of the world's 6,900 languages are endangered, and one language disappears every two weeks on average. If nothing is done, 90 percent of the world's languages could go extinct in the next two centuries. The loss does not just extend to oral traditions. Written traditions are suffering neglect and, in some cases, physical disintegration. Like biodiversity in many parts of the planet, linguistic diversity is declining fast, but the media have done a better job of publicizing the former than the latter.

Q: What does the writer suggest about linguistic diversity?
(a) Its loss is an unstoppable trend.
(b) It is closely linked with biodiversity.
(c) It does not receive the attention it deserves.
(d) Its decline is mainly due to human arrogance.

Part III   **Questions 38 — 40**

Read the passage. Then identify the option that does NOT belong.

38. Several Spanish radio stations are available in this region for Spanish speakers. (a) KABQ features Spanish and English programming with news items in Spanish and English every hour. (b) KA's Channel 12 cable programming includes reruns of *Bonanza* and *The Rockford Files*. (c) KALY features top 40 Spanish pop music with commentary in either English or Spanish. (d) And KARS is a country music station whose programming is exclusively in Spanish.

39. In creating sculptural artwork to celebrate rock music, Shinro Ohtake decided to dispense with people. (a) The 43-year-old Japanese artist's installation features three electric guitars, a drum kit and some Marshall amps. (b) Marshall amps are a standard in the music industry, known for their quality and solid construction. (c) On a wooden stage, the instruments are connected to stands and are played by robotic arms attached to cables. (d) When operating, the installation gives an automated musical performance in honor of rock music.

40. Taking notes is very important in business negotiations. (a) Writing information down during negotiations engages other parts of your brain as well as your eyes and fingers while you listen. (b) This helps with concentration and remembering salient points, which might be difficult otherwise. (c) When you write, be sure to make your notes legible so you can go over them and reconstruct the negotiation in your head. (d) The legibility of your writing will invariably affect the faith and confidence your potential employers have in you.

This is the end of the Reading Comprehension section. Please remain seated until the proctor has instructed otherwise. You are NOT allowed to turn to any other section of the test.

Listening Comprehension

Grammar

Vocabulary

Reading Comprehension

LISTENING COMPREHENSION

DIRECTIONS

1. In the Listening Comprehension section, all content will be presented orally rather than in written form.

2. This section contains 4 parts. In parts I and II, each passage will be read only once. In parts III and IV, each passage and its corresponding question will be read twice. But in all sections, the options will be read only once. After listening to the passage and question, listen to the options and choose the best answer.

Part I **Questions 1—15**

You will now hear fifteen conversation fragments, each made up of a single spoken statement followed by four spoken responses. Choose the most appropriate response to the statement.

Part II **Questions 16—30**

You will now hear fifteen conversation fragments, each made up of three spoken statements followed by four spoken responses. Choose the most appropriate response to complete the conversation.

Part III　**Questions 31—45**

You will now hear fifteen complete conversations. For each item, you will hear a conversation and its corresponding question, both of which will be read twice. Then you will hear four options which will be read only once. Choose the option that best answers the question.

Part IV　**Questions 46—60**

You will now hear fifteen spoken monologues. For each item, you will hear a monologue and its corresponding question, both of which will be read twice. Then you will hear four options which will be read only once. Choose the option that best answers the question.

GRAMMAR

DIRECTIONS

This part of the exam tests your grammar skills. You will have 25 minutes to complete the 50 questions. Be sure to follow the directions given by the proctor.

Part I   **Questions 1—20**

Choose the best answer for the blank.

---

1. A: Who do you think is our club's best tennis player?

B: Jonathan Coleman. He just keeps __________.

(a) wins
(b) to win
(c) winning
(d) having won

2. A: Let's meet at 2 o'clock in front of the mall entrance.

B: OK, __________ you there.

(a) I see
(b) I'll see
(c) I've seen
(d) I'm seeing

3. A: What's the name of that singer on the radio?

B: Sorry, I have no idea __________ the singer is.

(a) who
(b) which
(c) whom
(d) whatever

4. A: Why are you smiling?

B: I was thinking of a joke __________.

(a) me my brother told
(b) my brother told me
(c) my brother to me told
(d) to me my brother told

5. A: Good afternoon. I'm Brian. I called earlier about your job ad.

B: Of course. __________ you.

(a) I expect
(b) I'm expecting
(c) I've been expecting
(d) I'll have been expecting

6. A: I'm too sick to go on the school field trip today.

B: Then, I'll tell your teacher __________.

(a) your coming to it not
(b) to it your not coming
(c) aren't you coming
(d) you aren't coming

7. A: I think I'll submit these photos to the model agency.

B: But not one of them __________ a full-body shot.

(a) is
(b) are
(c) was
(d) were

8. A: Susan can't go to the mall with us today.

B: Really? That's __________.

(a) shame
(b) a shame
(c) the shame
(d) one shame

9. A: Will you come skiing this weekend?

    B: Well, I probably __________, if not for an assignment I have due.

(a) will
(b) was
(c) would
(d) am going to

10. A: Can I use your calculator?

    B: Only if you promise __________ me your class notes.

(a) lend
(b) to lend
(c) lending
(d) to have lent

11. A: What do you think of the government's new tax proposal?

    B: I __________.

(a) approve it not at all
(b) don't at all approve it
(c) approve not at all of it
(d) don't approve of it at all

12. A: Can you help me with this calculation?

    B: Sorry, I'm not __________ good at math.

(a) far
(b) any
(c) such
(d) rather

13. A: Do you know __________ at the ceremony?

    B: We have to be there by 6 pm.

(a) are we when expected to arrive
(b) we are expected to arrive when
(c) when we are expected to arrive
(d) to arrive when we are expected

14. A: Enjoy your trip, and don't forget to call.

    B: Don't worry. I'll phone you as soon as I __________.

(a) am arriving
(b) will arrive
(c) arrived
(d) arrive

15. A: What did the President say in his speech?

    B: I didn't hear it, so I have no idea __________.

(a) what was about it
(b) what it was about
(c) that it was of what
(d) of what about it was

16. A: Do I need to take any tests, Doctor?

    B: No, you __________.

(a) don't need
(b) don't need to
(c) don't need to do
(d) don't need to take

17. A: I mentioned to Bradley that you're planning to quit your job.

    B: But I didn't want him to know. You __________ have told him.

(a) mustn't
(b) couldn't
(c) wouldn't
(d) shouldn't

18. A: The kids are making too much noise.
   I can't read.

   B: OK, I'll go ___________ .

   (a) ask be quiet to them
   (b) to be quiet ask them
   (c) ask them to be quiet
   (d) to them ask to be quiet

19. A: What power management options
   does this laptop have?

   B: It can run on battery power
   ___________ 10 hours.

   (a) during
   (b) across
   (c) until
   (d) for

20. A: All political candidates are primarily
   concerned about the public good.

   B: Oh, come on, you ___________ .

   (a) expect we can't believe
   (b) can't expect us believe that
   (c) can't expect us to believe that
   (d) can't expect we are of that belief

Part II **Questions 21—40**

Choose the best answer for the blank.

---

21. The ancient Samnites ___________ as
barbaric people in history textbooks.

   (a) portrayed
   (b) had portrayed
   (c) have been portrayed
   (d) will have been portrayed

22. Always keep some business cards
handy to give to people so that they can
___________ .

   (a) to you contact more easily
   (b) more easily to you contact
   (c) more easily you contact
   (d) contact you more easily

23. To avoid hurting someone's feelings, it
is better to leave some things
___________ .

   (a) unsaid
   (b) to unsay
   (c) unsaying
   (d) have unsaid

24. The pay rate at our company is similar
to ___________ of other companies.

   (a) this
   (b) one
   (c) that
   (d) those

25. _____________ the basics of algebra, the boy struggled to finish his math homework.

(a) Not to have known
(b) Having known not
(c) Not knowing
(d) Not to know

26. Rebecca loves to chat with her sister, _____________ ideas are always interesting.

(a) which
(b) whom
(c) whose
(d) of which

27. Hardly _____________ before noon.

(a) ever arrives the mail
(b) the mail ever arrives
(c) does the mail arrive ever
(d) ever does the mail arrive

28. Consistency and predictability _____________ essential to maintaining discipline.

(a) is
(b) are
(c) is to be
(d) are to be

29. In most cultures, there are differing opinions _____________ correct and proper social conduct.

(a) on what constitutes for
(b) for what constitutes on
(c) on what constitutes
(d) what constitutes

30. Low-income families cannot pay for _____________ like piano lessons or golf lessons for their children.

(a) luxury
(b) luxuries
(c) the luxury
(d) other luxuries

31. A bottle of wine together with some chocolates _____________ a nice birthday gift.

(a) are being
(b) is being
(c) are
(d) is

32. Exports from the New World were principally sugar, coffee, tobacco, chocolate and cotton, all of _____________ required heavy labor to produce.

(a) that
(b) who
(c) which
(d) whom

33. The couple was late for breakfast, but it _____________ in the hotel restaurant when they walked in.

(a) will still be served
(b) has still been served
(c) had still been served
(d) was still being served

34. The professor requires that our working outline _____________ continually revised in the process of writing the essay.

(a) had been
(b) being
(c) was
(d) be

35. The cookie jar was put __________ the shelf above the table so that the children could not reach it easily.

(a) at
(b) to
(c) in
(d) on

36. Since the piece was so unpopular, the violinist thought __________.

(a) learning not worth her time
(b) it to learn not worth her time
(c) it was not worth her time to learn
(d) learning it not her time worth

37. Calls from public phone booths will cut out after a warning beep __________ you put more coins in the slot.

(a) if
(b) till
(c) once
(d) unless

38. Many people believe that taking __________ for relaxation after work is necessary for the sake of good mental health.

(a) time
(b) a time
(c) one time
(d) every time

39. __________, the man left the casino in despair, worried about how he was going to pay his bills.

(a) Lost all of his money
(b) Had lost all of his money
(c) His losing all of his money
(d) Having lost all of his money

40. __________ should appropriate music and video in the way he did for such a subtle critique of capitalism.

(a) How it was astounding that the artist
(b) How astounding it was the artist
(c) How astounding for the artist
(d) How the artist astounding

Identify the option that contains an awkward expression or an error in grammar.

41. (a) A: How was the club picnic on Saturday?
    (b) B: It is cancelled because not enough people could go.
    (c) A: That's too bad. It would've been fun.
    (d) B: I know. But we can always schedule another.

42. (a) A: It looks like we're going to be late for the concert.
    (b) B: Don't worry. We can get to the concert hall in time.
    (c) A: Are you sure? The traffic is much heavy in this area.
    (d) B: It's OK. I know a shortcut that will get us there quickly.

43. (a) A: Any idea what tomorrow's staff meeting is about?
    (b) B: I'm not sure, but it can be good news.
    (c) A: Do you suppose it's about a new engineering department?
    (d) B: Possibly, since that's been on the agenda for a while.

44. (a) A: Mister Governor, what's your opinion of what the senator said about you?
    (b) B: I can't excuse it, and I'll never accept his apologize for it.
    (c) A: Is that because of the personal nature of the senator's remarks?
    (d) B: Yes, they were shameful and not becoming of a public official.

45. (a) A: Growing up, my mother encouraged me to play sports.
    (b) B: So, what did you play, some kind of team sport?
    (c) A: No, I liked individual sports, especially tennis.
    (d) B: Oh, I can play tennis, too. We should have a game sometime.

Part IV   Questions 46—50

Identify the option that contains an awkward expression or an error in grammar.

46. (a) California's Salton Sea is an inland lake created nearly a century ago when floodwaters filled up a dry basin in the desert. (b) Since then, salt from desert soil and fertilizers from nearby farms have been washed into it. (c) This has caused the lake to become about 25% salty than the Pacific Ocean. (d) Some experts warn that, if conditions worsen as expected, all fish species in the lake will die off within 15 years.

47. (a) George Washington's actions and achievements made him a central figure in the founding of the United States of America. (b) Washington led the Continental Army to victory over Britain in the American Revolutionary War, which ended in 1783. (c) He was also of the first United States President from 1789 to 1797. (d) Because of his central role in the founding of the US, Washington is called the father of his country.

48. (a) Some people still fall for alternative therapies regardless of the scientific evidence that might exist against them. (b) Many are fooled by the allure of words like "natural remedy," "safe alternative" or even "miracle cure." (c) The terminally ill, for example, attract to the false hope that trying something unconventional might save them. (d) Unfortunately, there is little evidence that alternative medicines can help them or anyone else with a truly serious medical problem.

49. (a) According to a recent productivity study at Harvard, taking a nap at work may be a productive thing to do. (b) Thirty people in the study were tested four times a day on how quickly they could process information. (c) It was found that the people who napped for half an hour during the day did better than those who stayed awake the whole day. (d) Indeed those who did not take a nap showed a decline of 50% in their ability to process information.

50. (a) Angela Rixon is a celebrated author of books about animals. (b) Her interest in animals, however, extends beyond authorial one. (c) She also works as a professional animal photographer for naturalist magazines. (d) So, she often goes on photographic safaris through Africa and South America.

This is the end of the Grammar section. Do NOT move on to the next section until instructed to do so. You are NOT allowed to turn to any other section of the test.

VOCABULARY

Part I Questions 1—25

Choose the best answer for the blank.

1. A: You won't be able to take that bag on board our flight. It won't fit into the overhead compartment.

B: Why not? It's not that __________.

(a) fat
(b) big
(c) great
(d) rough

2. A: I'm not sure where we can catch the airport bus.

B: Wait. I'll ask at the information __________.

(a) title
(b) desk
(c) suite
(d) block

3. A: Hi Alice! I haven't seen you for a while.

B: Oh, well, I've been __________ busy.

(a) doing
(b) holding
(c) keeping
(d) enjoying

4. A: Do you need a bag for your groceries?

B: No, I've __________ my own.

(a) raised
(b) traced
(c) sought
(d) brought

5. A: Excuse me. Can you tell me where the closest post office is?

B: On the lower __________ of the mall.

(a) rank
(b) level
(c) layer
(d) surface

6. A: Let's see Charlie before he goes overseas.

B: Yes, we shouldn't __________ saying goodbye.

(a) miss
(b) pass
(c) lose
(d) fail

7. A: It's $99 a year to get the *Times* newspaper delivered.

B: Wow. That's an expensive __________.

(a) registration
(b) information
(c) subscription
(d) membership

8. A: Ever since Judy gained weight, she's become more __________.

B: Yeah. She seems to avoid going out with people.

(a) invalid
(b) indulgent
(c) introverted
(d) inexplicable

9. A: I'd like to open a savings account.

B: OK. Please __________ this form.

(a) fill out
(b) sign in
(c) turn up
(d) sort out

10. A: How come you got home so late?

B: I'm sorry, I was __________ at the office.

(a) delayed
(b) caught
(c) seized
(d) fixed

11. A: Why do birds __________?

B: To get to warmer regions where there is food.

(a) glide
(b) hover
(c) journey
(d) migrate

12. A: Professor, could you tell us when our assignment is __________?

B: You must hand it in by next Wednesday.

(a) set
(b) due
(c) over
(d) final

13. A: Our credit card debt is too high.

B: I know. We should cut back on __________.

(a) expenses
(b) accounts
(c) budget
(d) prices

14. A: Are you sure you can't finish your thesis by next month?

B: I'm afraid so. It's not __________.

(a) flexible
(b) feasible
(c) credible
(d) malleable

15. A: The TV screen is too bright.

B: Then, just __________ the contrast.

(a) place
(b) adjust
(c) stretch
(d) tighten

16. A: I can help you put your new bookshelves together.

B: Thanks, I have no idea how they should be __________.

(a) jointed
(b) knotted
(c) composed
(d) assembled

17. A: That opera was great, wasn't it?

B: Yes, it deserved a standing __________.

(a) ovation
(b) attention
(c) recognition
(d) confirmation

18. A: Hi, I'm calling to speak to Richard Swain. Is he in his office?

B: He just went out for a lunch __________.

(a) term
(b) break
(c) phase
(d) session

19. A: When did you start snowboarding?

B: Oh, I __________ last winter.

(a) set it out
(b) took it up
(c) shoved it off
(d) played it down

20. A: We need to encourage our employees to work hard.

B: Perhaps we should offer more __________, then.

(a) potentials
(b) incentives
(c) disciplines
(d) credentials

21. A: Why does Eliot have to see a psychiatrist?

B: Because he still has __________ of depression.

(a) gouts
(b) strains
(c) shields
(d) episodes

22. A: Looking back, what do you think of your time at college?

B: In __________, I should've majored in something else.

(a) forecast
(b) hesitance
(c) hindsight
(d) compromise

23. A: After I lost my job, I found an even better one.

B: In that case, losing your job was __________.

(a) salt in the wound
(b) a shot in the dark
(c) beating a dead horse
(d) a blessing in disguise

24. A: I can't believe John still hasn't decided on which car to buy.

B: I know. He's been __________ between two options.

(a) identifying
(b) vacillating
(c) resisting
(d) settling

25. A: Alec seems to be short of money all the time.

B: It's because he lives beyond his __________.

(a) means
(b) accord
(c) prestige
(d) supplies

26. All of the latest DVD releases are now ___________ on our website.

  (a) available
  (b) treatable
  (c) possible
  (d) reliable

27. Unlike traditional golf, speed golf ___________ about an hour to play.

  (a) takes
  (b) goes
  (c) puts
  (d) gets

28. The old woman had never flown in a plane before, so she was feeling nervous and ___________.

  (a) bored
  (b) frozen
  (c) beaten
  (d) scared

29. China's rapid economic growth has greatly ___________ the economies of other countries around the world.

  (a) forced
  (b) scaled
  (c) affected
  (d) managed

30. Your blood type is the result of the gene combination that you ___________ from your parents.

  (a) assigned
  (b) inherited
  (c) deserved
  (d) appointed

31. A student who repeatedly violates the student code of behavior should be ___________ from the school.

  (a) chased
  (b) banned
  (c) separated
  (d) discouraged

32. Take note that the skins of refrigerated bananas will ___________ black.

  (a) age
  (b) turn
  (c) come
  (d) switch

33. Woodwork, folk painting and pottery are ___________ in which the artist has a great deal of talent.

  (a) crafts
  (b) makes
  (c) articles
  (d) products

34. The king's son __________ to the throne after the death of the king.

(a) inclined
(b) acceded
(c) inspired
(d) attached

35. Until more __________ can be raised, development of the rapid transit train and other costly projects will have to be suspended.

(a) funds
(b) trusts
(c) charities
(d) currencies

36. The government should __________ a voucher system to help unemployed people pay for job training.

(a) implant
(b) deprive
(c) initiate
(d) reckon

37. Air quality is __________ in big cities of developing countries, where environmental care is often sacrificed for economic wealth.

(a) defusing
(b) corrupting
(c) extenuating
(d) deteriorating

38. Studies on identical twins have found a strong __________ between genetics and obesity.

(a) correlation
(b) implication
(c) justification
(d) contradiction

39. Opponents of capital punishment say that it does not necessarily __________ crime.

(a) deter
(b) arrest
(c) foster
(d) defend

40. The luncheon was a great success with much laughter and __________ because of the many humorous stories told.

(a) piety
(b) gaiety
(c) sobriety
(d) instability

41. Although the medieval cornet evolved into what we call a trumpet, it differed immensely from its modern __________.

(a) identity
(b) emulator
(c) illustration
(d) counterpart

42. This street is __________ as a vehicle-free zone on weekends from 8 am to 9 pm.

(a) imposed
(b) resolved
(c) confined
(d) designated

43. The samurai culture that emerged in 12th-century Japan __________ prominent well into the modern era.

(a) held
(b) lasted
(c) pressed
(d) remained

44. Even though the volunteer army was insufficiently trained, they were able to __________ the enemy and claim victory.

(a) impel
(b) defeat
(c) scrape
(d) agitate

45. Candidate Brown demonstrated his quick wit once again with a brilliant __________ against his opponent's argument.

(a) retort
(b) fallacy
(c) conjecture
(d) controversy

46. The CEO __________ the employee for his excellent accomplishments.

(a) lauded
(b) melded
(c) exerted
(d) boasted

47. In the midst of the scandal, Senator Daniels made several misleading statements that further __________ the truth.

(a) demystified
(b) obfuscated
(c) irradiated
(d) abhorred

48. Fans of the novelist will no doubt be __________ to learn that his latest effort is hugely disappointing.

(a) corpulent
(b) audacious
(c) distraught
(d) annihilated

49. Maurice was severely __________ by the military tribunal because he had left the army base without permission.

(a) rebuked
(b) inhibited
(c) smudged
(d) depreciated

50. Although the piranha is known as a __________ predator, its threat to humans has been exaggerated.

(a) combustive
(b) ferocious
(c) noxious
(d) tedious

This is the end of the Vocabulary section. Do NOT move on to the Reading Comprehension section until instructed to do so. You are NOT allowed to turn to any other section of the test.

READING COMPREHENSION

Read the passage. Then choose the option that best completes the passage.

---

1. Many valuable archaeological discoveries _________________________. For example, in 1940, when four boys were exploring the woods in southwestern France, they came across a small hole in the ground. Upon entering the hole, they discovered a narrow pathway that guided them to an array of underground rooms with animal paintings on the walls and ceilings. This chance discovery was of what we now know as the caves at Lascaux, which represent some of the most significant prehistoric paintings around the globe.

(a) are buried underground
(b) are turning out to be fakes
(c) are discovered by chance
(d) are being destroyed by humans

2.

Dear Circulation Editor:

I wish to cancel my subscription to *The Coloradoan.* The reason I do not wish to continue receiving your newspaper is that its delivery is always late. I spoke on the phone to one of your staff members, Karl Madsen, two weeks ago about this problem, and he assured me that he would sort it out. However, your newspaper is still _______________________.

Sincerely,
Thomas Stone

(a) much too expensive
(b) of the lowest quality
(c) not stating the real facts
(d) not being delivered on time

3. In order to design better waterproof fabrics, scientists examined the waxy surface of the lotus leaf, one of nature's most waterproof materials. They found that it had many microscopic bumps that trap air and prevent water from sticking to its surface. Eventually, they were able to create a similar effect by making a coating with anti-wetting properties, but the way it was done was expensive. Then, a team of Turkish scientists found a cheaper way, creating a gel coating that _______________________.

(a) makes Turkish fabrics last longer
(b) mimics the surface of a lotus leaf
(c) makes fabrics more breathable
(d) is able to absorb a lot of water

4. Twenty years ago, on the streets of Philadelphia, a nun called Sister Mary Scullion decided to create an organization to provide shelter for all of Philadelphia's homeless people. "We can't walk by people living on the street and think that it's OK," she once told reporters. "It's not OK. It degrades me as well as the person who's on the street." The organization she founded was a great success. It helped reduce

_______________________.

(a) the number of unemployed people
(b) the high rate of crime in Philadelphia
(c) the social causes that lead to homelessness
(d) the city's homeless population significantly

5. In the late 1600s, ships would arrive at the West African port of Whydah with the purpose of _______________________. Captains and crews would be welcomed by the king of Whydah and then taken to his residence. It was there that a price for slaves, who had often been captured by fellow Africans, was negotiated. Once a price was established, the ship's doctor would carefully inspect the naked captives to be sure that they were of sound body, young and free of disease. The slaves were then shipped to the New World.

(a) purchasing slaves
(b) exploring Africa's interior
(c) establishing another colony
(d) negotiating an end to slavery

6. In the Chicago Metropolitan area, _________________________________. After an early spell of warm spring weather, the cold temperatures and flurries Wednesday caught many off-guard. Gusty winds throughout the area sent plant owners rushing to shield spring bulbs from the cold. According to the National Weather Service, temperatures of around 30 degrees Fahrenheit will continue through to the weekend and will gradually reach up to 50 degrees Fahrenheit by early next week.

(a) a storm has left citizens without power
(b) cold weather has returned for the week
(c) spring has finally arrived to warm things up
(d) low temperatures mark the beginning of winter

7. The Ellison Academy is once again _________________________________. All applicants are welcome. We are looking for promising young actors anxious to develop their craft in a play of social importance. The story revolves around the play's namesake, a performer named Dinah who worked at the Sahara Hotel in Las Vegas in the 50s. After being turned away at the "whites-only" entrance, Dinah comes to head an anti-racism protest. Call 123-3245 by October 12th for more detail on the time and date as well as the venue for the audition.

(a) gearing up for its annual fall production of Dinah
(b) holding auditions for those who wish to attend the academy
(c) organizing a large protest in the memory of Dinah
(d) set to stage a historic reenactment in Las Vegas

8. Traditional print newspapers were initially slow to embrace the Internet. Some were ignorant or skeptical of its potential and ignored it; others saw it as a threat but were too slow to act. Consequently, none was ready for the massive social shift away from print media to online news. Some collapsed and others were sold, while the survivors poured resources into the online side of their businesses. Some are still catching up. Certainly now, the industry _________________________________.

(a) realizes that nothing can replace good journalism
(b) seeks to attract readers back to print newspapers
(c) makes huge sums of money through advertising
(d) recognizes that the new frontier is online news

9. Charles Rosen's *The Classical Style* is a must-have for all classical music lovers. In the book, Rosen concentrates on the compositions of Haydn, Mozart and Beethoven to identify the characteristics of the classical style. He analyzes different genres and musical forms with unparalleled expertise to create a multi-faceted picture of how these three great composers helped develop the classical style by solving the musical and formal problems of the earlier Baroque period. This book ___________________________.

(a) will be enjoyed more by laypeople than music lovers
(b) is so complex that at times it is difficult to get through
(c) will satisfy readers interested in biographical highlights
(d) is highly recommended as a milestone in musical analysis

10. In a polar wasteland, where there is extreme variation in daylight hours, it is not easy to guess the time of day. But knowing the precise time is paramount for polar explorers for tasks such as accurate navigation. That is why the Time Explorer is their timepiece of choice. Instead of a regular 12-hour revolution of the hour hand, Time Explorer's hour hand completes a revolution every 24 hours. This allows you to _______________________________. With a Time Explorer, you can know what time it is no matter where you are.

(a) tell the time in a different time zone
(b) use it as you would use a compass
(c) use the watch in any temperature
(d) tell whether it is night or day

11. The majority of the personages that we see in Wordsworth's poems are lonely in one way or another. They do not share common features with the social types found in the poetry of other Romantic poets, types like Byron's Don Juan or Childe Harolde. Maybe it is because Wordsworth himself was a fairly solitary individual. While he did enjoy interacting with a select few individuals such as his beloved sister Dorothy, he seemed happiest _____________________________.

(a) if literary critics praised his poetry
(b) among other poets whom he respected
(c) when his only company was himself
(d) in the company of family members

12. Recently, a study was done in Britain on ________________________________. The study, which looked at 2,954 high schools and 979 primary schools, showed that boys and girls performed better academically at single-sex schools than their peers at co-ed ones. It further showed that students in single-sex schools tended to perform better in subjects not traditionally associated with their gender; girls' skills in math and science improved, as did boys' skills in subjects like arts and literature.

(a) the ways boys and girls differ in school
(b) the way single-sex classrooms affect girls
(c) how single-sex schools benefit boys and girls
(d) how to improve weak subjects for boys and girls

13. I was ten years old when packaged instant noodles were introduced in Japan. I dismissed them as impractical luxury items because they cost 35 yen, six times the cost of a bowl of fresh noodle soup at our neighborhood eatery. But now, 40 years later, the contrary is true. Today, a bowl of fresh noodles in Tokyo costs around 800 yen, while I can buy a packet of ramen for 100 yen. ________________________________, instant ramen is very easy to cook, which is why I always have a stock of it in my pantry.

(a) Besides being so cheap and practical
(b) Now that it is not considered a luxury item
(c) Although something that I did not enjoy that much
(d) Even though its price has become three times higher

14. An emerging field of neuroscience concerns how ________________________________. Central to this field are "mirror neurons," a class of brain cells that appear to help us sense what others might feel. When we perceive or sense the emotion or even intentions of another person, these neurons stimulate the parts of our brain associated with what we have perceived or sensed. In a way, the behavior of others is replicated or "mirrored" within our own minds by these neurons. Mirror neurons may explain our feelings of empathy and our understanding of the feelings of another person.

(a) people manipulate each other's feelings
(b) social networking is handled by the brain
(c) neurons are to blame for emotional stress
(d) one person's emotion may affect another's

15. Investing with Triple Top Investments could be the best choice you ever
make. Our investment packages have a proven track record and can make up
to 20% annually for our customers, depending on their investment portfolio.
___________________________________, all of our packages are registered, meaning that
investors can feel assured by our pledge to protect them against any loss. Triple Top
Investments—making profit the smart way.

(a) And yet
(b) In addition
(c) For instance
(d) Despite that

16. In spite of America's so-called "War on Drugs," the demand for cocaine is still high, and
the drug has become less expensive. Drug lords have discovered creative channels to
eliminate middlemen, and dealers will readily work the street corners for lower pay.
___________________________________, the Free Trade Agreement has made smuggling
easier, as drugs transported in trucks and commercial vehicles continually move across
the Mexican border undetected.

(a) As a result
(b) Meanwhile
(c) By contrast
(d) Nevertheless

> **Part II** **Questions 17—37**
>
> Read the passage and the question. Then choose the option that best answers the question.

17. Arkansas annually attracts over 30,000 visitors from across the nation and abroad. They are drawn to many outdoor adventures and to its natural beauty, as seen in the state's waterfalls, forested mountain trails and scenic drives. You can even dig for keeper diamonds at a public diamond mine. Arkansas, The Natural State, is a must-see vacation destination.

Q: What is the advertisement mainly about?
(a) Attractions of Arkansas
(b) A public diamond mine
(c) Nature parks in Arkansas
(d) An adventure tour package

18. Some critics have stated that the Peter Shaffer and Milos Forman film on Mozart, *Amadeus*, led us to a deeper appreciation of the composer and his art. I beg to differ. The film was essentially based on popular myths and Mozart's letters, which are hardly the sum of the man. The resulting depiction of Mozart will leave most with the impression that he was childish and vulgar. If you hope for a better understanding of Mozart and his genius, you will not find it in *Amadeus*. It has no deeper purpose other than to entertain, as the film makers intended.

Q: What is the main idea about *Amadeus* in the passage?
(a) It gives a distorted portrait of Mozart.
(b) It deviates from the details in Mozart's letters.
(c) It accurately presents aspects of Mozart's daily life.
(d) It is as entertaining as the film-makers had intended.

19. When hiking on long treks over rough, winter terrain, weather conditions and the nature of the terrain will generally dictate the distance you travel. With good weather over gentle terrain, you can cover 20 miles in a day. However, if the weather changes for the worse and if you strike snow flurries and slippery terrain, you might be lucky to go five miles. So, don't bank on making it to any preplanned destination at a set time. Also, to protect yourself against unforgiving elements, always carry your shelter with you.

Q: What is the main point about winter hiking?
(a) Arrange for lodgings ahead of time.
(b) Make sure you take the best equipment.
(c) Be prepared to be delayed by bad weather.
(d) Do not go trekking if the weather is severe.

20. The University of Chicago changed education in the US by establishing the country's first university extension program for adults. It was the brainchild of the university's first president, William Harper, who believed that education was "evidence of, and the surest means toward, the higher civic life." The program embodied Harper's desire to extend teaching, research and intellectual discussion into the broader community by opening classes to the public. Thus, in October, 1892, those in the community who had difficulty in getting a higher education were able to partake in university classes for the first time.

Q: What is mainly being discussed about the University of Chicago in the passage?
(a) Its efforts to improve the lives of people
(b) Its continued support of community groups
(c) Its introduction of extended education to the public
(d) Its beginnings under the leadership of William Harper

21. Although the demise of every civilization is unique, striking similarities exist in the causal processes and the human response to them. For example, human societies have tended to be fixed in their responses to ecological conditions around them, losing the ability over time to react or adapt to environmental change. They have sometimes failed to foresee or reverse unsustainable behavior, helplessly applying small-scale, short-term solutions to large-scale problems. Thus, for many civilizations, decline was inevitable—it was just a matter of time.

Q: What is the main topic about human societies in the passage?
(a) They invariably ignore large-scale ecological problems.
(b) They respond to problems by believing things will get better.
(c) They are responsible for the protection of Earth's environment.
(d) They bring on their own demise by reacting too quickly to change.

22. The sixteenth and seventeenth centuries saw dramatic changes in Europe. Reformation ideas, with their emphasis on individual liberty, were applied to areas outside of religion, and this led to social and political dissent. For example, concepts of individualism threatened monarchic rule, prompting political philosophers to justify the monarchy's authority by citing two doctrines: "natural law" and "the Divine Right of Kings." Both doctrines upheld the idea of absolutism, where a monarch rules with unshared power. However, such doctrines could not soften the impact of the Reformation or mend the political and social divisions it created.

Q: What is the main idea of the passage?
(a) Reformation changes had a profound effect on political thinkers.
(b) Political dissenters were responsible for creating the Reformation.
(c) Philosophers during the Reformation sought to justify absolutism.
(d) Reformation concepts gave rise to political unrest and social change.

23. Established in 1701 by French fur traders, Detroit is the largest city in the American state of Michigan. Located in Wayne County, Detroit is an important port city on the Detroit River in the American Midwest. In 2005, Detroit ranked 11th among the most populous cities in America, with a population of 886,675. However, this is less than half the number it boasted in 1950, and in fact the city now leads the nation in declining urban population.

Q: Which is correct about Detroit according to the passage?
(a) It was founded by the Michigan Indians.
(b) It was the 11th largest US city in 1950.
(c) It has fewer residents than it used to have.
(d) It is located in the west of the United States.

24. Many students dream of taking extravagant vacations after graduating from college. But when Alex Tehrani graduated from the Tisch School of the Arts' photography program, he headed for the war-ravaged country of Angola. After 30 years of civil war, the country was finally at peace, and Tehrani's plan was to photograph the first democratic election ever to be held there. However, peace did not last long, and he ended up photographing the country's descent into more violence. In the process, he gained a reputation for merging artistic elegance with a documentary style.

Q: Which of the following is correct about Alex Tehrani?
(a) He photographed violent conflicts in Angola.
(b) He went to Angola to report on a civil war.
(c) He vacationed in Angola after graduating.
(d) He studied photography while in Angola.

25.

Dear Kathy,

Sorry for the delayed response to your invitation of a few days ago. I didn't reply straight away because I wanted to find out whether my wife was able to attend. We are both glad that you invited us on your annual ski trip, but, while we would like nothing more than to join you again this year, we are going to have to pass. Unfortunately, my wife's asthma is proving to be quite a burden. Hopefully things will be better next year and we'll be able to join you then.

Bye for now,
Eric

Q: Which of the following is correct according to the email?
(a) Eric will attend Kathy's ski trip.
(b) Kathy hosts a ski trip every year.
(c) Eric's wife is slowly recovering from asthma.
(d) Kathy sent an invitation to Eric's wife a week ago.

26. A Bangladeshi economist, Muhammad Yunus, and the bank he founded 30 years ago were jointly awarded the Nobel Peace Prize in 2006. Yunus founded his banking system so that tiny loans could be given to millions of people that no commercial bank would bother with, mainly the rural poor in Bangladeshi villages. Most of the low-interest microloans, as they are called, go to women, who use them to start their own profit-making enterprises, mainly in agriculture, crafts or services. Yunus' banking success in combating poverty has inspired similar schemes across the developing world.

Q: Which of the following is correct about Muhammad Yunus' bank?
(a) Its loans go exclusively to women.
(b) It lends money to the poor interest-free.
(c) It has given farmland to villagers in Bangladesh.
(d) Its methods are being copied in other poor nations.

27.

> To Whom It May Concern:
>
> I am responding to your newspaper advertisement for a Managing Editor. As you can see from my résumé, I have many years of experience as an editor, proofreader and layout designer. My résumé also shows that I have worked as a copy editor for sports and technology magazines. I am currently Production Editor at *Newsline Magazine*, but I feel that it is time to advance my career to a managerial position. I am confident I would be ideal for the position of Managing Editor at your magazine. Thank you for your consideration, and I look forward to hearing from you.
>
> Sincerely,
> April Armond

Q: Which of the following is correct about the writer?
(a) She wants to work for a magazine publisher.
(b) Her experience as a proofreader is limited.
(c) Her goal is to become a production editor.
(d) She writes articles for several magazines.

28. More than three decades after Chicago banned phosphate-laden detergents that caused foul-smelling algae to flourish and choke up lakes and rivers, dish-washing liquids containing phosphates are still on supermarket shelves. The ban on phosphates was implemented by Mayor Richard J. Daley in 1971, and it became the model for efforts that helped revive the Great Lakes. However, the city's current administration rarely enforces the ban, even though its mayor promotes Chicago as one of the nation's most environmentally friendly cities.

Q: Which of the following is correct about Chicago according to the passage?
(a) Its current mayor is working to revive the Great Lakes.
(b) Its stores no longer sell phosphate-laden detergents.
(c) Its lakes were choked with algae in the early 1970s.
(d) Its rivers recently started emitting foul odors.

29. Recently, a small number of psychologists began to consider fame as more than a shallow cultural phenomenon, exploring it as a significant motivator of human behavior. By ranking fame with other goals and measuring its psychological effects, they found that people with an overriding desire to be widely known differ from those who primarily covet wealth and influence. Fame-seeking behavior appears rooted in a desire for social acceptance and reassurance promised by wide renown.

Q: Which of the following is correct according to the passage?
(a) Fame has long been studied by psychologists.
(b) Desire for fame is linked to a desire for wealth.
(c) People seek fame due to a longing for acceptance.
(d) Fame is the strongest motivator in human societies.

30. Lakewood City Council has enacted a smoking ban for public places, including parks, Forest Park Beach and Market Square, effective February 1. The ordinance further prohibits smoking in all enclosed public areas and places of employment. Excluded from the ban are public sidewalks and parking lots. A smoking ban for all clubs, bars and restaurants is being considered for next spring. This ban is similar to legislation enacted in a number of communities throughout the State of Illinois.

Q: Which of the following is correct as of February 1 according to the passage?
(a) Smoking is banned in Lakewood's enclosed public areas.
(b) Smoking bans are now in effect throughout Lakewood.
(c) Smoking in Lakewood's parking lots is prohibited.
(d) Smoking is banned in Lakewood's bars and clubs.

31. In 1940, Walt Disney released *Fantasia*, a movie combining the music of Tchaikovsky, Stravinsky, Beethoven and others with imaginative and artistically-choreographed animation. The reviews were generally positive, but the film performed poorly at the box office. Some griping about Disney ensued as well, not least from Stravinsky, who was outraged that Disney had used a cut version of his *Rite of Spring* for the film. But Disney dismissed this criticism, saying that Stravinsky had originally approved of the use of his music in the film.

Q: Which of the following is correct according to the passage?
(a) Disney had new songs composed for *Fantasia*.
(b) *Fantasia*'s animation was too outdated for audiences.
(c) Stravinsky's music was used without his permission.
(d) Film reviewers gave *Fantasia* good reviews for the most part.

32. Stuttering, an ailment characterized by disturbances in speech fluency, afflicts an estimated 3 million Americans. It is usually treated through speech therapy, but now scientists have developed a promising drug called pagoclone to control it. It works by reducing anxiety and the brain's dopamine levels, thus allowing for a more free-flowing thought process. These actions enable stutterers to have fewer inhibited speech patterns. Although not the first stuttering drug developed, pagoclone does not have the side-effects other drug treatments have.

Q: Which of the following is correct according to the passage?
(a) Pagoclone works best in conjunction with therapy.
(b) Previous drug treatments produced similar side-effects.
(c) Pagoclone helps stutterers by lowering their anxiety levels.
(d) Non-stutterers have higher dopamine levels than stutterers.

33. Near the end of the 1800's, an extreme religious organization endeavored to drive Christians and foreigners from China. This organization called itself the Fists of Righteous Harmony, since its members were skilled in a conventional type of hand-to-hand combat, but they became better known simply as the Boxers. Their members practiced clandestine ceremonies held exclusively for members, including one practice that was supposed to make their bodies bulletproof. Such rituals and beliefs contributed to making them fearless and impetuous fighters.

Q: Which of the following is correct about the Boxers?
(a) They preferred Christians to other foreigners.
(b) They trained to fight in the boxing ring.
(c) They believed that bullets could not harm them.
(d) They wished to preserve Chinese martial arts.

34. My twelve-year-old daughter won a writing contest last year, and she wants to do it again this year. I'm thrilled to see her so excited about writing because I work as a writer myself. But as a writer, I know about winning contests and about losing them. I know how upsetting it is when something I've worked on so hard is rejected by publishers. What if my daughter doesn't win the contest again? It'll upset her, sure, yet it'll be good for her, too. It'll help her learn what being a writer is all about.

Q: What can be inferred about the writer?
(a) She is embarking on a new career as a writer.
(b) She is hopeful her daughter will give up the contest.
(c) She has faced challenges during her writing career.
(d) She fears her daughter's writing is better than her own.

35. The disability of dyslexia, characterized by difficulties in reading, writing and spelling, was misunderstood in the past. Some people blamed it on a lack of intelligence, but dyslexic people can be highly intelligent and gifted in many areas. Other people blamed dyslexia on a lack of motivation. However, we now know that it is a biological condition, and scientists are getting closer to confirming the key areas of the brain that are associated with it. This will lead to new insights which will help in developing new therapies.

Q: What can be inferred from the passage?
(a) Dyslexia can be prevented with early diagnosis.
(b) Research has changed people's opinions on dyslexics.
(c) Symptoms of dyslexia can vary from person to person.
(d) Motivation training can reduce the symptoms of dyslexia.

36. With the rise of globalization and technology, few cultures now stand truly isolated. In fact, few places exist in the world where one could be born and remain ignorant of other cultures and practices. A few centuries ago, a cultural map of the earth showed large patches of color, distinct from one another, with fairly sharp edges; but in years to come, such a map will likely have blurred lines, with colors merged and only faint blushes of pure color remaining in a few isolated enclaves.

Q: What can be inferred from the passage?
(a) Cultures worldwide are tending toward integration.
(b) Fewer primitive societies exist today than ever before.
(c) Some cultures will fight to maintain their cultural identity.
(d) It is unlikely one culture will emerge to dominate the world.

37. By quoting experts, a writer can make a convincing case without having to provide all the data supporting their claim. However, to be acceptable, citations must be legitimate. First, they need to be academic and informative—no vague and hollow statements such as "Disarmament is a splendid idea." Second, quotes from reputable authorities must concern their areas of expertise. For example, an anthropological expert may be cited on anthropology, but comments that person made about physics should not be quoted.

Q: What can be inferred from the passage?
(a) Utilizing quotations relieves some of the writer's burden.
(b) A florid style is more compelling than cited testimonials.
(c) Providing supporting data is more common than quoting.
(d) Some conclusions in physics conflict with those in anthropology.

38. Alcohol rapidly affects our body once swallowed. (a) That's because, unlike most foods and drinks, it does not require digestion and so flows directly into the bloodstream. (b) Within minutes after consumption, it reaches the brain and starts to have an impact on the drinker. (c) It is known to be a major cause of accidents, leading to thousands of fatalities each year. (d) The major impact alcohol has on people is slowing down and impairing bodily functions—both mental and physical.

39. The *Apollo Music Encyclopedia* has become the standard comprehensive resource for Western music in English. (a) Though compiling information was practiced well before the 16th century, the term encyclopedia was not used until that time. (b) It contains comprehensive entries on music history, musicians, theory, practice and instruments. (c) The longer biographical entries include comprehensive details on composers, musicians and instrument makers. (d) Although this edition caters primarily to the needs of music scholars, its unrivaled coverage of classical music will delight enthusiasts.

40. Racism has been around for many thousands of years in various forms. (a) It is different from ethnocentrism, which is a tendency to judge other cultures by the standards of your own. (b) One form of racism developed in early America, as a part of the moral justification that was applied to slavery. (c) Ironically, once slavery was abolished, racism actually intensified because blacks were then regarded as posing an economic threat. (d) It began to decline in the 1960s, and now laws exist against racism so that everyone has equal rights and receives fair treatment.

This is the end of the Reading Comprehension section. Please remain seated until the proctor has instructed otherwise. You are NOT allowed to turn to any other section of the test.

Listening Comprehension

Grammar

Vocabulary

Reading Comprehension

LISTENING COMPREHENSION

DIRECTIONS

1. In the Listening Comprehension section, all content will be presented orally rather than in written form.

2. This section contains 4 parts. In parts I and II, each passage will be read only once. In parts III and IV, each passage and its corresponding question will be read twice. But in all sections, the options will be read only once. After listening to the passage and question, listen to the options and choose the best answer.

Scripts P 296 / 정답 P 329

Part I **Questions 1—15**

You will now hear fifteen conversation fragments, each made up of a single spoken statement followed by four spoken responses. Choose the most appropriate response to the statement.

Part II **Questions 16—30**

You will now hear fifteen conversation fragments, each made up of three spoken statements followed by four spoken responses. Choose the most appropriate response to complete the conversation.

Part III   **Questions 31—45**

You will now hear fifteen complete conversations. For each item, you will hear a conversation and its corresponding question, both of which will be read twice. Then you will hear four options which will be read only once. Choose the option that best answers the question.

Part IV   **Questions 46—60**

You will now hear fifteen spoken monologues. For each item, you will hear a monologue and its corresponding question, both of which will be read twice. Then you will hear four options which will be read only once. Choose the option that best answers the question.

GRAMMAR

DIRECTIONS

This part of the exam tests your grammar skills. You will have 25 minutes to complete the 50 questions. Be sure to follow the directions given by the proctor.

Part I   Questions 1–20

Choose the best answer for the blank.

1. A: Would you like chicken or fish for dinner?

   B: ___________ will be fine.

   (a) One
   (b) Some
   (c) Either
   (d) Another

2. A: I don't feel comfortable about asking my boss for a raise.

   B: You deserve it, so don't delay ___________ to her any longer.

   (a) talk
   (b) talked
   (c) to talk
   (d) talking

3. A: Chris seems to know a lot about the history of our city's buildings.

   B: No wonder. He majored in ___________ at university.

   (a) architecture
   (b) an architecture
   (c) the architecture
   (d) some architecture

4. A: This radio is out of order.

   B: Oh, yes, ___________.

   (a) so it is
   (b) it so is
   (c) so is it
   (d) is so it

5. A: Do you have any running shoes?

   B: Yes, we have many different ___________.

   (a) size and price
   (b) size and prices
   (c) sizes and price
   (d) sizes and prices

6. A: Are you going to read this letter right away?

   B: Not until I ___________ my dinner.

   (a) finish
   (b) finished
   (c) will finish
   (d) will have finished

7. A: Do you like the band Devil's Top?

   B: To be honest, I've ___________.

   (a) never heard of it before
   (b) heard of it never before
   (c) ever before not heard of it
   (d) before not ever heard of it

8. A: Do you think the team lost the game because Ben didn't play?

   B: Of course! Having him play in that game ___________ all the difference.

   (a) makes
   (b) had made
   (c) would make
   (d) would have made

9. A: It's already dark outside. Let me
    accompany you.
    B: That's OK. You don't need

    ___________.

    (a) taking me home
    (b) to take me home
    (c) taking me to home
    (d) to take me to home

10. A: I wish you'd stop swearing all the
    time. It's really annoying.
    B: I didn't realize it was __________ a
    nuisance to you.

    (a) so
    (b) that
    (c) such
    (d) much

11. A: You shouldn't stay out too late.
    B: I think I'm old enough __________
    as late as I like.

    (a) to stay out
    (b) staying out
    (c) having stayed out
    (d) to have stayed out

12. A: Did you have an expert evaluate
    your antique chair?
    B: Yeah, and it wasn't worth as much
    as I __________.

    (a) am expecting
    (b) had expected
    (c) have expected
    (d) will be expecting

13. A: What do you think of the philosophy
    class?
    B: I find it quite __________.

    (a) interest
    (b) interested
    (c) to interest
    (d) interesting

14. A: How did I do in my presentation?
    B: Unfortunately, you left out
    __________ I was hoping to see.

    (a) the important points of some
    (b) some of the important points
    (c) some of the points important
    (d) the points of importance some

15. A: Where can I find the information for
    our report for tomorrow's meeting?
    B: Some __________ in these files.

    (a) is
    (b) are
    (c) has
    (d) have

16. A: How can I find out if I __________
    the scholarship?
    B: You'll be notified of our decision by
    mail.

    (a) had awarded
    (b) have awarded
    (c) had been awarded
    (d) have been awarded

17. A: Do you think Jason will be late for work again today?

B: He __________ unless he wants to lose his job.

(a) wouldn't dare
(b) wouldn't dare do
(c) wouldn't dare late
(d) wouldn't dare be it

18. A: Can I see Dr. Russell next week?

B: Yes, he __________ back from his vacation by then.

(a) is
(b) will be
(c) has been
(d) had been

19. A: Do you know who invented __________?

B: Antonio Meucci is officially credited.

(a) a telephone
(b) the telephone
(c) one telephone
(d) some telephone

20. A: What will you do about the job offer?

B: I've given __________, but I can't make up my mind.

(a) a lot of thought it
(b) it a lot of thought
(c) to it a lot of thought
(d) a lot of thought for it

Part II **Questions 21—40**

Choose the best answer for the blank.

---

21. Broadway is always crowded __________ it has world-class theaters.

(a) while
(b) when
(c) though
(d) because

22. No one was able to figure out how __________ to perform the trick.

(a) the magician managed
(b) managed the magician
(c) did the magician manage
(d) the magician did to manage

23. With few exceptions, the little research __________ has been done on Baltic Latvian history is far from enlightening.

(a) in which
(b) of which
(c) what
(d) that

24. Adding to the complex political situation arising in Europe following World War I during the 1920s and 1930s __________ the postwar economy's instability.

(a) is
(b) are
(c) was
(d) were

25. Not only __________ to hand in the report on time but also made many mistakes in it.

(a) Susan failed
(b) did Susan fail
(c) failed had Susan
(d) Susan had failed

26. Bill sat in the front row, anxiously __________ his music teacher.

(a) await
(b) awaited
(c) to await
(d) awaiting

27. The company is facing bankruptcy, __________ its sales figures have steadily moved downward.

(a) as if
(b) in case
(c) inasmuch as
(d) notwithstanding

28. A new vocational aptitude test for adolescents is set to become an integral tool __________.

(a) assesses their career potential
(b) for assessing their career potential
(c) that their career potential assesses
(d) assessing for their career potential

29. A confederate system of government involves states having power over the matters __________ concern them.

(a) what
(b) which
(c) of which
(d) to whom

30. The book is written so clearly that __________.

(a) even children can understand it
(b) children can understand even it
(c) even it can understand children
(d) it can understand even children

31. Until now, the growth in Japan's trade with China __________ by China's economic boom.

(a) is driven
(b) will be driven
(c) has been driven
(d) had been driven

32. Jim's mother finally approved __________ a girl he had met at work.

(a) him marry
(b) of him to marry
(c) him of marrying
(d) of him marrying

33. __________ in the late 1980s, the transition from socialist to capitalist economic policies changed Russian society.

(a) Started
(b) To start
(c) Starting
(d) Had started

34. Some people believe that the Internet has turned the world into one big outlet store __________ middlemen are not needed.

(a) that
(b) which
(c) whose
(d) where

35. Despite a long and exhausting trip, the traveler's spirits rose __________ the thought of home.

(a) in
(b) at
(c) on
(d) for

36. Specialty shops __________ a particular kind of customer by providing personalized service and unique merchandise.

(a) generally cater to
(b) cater to generally
(c) are generally catered to
(d) are catered to generally

37. It seems that only one student __________ that an incorrect number was used in the algebraic equation.

(a) notices
(b) noticed
(c) had noticed
(d) will have noticed

38. __________ any response to the letter she had sent a month before, the girl decided to send another one.

(a) Not to receive
(b) Not have received
(c) Not having received
(d) Not to have received

39. The general argued that despite his deep regret for the civilian casualties, he was sure his troops __________ not have harmed civilians on purpose.

(a) need
(b) might
(c) would
(d) should

40. The woman wanted __________ the murderer of her father.

(a) herself avenge to
(b) herself to avenge on
(c) to avenge on herself
(d) to avenge herself on

41. (a) A: I think you'll definitely like my brother.
(b) B: Really? How can you be so sure?
(c) A: He's smart and funny, and always smile.
(d) B: Yeah, that's the kind of guy I like.

42. (a) A: Is it true that everyone at your company got a pay raise?
(b) B: Yes, management has increased salaries recently.
(c) A: That's amazing. I rare hear of a company doing that.
(d) B: I know. My company cares about its employees.

43. (a) A: Where did you put my gloves, honey?
(b) B: Right besides your hat, just like always.
(c) A: I've looked all around, but I can't find them.
(d) B: Well then, maybe they slipped onto the floor.

44. (a) A: I picked up a case of soft drinks for our party tonight.
(b) B: Thanks. I was hoping you'd be able to do that.
(c) A: It was no problem. I got it from a store on my way home.
(d) B: Well, I'm glad you wouldn't forget about it.

45. (a) A: What's up? You don't seem all that happy.
(b) B: My students have done what they promised to not.
(c) A: And what was that? Was it to stop making noise?
(d) B: No, they failed a class test they said they'd surely pass.

Part IV   **Questions 46—50**

Identify the option that contains an awkward expression or an error in grammar.

46. (a) Surrounding the Earth is a blanket of air called the atmosphere. (b) It provides the oxygen we need and protects us from the heat of the Sun. (c) The greater the distance from the Earth's surface, the more the atmosphere thins and temperature changes. (d) This continues until the atmosphere is reached into outer space, about 100 kilometers up.

47. (a) There are several methods available for determining a rock's age.
(b) Geologists can work out a rock's age from the sequence of geological events recording in the rock. (c) Paleontologists can look for fossils in a rock and figure out its age from them. (d) Geochemists can use dating techniques based on radioactive decay to determine a rock's age.

48. (a) In May 2004, the European Union admitted new ten member nations.
(b) This addition made the EU the world's biggest trading bloc, with a population of 455 million. (c) In addition, farming was strong in many of the new members' economies. (d) Thus, the total agricultural production in the EU was boosted significantly.

49. (a) If a child stood out from his or her peers as being highly aggressive, it will be wrong to assume that he or she will outgrow it. (b) Research has shown that aggressive behavior is something that needs to be treated at an early age. (c) If left untreated, aggressive behavior will invariably lead to other developmental problems and conflicts. (d) It will increase the likelihood of more violent acts of aggression and of financial, social and academic failure.

50. (a) Like humans, insects use their senses to assemble a picture of the world around them. (b) However, sight can be even more complicated for insects than for humans. (c) Insects rely on compound eyes that may have the total of 56,000 lenses. (d) Many insects also have ocelli, simple eyes that help with balance, flight and light detection.

This is the end of the Grammar section. Do NOT move on to the next section until instructed to do so. You are NOT allowed to turn to any other section of the test.

VOCABULARY

Part I   **Questions 1—25**

Choose the best answer for the blank.

1. A: Why were you late to class?

B: I forgot to __________ my alarm clock last night.

(a) set
(b) tick
(c) tune
(d) correct

2. A: How do you like your coffee?

B: I'll __________ mine with milk, please.

(a) use
(b) take
(c) catch
(d) contain

3. A: I'm so nervous about my audition.

B: Don't worry. I'm sure you'll do __________.

(a) solid
(b) high
(c) fine
(d) full

4. A: I'm doing two part-time jobs this semester.

B: Don't __________ yourself too hard, or you'll get stressed out.

(a) make
(b) push
(c) send
(d) pull

5. A: Thank you for the plaque you gave me at my retirement party.

B: It was just a small __________ of our appreciation for your service.

(a) idea
(b) token
(c) reward
(d) present

6. A: I'm going out for a walk.

B: Oh, can I __________ you?

(a) join
(b) bind
(c) show
(d) move

7. A: Didn't you say you were going shopping after lunch?

B: I did. But I __________ my mind.

(a) shifted
(b) adjusted
(c) renewed
(d) changed

8. A: How do you do?

B: How do you do, Lady Clarke? I'm __________ to meet you in person.

(a) eager
(b) honored
(c) desirable
(d) interested

9. A: I'd like to see the doctor today.
   Could you possibly fit me in?
   B: We might have a(n) __________
   later today. I'll check.

   (a) opening
   (b) filling
   (c) break
   (d) dent

10. A: Hello, could you please put me
    through to extension 210?
    B: Certainly, please stay on the
    __________.

    (a) call
    (b) line
    (c) station
    (d) machine

11. A: Is there a shortcut to City Hall from
    here?
    B: I'm afraid there is no __________
    way to get there from here.

    (a) loose
    (b) quick
    (c) thorough
    (d) immediate

12. A: Only a few members of the union
    have agreed to go on strike.
    B: They're definitely in the
    __________.

    (a) primary
    (b) insanity
    (c) quantity
    (d) minority

13. A: Welcome to Towermont Hotel. Can
    I help you?
    B: Yes, do you have any __________
    for two days?

    (a) facility
    (b) vacancy
    (c) appliance
    (d) equipment

14. A: How much do you sell this crystal
    glass for?
    B: Let's __________ it ten bucks.

    (a) offer
    (b) give
    (c) call
    (d) get

15. A: Jill seemed very agitated yesterday.
    B: She got __________ from her job.

    (a) laid off
    (b) let down
    (c) caught up
    (d) taken aback

16. A: How long has this cheese been
    sitting in the fridge?
    B: Why? Is it __________?

    (a) moldy
    (b) misty
    (c) rusty
    (d) dirty

17. A: I don't think my diet is giving me
    the vitamins I need.
    B: Why not start taking __________?

    (a) sedatives
    (b) additives
    (c) supplements
    (d) prescriptions

18. A: Did you accept the invitation to be a keynote speaker at the conference?

B: No, I had to ___________.

(a) concede
(b) resume
(c) confess
(d) decline

19. A: Jane always seems to get other people to do whatever she wants.

B: Yes, she's good at ___________ people.

(a) manipulating
(b) perpetuating
(c) collocating
(d) acquiring

20. A: Our flight's been delayed by four hours.

B: Oh, no! That means we're going to miss our ___________ flight as well.

(a) transmitting
(b) interlocking
(c) exchanging
(d) connecting

21. A: My father has had a long career as a doctor.

B: Are you going to ___________?

(a) follow suit
(b) pull strings
(c) jump the gun
(d) bury the hatchet

22. A: I know I should spend more time with my kids, but I'm too busy at work.

B: I think you should get your ___________ in order.

(a) priorities
(b) necessities
(c) alternatives
(d) requirements

23. A: I don't think I can manage this workload much longer.

B: Tell me about it. I can't keep up with this ___________, either.

(a) pace
(b) range
(c) burden
(d) diversion

24. A: Some baseball players make a lot of money, don't they?

B: Yes, they usually get very ___________ contracts.

(a) pricey
(b) eminent
(c) lucrative
(d) mercantile

25. A: Learning new things is always built on prior learning, I believe.

B: That's right. Learning is a(n) ___________ process.

(a) iterative
(b) relational
(c) cumulative
(d) precipitous

Part II   Questions 26—50

Choose the best answer for the blank.

26. The National Park Service must ___________ the number of visitors in order to protect the caves' ecosystems.

(a) limit
(b) excel
(c) break
(d) release

27. Sesame seeds come in a ___________ of colors, including brown, red, black, yellow and the most common, ivory.

(a) kind
(b) type
(c) shade
(d) variety

28. When the vampire bat drinks the blood of domestic livestock, it can ___________ the animals with rabies.

(a) spoil
(b) infect
(c) decay
(d) impair

29. In this recipe, cream can be ___________ for milk.

(a) manufactured
(b) substituted
(c) fabricated
(d) appended

30. A factor that attracts many students to online courses is a(n) ___________ schedule that allows them to learn any time.

(a) mobile
(b) flexible
(c) tentative
(d) intensive

31. The ancient Greeks believed that music was able to ___________ a listener's moral character.

(a) relive
(b) endure
(c) cultivate
(d) persuade

32. Congress tried to ___________ restrictions on the President's decision-making process in order to reduce spending.

(a) discharge
(b) interact
(c) impose
(d) deport

33. With many people in China relocating to cities, there has been a(n) ___________ growth in urban populations.

(a) implicit
(b) prudent
(c) resistant
(d) explosive

34. Many species of birds in North America ____________ south for the winter.

(a) transfer
(b) migrate
(c) exhume
(d) dispatch

35. Eric's essay was ____________ in that each point flowed nicely into the next point.

(a) choppy
(b) succinct
(c) jumbled
(d) cohesive

36. In the 18th century, the majority of women writers used ____________ for their real names to be kept unknown.

(a) acronyms
(b) anagrams
(c) monograms
(d) pseudonyms

37. The steady growth of the printing industry in Canada has ____________ that of the national economy.

(a) paralleled
(b) managed
(c) replaced
(d) erased

38. If the mayor refuses to listen to different opinions, he will eventually ____________ his colleagues and supporters.

(a) extend
(b) digress
(c) confine
(d) alienate

39. A cruise on our ocean liner will offer you a complete ____________ from your normal routine.

(a) rejection
(b) dismissal
(c) departure
(d) elimination

40. The terrorist attack did ____________ damage to the building, and it soon collapsed.

(a) benign
(b) consensual
(c) irreparable
(d) resounding

41. We urge the public to raise awareness of wildlife smuggling and fight against the ____________ of our native animals.

(a) detention
(b) trafficking
(c) profiteering
(d) consternation

42. The great breakthrough in perfumery came with the method of ____________ perfume oils from plants and flowers.

(a) restoring
(b) extracting
(c) disclosing
(d) presuming

43. Drug companies have announced that they will ____________ joint investigations into the counterfeiting of prescription drugs around the world.

(a) seize
(b) pacify
(c) discern
(d) conduct

44. The ability to make art for art's sake is one of humankind's __________ characteristics from other animals.

(a) prudential
(b) distinctive
(c) integrative
(d) contentious

45. This bridge allows a vertical __________ of 37 feet at mean high water.

(a) clearance
(b) drought
(c) width
(d) load

46. You are requested to __________ receipt of this letter.

(a) deem
(b) perceive
(c) speculate
(d) acknowledge

47. When the US invaded Cambodia in 1970, America's college campuses were __________ by violent protests.

(a) ratified
(b) avouched
(c) convulsed
(d) repudiated

48. Films about troubled war veterans often depict past __________ through flashbacks to provide background to the mental trauma the veterans suffer.

(a) atrocities
(b) banalities
(c) clemencies
(d) magnanimities

49. The teacher suspected cheating when he noticed the normally mediocre student's __________ grammar and spelling.

(a) tedious
(b) sporadic
(c) corpulent
(d) impeccable

50. The debate over __________, or allowing the terminally-ill to die painlessly, continues to be controversial.

(a) dyslexia
(b) dichotomy
(c) euthanasia
(d) postmortem

This is the end of the Vocabulary section. Do NOT move on to the Reading Comprehension section until instructed to do so. You are NOT allowed to turn to any other section of the test.

READING COMPREHENSION

Part I **Questions 1—16**

Read the passage. Then choose the option that best completes the passage.

---

1. "Children's street culture" is a generic expression used to explain a phenomenon where children create games, songs and rhymes that are then handed down to the next generations of children. It is oftentimes most prominent in places where there is a significant concentration of blue collar city dwellers. In these heavily populated areas, there are more opportunities for children to interact with each other socially. What anthropologists consider most intriguing is that these street cultures are almost universal. Wherever there are a lot of working class people, _______________________________.

(a) there is a thriving children's street culture
(b) children are not given a good education
(c) children will likely cause many problems
(d) there are fewer opportunities for children

2.

Dear Mr. Brigand,

I congratulate you on recognizing our company's safety issues at last, but obviously, as CEO, you should have done so long ago. You are playing catch-up, and it was at the cost of two lives that you admitted to the mining operation's poor safety regulations. You mention devotion to improvement, but a great deal of money needs to be invested. It is time now for the company to demonstrate a financial dedication to solving this issue. I therefore suggest we get together soon to

_______________________________.

Regards,
Stan Walton
Union Leader, Brigand Mining Corporation

(a) acknowledge my investment portfolio
(b) discuss how to invest in better safety
(c) arrive at a solution to the pay dispute
(d) help improve safety in the local area

3. A dominant tendency in Western culture in general and in the US in particular is a
_________________________________. This adversarial frame of mind is based on the
assumption that winning is achieved by opposition. The best way to discuss an idea is to
debate it; the best way to settle disputes is through a lawsuit; the best way to begin an
essay is to attack an idea; and the best way to win an argument is to criticize. According
to some experts, this atmosphere of unrelenting contention can distort people's
perceptions.

(a) desire to win in every area of life
(b) need to assert one's political views
(c) combative approach to social discourse
(d) belief in the superiority of Western thinking

4. Our exclusive online sale features huge savings on the hottest brands and is available to
members only, so make sure you register at cooldesignerz.com. Registering will give you
access to the sale, which begins on April 1 and ends on April 30. As a member, you will
receive massive online discounts on premium denim including JeanGroove, Brad, Denim
Shade and more. You can also buy Lily Vanilla tops, Rose Couture jackets and much
more. Remember, _________________________________, so sign up now before it's too
late!

(a) the sale has only one day to go
(b) everyone has a chance of winning
(c) we can arrange your tour package
(d) you have to be a registered member

5. Up to two thirds of the population of European cities died of the plague in the 14th
century. The plague spread rapidly in cities because of _________________________________,
which made the transmission of disease easier. Cities at the time were also filthy,
infested with lice, fleas and rats, and subject to diseases related to malnutrition and poor
hygiene. On the other hand, some rural areas like eastern Poland and Lithuania were so
isolated and sparsely populated that the plague made little impact there.

(a) people's religious view against bathing
(b) the lack of adequate medical assistance
(c) people's little awareness of harmful insects
(d) high population density and close living quarters

6. Harriet Beecher Stowe was outraged by the Fugitive Slave Act. In response, she wrote *Uncle Tom's Cabin*, a fictional book depicting what she perceived as the evils of slavery. Furiously denounced in the South, the book became an overnight bestseller in the North. It was responsible for ________________________. Lincoln himself believed the novel was instrumental in building support to end slavery.

   (a) stirring up even more racial conflict
   (b) setting many in opposition to slavery
   (c) helping slaves enjoy their new freedom
   (d) convincing people to vote for the legislation

7. Work will begin Monday on a project to ________________________ the nearly two-mile hike to the summit of the Arrowhead Mountain in Honolulu. Although there have been no accidents in the dark areas, a park spokeswoman said that the rapidly increasing number of visitors walking on the dimly-lit path raised safety concerns.

   (a) light dark sections of
   (b) build rest areas along
   (c) put crosswalk signs up on
   (d) create a promotional video of

8. Between 1948 and 1978, successive governments in Britain provided funds through the Arts Council to encourage the growth of culture and the arts. This continued until the 1979 election of the conservative government, which reduced or else withdrew state subsidies for the arts. It was a government that promoted individualism, private enterprise and marketplace values in almost every area of society. Under these conditions, the arts ________________________. Plays, films and exhibitions could not be produced unless they could turn a profit in a competitive market.

   (a) had to be treated as any other business
   (b) became a valuable aspect of everyday life
   (c) were supported by the Arts Council instead
   (d) received the support and funding they needed

9. The Peuster Silver Lizard Brooch was made for people who adore high quality, handcrafted accessories at a reasonable price. Featuring a green and gold color scheme, this brooch goes well with all of your favorite clothes and is especially great for spicing up an outfit that requires an extra kick. Made from silver tone metal and studded with diamond-colored rock crystals, the Peuster Silver Lizard Brooch ________________________________.

(a) will definitely be worth its high retail price
(b) is comprised of the finest gems available
(c) matches well with items of similar color
(d) gives your whole wardrobe a touch of flair

10. Washington State's plan to deepen the channel of the Columbia River from 40 to 50 feet will provide new export opportunities for the state. While ten feet of dredging may not seem like a lot, its economic impact will be tremendous. Previously, larger ships weighed down with cargo were discouraged from visiting Columbia's seaports because it was dangerously shallow. The state's plan, however, will allow ________________________________. Farmers, ranchers and manufacturers will better be able to keep up with the global economy with a resulting reduction in shipping costs.

(a) large ships safe passage all along the Columbia river
(b) people better access to the river for boating activities
(c) families the opportunity to live along the scenic riverfront
(d) more frequent shipping without harming the environment

11. It is tempting to ________________________________. In dinosaurs, the brain represents 1/100,000th of the body's weight, in whales 1/10,000th, in elephants 1/600th and in humans 1/45th. The principle, going by these examples at any rate, seems sound, but this initial judgment may be misleading. In mice, the brain is 1/40th of the body's weight, and in marmosets 1/25th. By our brain ratio principle above, the marmoset would have to be one of the world's most intelligent creatures, and humans would not be able to even outthink mice.

(a) predict an animal's brain size through its body composition
(b) assume intelligence determines vulnerability to extinction
(c) generalize on intellectual superiority based on brain size
(d) create a classification system based on brain capacity

12. In dream analysis, doorways may be especially compelling, for they may reflect _________________________________. Someone knocking on your front door in a dream may reflect a recent possible development in your life. Since each new opportunity accompanies both positive and negative possibilities, emotions and imageries surrounding doorways are often mixed. You might want to greet the strange man at the door readily, for he is attractive or charming, but also feel it is improper for him to request entrance into your home. Indeed, undesired changes in our lives are frequently portrayed in dreams as intruders or strangers coming to the door.

(a) different paths one may choose in life
(b) both new opportunities and their risks
(c) possible chances to meet new people
(d) your past and future simultaneously

13. Young political reporters fear that the use of the most direct language about a politician occupying a high office will make them vulnerable to complaints of bias and leave them subject to retaliation. But, political reporters with a wealth of media experience _________________________________. They recognize that the relationship between the media and politicians is a kind of game and that politicians know tough talk in the media is all a part of the game.

(a) know that those fears are largely unfounded
(b) emphasize that the key is to remain impartial
(c) acknowledge that most politicians are dishonest
(d) understand that reporting can be a dangerous job

14. Do you have experience as a _________________________________? We are offering a full-time position with a salary of $3,175-$5,716 each month, depending on qualifications and experience. Under the guidance of the Associate Director of Technology and Development, you will be in charge of developing and providing training sessions and technical support to our staff and customers (schools, students, parents, partner organizations) on how to operate our latest Learning Management System (Whiteboard) and our Enrollment and Academic Portfolio System (EAPS).

(a) developer of high-end database software programs
(b) instructor, trainer and technical support specialist
(c) director in the field of technology and development
(d) supervisor in the field of high-tech human resources

15. Influenza and the common cold are often confused, since they display many common
symptoms. An individual with a runny nose or a sore throat, for example, could have
either a cold or the flu because these symptoms are characteristic of both diseases.
________________________________, the distinction is crucial, in particular for sufferers
of chronic heart or lung diseases. For them, the flu is not simply a week-long
aggravation; as they are prone to such complications as pneumonia, pulse irregularities
and congestive heart failure, catching the flu could spell death for them.

(a) Besides
(b) However
(c) Likewise
(d) Furthermore

16. The characteristics of successful supervisors have been studied to determine whether
effective performance or self-promotion is a better determiner of ultimate career success.
The study revealed that the relative importance of these two factors varies from company
to company. ________________________________, the qualities and skills demanded for
effective performance in the present management job are not always identical to those
necessary at a higher level of management.

(a) By contrast
(b) Thereafter
(c) Otherwise
(d) Moreover

Part II   **Questions 17—37**

Read the passage and the question. Then choose the option that best answers the question.

---

17. If you are having difficulty falling asleep on the eve of an exam, try calming yourself down by using psychological imagery. To accomplish this, you need to come up with your own peaceful scene. It can be real or make-believe—the beach, the woods or the mountains—as long as it is a setting in which you would feel completely calm and peaceful. Use your five senses to guide your imagination: what would you see, hear, taste, smell and feel if you were there?

Q: What is the topic of the talk?
(a) What to imagine before sleeping
(b) What to do the day before an exam
(c) How to use mental imagery to relax
(d) How to keep yourself in good shape

18. Moderate use of alcohol is said to be linked with a lowering of cholesterol. However, the benefit is not great enough for authorities to recommend drinking alcohol as a way to improve health. Increased consumption of alcohol has many health risks such as high blood pressure and liver cirrhosis. Given the potential dangers, the American Heart Association cautions people against controlling cholesterol through increasing their alcohol intake or starting to drink if they have not already done so.

Q: What is the passage mainly saying about alcohol?
(a) It is associated with many health benefits.
(b) It is the main cause of high blood pressure.
(c) It is healthy if consumed in small amounts.
(d) Its dangers to health outweigh its benefits.

19. In winter, it is harder for birds to find food, so there is no better way to attract birds into your backyard than by providing a regular supply of food. Seeds, nuts, kitchen scraps and water will entice the birds and allow you to watch them at close quarters. You might even be able to persuade birds to stay for the summer by giving them somewhere to nest. Bird houses placed carefully beyond the reach of cats make valuable homes for various birds.

Q: What is the best title for the passage?
(a) Helping Birds Stay Safe
(b) How to Make a Good Bird Nest
(c) What Kinds of Foods Birds Like
(d) Attracting Birds to Your Backyard

20.

Dear Sir/ Madam,

Enclosed is a parking ticket which I don't think should have been issued to me. The ticket was placed on my vehicle, in my presence, at the corner of 5th Avenue and Broadway on Friday, May 4 at 8 pm. At that time, I explained to the meter maid that my car had stalled and I was waiting for a tow truck. However, she replied that she could make no exception of my case. This is outrageous and unfair. I am positive you will agree that, given my situation, the ticket was unjustly handed out and should be withdrawn.

Yours sincerely,
Ian Rutgers

Q: What is the purpose of the letter?
(a) To explain a car accident
(b) To appeal against a parking fine
(c) To file a lawsuit against the city
(d) To compliment a meter maid

21. The Roman Colosseum is a monument not only to the grandeur of the Roman Empire but also to its cruelty. Ancient Roman festivities held there opened with a series of wild animal fights, featuring contests among tigers, lions, elephants, giraffes and humans. Midday brought the morbid spectacle of public executions before the main event the gladiator matches. Depending on the day's structure, however, these events were sometimes combined in one long, chaotic battle. Eventually, Christian leaders ensured that the Colosseum's entertainments no longer featured human executions, but animal slaughters continued until around AD 524.

Q: What is the passage mainly about?
(a) Cruelties to animals that ancient Roman citizens watched
(b) Acts of cruelty once practiced at the Roman Colosseum
(c) Sacrifices made in the name of the Roman Empire
(d) Carnivals held at the Colosseum of ancient Rome

22. In-store merchandising is a method for maximizing sales by displaying a product effectively in the store. It can be applied to promoting home accessory sales. For instance, picture frames should be displayed as they would appear in a home. Display the frames with photos in them—pictures of children and dogs are recommended. If possible, place them next to flowers, candles or other household items. This will further help the customer visualize how the frame will look in his or her home. This concept of creating a homey setting to entice customers can be applied to any home accessory.

Q: What is the main point of the passage?
(a) Better display of home accessories can increase sales.
(b) Home accessory is one of the fast growing businesses.
(c) Frames displayed as if in a real home sell more quickly.
(d) Decorating a store with household items can promote sales.

23. When I was young, I commuted to school by bus. Each day my friends and I would get off at the bus stop and cross the street to spend a few minutes with the Doves, an elderly couple in our neighborhood. Every afternoon, Mrs. Dove would happily prepare freshly squeezed lemonade or iced tea to drink and an afternoon snack to nibble on. We would end up spending hours listening to their stories and tidbits of wisdom. Recalling those afternoons on the back porch with the Doves always makes me smile.

Q: Which of the following is correct about Mrs. Dove?
(a) She sold lemonade and iced tea to her neighbors.
(b) She enjoyed giving students something to eat.
(c) The students sometimes considered her boring.
(d) She liked to listen to stories from the students.

24.

Dear Mr. Dipola,

I am writing to express some concerns I have about my son's performance in your science class. John's grades have never fallen as low as they are now. He has fallen behind in all of his classes, but he is furthest behind in yours. I tried to help John with his homework, but the material he is studying was too advanced for me. Do you have any suggestions that might help improve my son's grades? I look forward to hearing from you soon.

Regards,
Margaret Scully

Q: Which of the following is correct according to the letter?
(a) John's homework is too advanced for his grade level.
(b) Mr. Dipola is being blamed for John's poor performance.
(c) Mr. Dipola is being asked to help John with his homework.
(d) John is having problems keeping up with his classes at school.

25. The collective nature of Christianity called for an architectural style distinguishing itself from the religious architecture of Greece and Rome. Whereas temples from those cultures had functioned as storehouses and backgrounds for outdoor rituals, Christians honored God and prayed together inside their churches. Thus, the builders of the first churches borrowed the design not belonging to temples, but to Roman public halls called basilicas. The basilica scheme offered open space for Christians to gather and windows to illuminate the inside, a style that is still prominent in modern churches.

Q: Which of the following is true according to the passage?
(a) The first Christian churches were built in a Greek temple style.
(b) Early Christian worshipers utilized temples as their gathering place.
(c) The basilicas had enough space for the worshipers to gather inside.
(d) Modern Christian churches are built in a different style from basilicas.

26. Since 1958, *Sources of Indian Tradition* has been one of the most significant and broadly used textbooks on societies and cultures of South Asia (now the nation-states of India, Pakistan, Bangladesh, Sri Lanka and Nepal). It has helped countless students and readers understand how foremost thinkers in South Asia have viewed life, the customs of their forefathers and the world they live in. This second version of the book has been extensively modified, with prefacing essays describing the specific environments in which these thinkers have surfaced.

Q: Which of the following is correct about *Sources of Indian Tradition*?
(a) The country that receives most attention in the book is India.
(b) It shows how Westerners have misunderstood Indian traditions.
(c) The second edition covers thinkers not included in the first edition.
(d) It outlines the ideas of respected thinkers in the South Asia region.

27. Why do some sales teams succeed and others don't? We know why, and we can show you the reason at our annual sales seminar. This two-day seminar will help sales managers in particular focus on developing solutions to make their sales teams more efficient. In this seminar, you will learn how to effectively organize staff, maximize both customer and salesperson loyalty, and generate desired sales results from each member of your sales team. This seminar is designed for anyone working in sales management or anyone who intends to become a sales manager in the future. Don't miss out. Register online today at salesseminar.com.

Q: Which of the following is correct about the seminar?
(a) It will help sales managers achieve high sales figures.
(b) It will include an educational program for customers.
(c) It is intended for new sales staffs that need extra training.
(d) It requires participants to take an online class in advance.

28. Ginkgo extracts are swiftly joining the mainstream of the field of medicine worldwide. The usage of ginkgo leaf extracts is known to originate from Chinese medicine. Over time, it has been developed into a widely used herbal remedy that enhances memory, learning, alertness and mood. German health officials recently approved the extract for dementia treatment. In America, the National Institute on Aging is currently promoting a clinical trial to assess the effectiveness of ginkgo in treating the symptoms of Alzheimer's disease.

Q: Which of the following is correct according to the lecture?
(a) Germany plans to market ginkgo medicines.
(b) Ginkgo is currently a treatment for dementia.
(c) Ginkgo is able to slow down the aging process.
(d) Western medicine still has not embraced ginkgo.

29. The idea of rules governing warfare seems illogical; yet, all combative nations that signed the Geneva Conventions are supposed to abide by its rules of engagement. These international laws are meant to prevent actions that cause unnecessary suffering, although admittedly, they seldom prevent criminal behavior in warfare. However, they have been invoked by International War Crimes Tribunals to try individuals involved in the Holocaust, the Nanking Massacre and genocides in Yugoslavia, Rwanda and Cambodia. So, while not a strong deterrent, at least these rules can help bring war criminals to justice.

Q: Which of the following is correct according to the passage?
(a) Rules governing war actively prevent most war crimes.
(b) International Tribunals decide what rules govern warfare.
(c) War Crimes Tribunals helped end the genocide in Rwanda.
(d) The Geneva Conventions gives rules on proper combat conduct.

30. Back pain has always been around, like the common cold. But now sufferers have wider treatment options to choose from. They can turn to alternative medicines or ever more aggressive conventional medications to alleviate their symptoms. In the worst cases, however, some may find that they are no better off for all the treatment they receive. For those severe cases, surgery is sometimes the only solution.

Q: Which of the following is correct about back pain?
(a) The costs for treating back pain are rising.
(b) Some sufferers have no alternative but surgery.
(c) More and more people are having back problems.
(d) Many sufferers are misled by alternative treatments.

31. Would you like to visit Japan to find out more about its citizens and culture? Since 1990, the Oregon Educational Homestay Program has been introducing American students to the marvelous culture of Japan via partnership alliances with several affiliated Japanese cities. This coming June, we are jointly putting together another three-week visiting program for 30-40 high school students as well as teachers, parents and any other volunteer adult chaperones. Having some familiarity with Japanese language and culture is desirable but not necessary. To register, please consult your local high school guidance counselor.

Q: Which of the following is correct about the homestay program?
(a) No adults are allowed to go on the trip to Japan.
(b) The next trip is for three weeks this coming June.
(c) It mainly introduces Japanese students to US culture.
(d) Students must speak Japanese in order to be eligible.

32. While the Ottoman Empire's strength in the 16th century was its military, ironically, the Empire's collapse resulted from misplaced confidence in this same institute. The Ottoman Army, which originally promoted soldiers based on merit, gradually adopted a system of inheriting officers' commissions. Hereditary rank led to ignorant officers and poorly trained forces unprepared for 20th century warfare. By the time the Ottoman army faced allied forces in the Arab theater during World War I, the decline of the army was evident, and defeat was swift. This loss ended the Empire and created modern day Turkey.

Q: Which of the following is correct according to the passage?
(a) Bad training led to officers who did not understand modern warfare.
(b) Rank in the Ottoman army was originally awarded based on heredity.
(c) The Ottomans had little confidence in the military before World War I.
(d) Allied forces were able to quickly conquer the Ottoman army in World War I.

33. Effective March 15, Meril Canada will be renamed InvestDirect. Although the name of the company and the look and feel of our website will change, the range of investment services we make available to clients will not be affected. In fact, you can expect to see even more quality services available. We are committed to increasing our range of services online in the near future in order to make your investing experience as seamless as possible.

Q: What can be inferred about Meril Canada?
(a) It is losing business to competitors.
(b) It plans to change its business focus.
(c) It is aiming to boost its online presence.
(d) It plans to downsize the number of staff.

34. Statistically speaking, we are in more danger now of street crimes than we were a decade ago due to an increase in muggings over the past several years. The growth in street crimes coincides with the rising popularity of small but expensive technology such as mobile phones and MP3 players, which have become the most commonly stolen objects. Aside from the fact that they are fashionable, police note that high-tech gear is easier to steal than a purse or wallet, and harder to trace back to the criminal than a credit card.

Q: What can be inferred from the passage?
(a) Openly carrying an MP3 player makes you a target for crime.
(b) You are more likely to be mugged if you appear to be rich.
(c) The weak and helpless are often the ones who get mugged.
(d) More people will start to carry firearms on the street.

35. New York hip-hop artist Paul Mayes is often called a hip-hop poet, a label that attempts to exalt him above the current conventionality of what was once America's most poetic, radical and creative music. Once described as the "black CNN" for its gritty news on the social malaise afflicting black America, so much of hip-hop now offers only a rigid backbeat to the dreary doggerel of sex, money, ego and brittle urban romance. With a breathless, galvanizing energy, Mayes is reclaiming hip-hop's poetic power. His lyrics go well beyond a ghetto news flash to give us a hyper-literate visionary polemic on the state of black America.

Q: What can be inferred about Paul Mayes?
(a) He falls short of the poetic styles of younger hip-hop artists.
(b) He is revitalizing a music genre that has lost its edge of late.
(c) He brings talents to hip-hop that are not part of its tradition.
(d) He ironically criticizes hip-hop by highlighting hip-hop clichés.

36. Pyramid fanatics have put forth arresting mathematical formulas from the heights, lengths and angles of the Great Pyramid of Cheops. They have discovered dimensions said to be based on the Earth's polar radius and its range from the sun in miles. Unfortunately, their figures do not hold up under close examination. One can experiment with any set of numbers and ultimately produce vaguely meaningful outcomes that were never anticipated. Martin Gardner proved this by working out the speed of light from the height and capstone weight of the Washington Monument.

Q: What can be inferred from the passage?
(a) Figures can be manipulated to deceive the unwary.
(b) The Great Pyramid is still a mystery to archaeologists.
(c) Pyramids were used by ancient Egyptians for astronomy.
(d) The speed of light was calculated incorrectly by Martin Gardner.

37. For reasons that are not well explained, the number of newly diagnosed cases of asthma in the US has risen sharply, up by 58.6 percent. Asthma deaths, too, are on the increase. Ironically, these increases are taking place at a time when irritants associated with asthma are better understood by medical specialists and are under better control. In an attempt to solve the mystery, some investigators are focusing their attention on the way modern homes and workplaces are tightly sealed, with the result that irritants and contaminants are trapped and recirculated.

Q: What can be inferred about asthma in the US?
(a) Asthma attacks will decrease in the future.
(b) Medical specialists will find a cure for asthma soon.
(c) Bad air in homes and offices is causing asthma attacks.
(d) New kinds of viruses are causing fatal asthma symptoms.

38. Heat removes the poisons from some plants. (a) Cooking can therefore make edible what would otherwise be dangerous to eat. (b) The bitter and poisonous manioc, for instance, became a staple food of the Amazon when natives learned about the effects of heat on plants. (c) When manioc roots are boiled, the poison seeps from them into the water. (d) Animals leave most poisonous plants untouched out of instinct.

39. How environmentally conscious are you when shopping for clothes? (a) Are you aware that, from the chemicals used in dry-cleaning to the energy required for washing, your clothes can indirectly harm the environment? (b) One solution is to avoid dry-clean-only garments and look for clothes that you can easily wash yourself. (c) Study the care labels carefully before you decide whether to dry-clean or wash expensive clothes. (d) Also, washing your clothes in cold water can help the environment since hot water wastes a lot of energy.

40. Puppet shows enjoy popularity around the world. (a) One reason for this is that they are mostly performed in small theaters. (b) This small venue allows for more intimate interaction between performer and audience. (c) Puppetry is a very specialized art and takes years of training to master. (d) As well, the stories they tell are quite simple and embrace universal themes recognizable to diverse audiences.

This is the end of the Reading Comprehension section. Please remain seated until the proctor has instructed otherwise. You are NOT allowed to turn to any other section of the test.

Listening Comprehension

Grammar

Vocabulary

Reading Comprehension

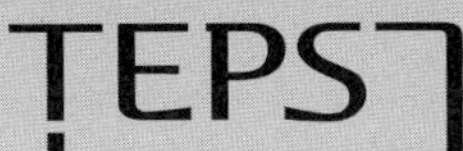

LISTENING
COMPREHENSION

DIRECTIONS

1. In the Listening Comprehension section, all content will be presented orally rather than in written form.

2. This section contains 4 parts. In parts I and II, each passage will be read only once. In parts III and IV, each passage and its corresponding question will be read twice. But in all sections, the options will be read only once. After listening to the passage and question, listen to the options and choose the best answer.

Part I **Questions 1—15**

You will now hear fifteen conversation fragments, each made up of a single spoken statement followed by four spoken responses. Choose the most appropriate response to the statement.

Part II **Questions 16—30**

You will now hear fifteen conversation fragments, each made up of three spoken statements followed by four spoken responses. Choose the most appropriate response to complete the conversation.

Part III Questions 31—45

You will now hear fifteen complete conversations. For each item, you will hear a conversation and its corresponding question, both of which will be read twice. Then you will hear four options which will be read only once. Choose the option that best answers the question.

Part IV Questions 46—60

You will now hear fifteen spoken monologues. For each item, you will hear a monologue and its corresponding question, both of which will be read twice. Then you will hear four options which will be read only once. Choose the option that best answers the question.

GRAMMAR

DIRECTIONS

This part of the exam tests your grammar skills. You will have 25 minutes to complete the 50 questions. Be sure to follow the directions given by the proctor.

Part I **Questions 1—20**

Choose the best answer for the blank.

1. A: I need to see some ID.

B: OK, ___________ driver's license.

(a) here my
(b) it is here
(c) here it is
(d) here is my

2. A: Good evening. Are you ready to order?

B: Not yet. ___________ you give us a little more time, please?

(a) Do
(b) Can
(c) May
(d) Shall

3. A: Hi, Jeremy. How's school going?

B: OK, except that there's so much ___________ I have to do.

(a) read
(b) reading
(c) to read
(d) having read

4. A: Are you sure you want to see this movie?

B: Yes, I ___________ want to see it.

(a) too
(b) very
(c) such
(d) really

5. A: Where's that report I asked you to do?

B: I put ___________ when you were in Mr. Russell's office.

(a) your desk
(b) it your desk
(c) on your desk
(d) it on your desk

6. A: Do you go to yoga every night?

B: Of course. I ___________ a class yet.

(a) will not miss
(b) hadn't missed
(c) am not missing
(d) haven't missed

7. A: Should I accept the job offer?

B: Yes. If I ___________ you, I would take it.

(a) am
(b) were
(c) will be
(d) would have been

8. A: Could you have someone come up and clean my suite?

B: Certainly, sir. Someone ___________ shortly.

(a) will be
(b) be there
(c) will be there
(d) there will be

9. A: _________ it be all right if I
       borrowed your car tomorrow?
    B: No, I need it to get to work.

    (a) Will
    (b) Can
    (c) Would
    (d) Could

10. A: I can't stand it anymore. You're
       getting on my nerves!
    B: Well, _________!

    (a) so are you
    (b) are you so
    (c) you so are
    (d) you are so

11. A: Is there a number I can call to reach
       you?
    B: Sure. Call my cell phone number,
       _________ is 011-877-4615.

    (a) that
    (b) who
    (c) what
    (d) which

12. A: How about playing a video game?
    B: I can't. I have work _________.

    (a) done
    (b) to do
    (c) doing
    (d) to doing

13. A: Guess what! While _________
       down the street, I ran into my old
       boyfriend.
    B: No kidding! Did he recognize you?

    (a) walk
    (b) to walk
    (c) walking
    (d) having walked

14. A: Hurry up, Alice!
    B: I am. I'm driving above _________.

    (a) speed limit
    (b) a speed limit
    (c) the speed limit
    (d) some speed limit

15. A: I'm too old to go jogging anymore.
    B: Well, no matter _________, you
       need to get some exercise.

    (a) what is your age
    (b) what your age
    (c) age you are at
    (d) your age is

16. A: Can I play some music?
    B: _________ you keep the volume
       low.

    (a) Even if
    (b) So that
    (c) As long as
    (d) Inasmuch as

17. A: I thought you were going to go
       fishing.
    B: I was _________, but I changed my
       mind.

    (a) to go
    (b) going to
    (c) going to do
    (d) going to go to

18. A: Where's Charlie?

    B: I don't know. He called a while ago to say he __________ in five minutes.

  (a) left
  (b) leaves
  (c) had left
  (d) was leaving

19. A: Are you ready to present the results of your experiment?

    B: Yes, __________.

  (a) all the data have I ready
  (b) all the data I have ready
  (c) I have all ready the data
  (d) I have all the data ready

20. A: Has the new medication proved effective?

    B: Yes, I've nearly recovered __________ my illness.

  (a) across
  (b) from
  (c) over
  (d) off

Part II Questions 21—40

Choose the best answer for the blank.

---

21. Since neither the horse __________ the rider has any experience, they are not favored to win the race.

  (a) or
  (b) yet
  (c) and
  (d) nor

22. __________ to measure one's progress in improving fitness.

  (a) It not being easy
  (b) It is not easy
  (c) Not easy is
  (d) Not easy

23. The driver was speeding on the highway when one of his front tires burst, __________ him to lose control of his car.

  (a) caused
  (b) causing
  (c) to cause
  (d) having caused

24. Since 60% of all campaign funds __________ on television, politicians try hard to master that medium.

  (a) spent
  (b) spending
  (c) are spent
  (d) are spending

25. __________ on stage, the short speaker could hardly be seen over the tall podium.

(a) Stand
(b) Standing
(c) To stand
(d) Having stood

26. As a result of his stroke last year, __________.

(a) it was unable to speak to Greg
(b) speaking to Greg was unable
(c) to speak Greg was unable to
(d) Greg was unable to speak

27. Vaccines are often made from small amounts of __________ microbes.

(a) weaken
(b) to weaken
(c) weakened
(d) weakening

28. After falling over, Jane stood up and continued on her way as if nothing __________.

(a) happens
(b) has happened
(c) had happened
(d) was happening

29. The aim of advertising is to establish the identity of a particular brand name __________ will be preferred over the competition.

(a) prominently that it
(b) that it prominently
(c) so that it prominently
(d) so prominently that it

30. In the human body, __________ detected by the immune system is attacked by antibodies.

(a) germ
(b) germs
(c) any germ
(d) one germ

31. Baking cookies and pies __________ what makes Mrs. Harold happy.

(a) is
(b) are
(c) was
(d) were

32. Often there is a character in a movie __________ no one wishes to identify.

(a) in that
(b) by whom
(c) with whom
(d) of whatever

33. After __________ happened between the Presidents, it is unlikely that the two countries will resolve their conflict anytime soon.

(a) that
(b) what
(c) anything
(d) something

34. Nowadays only crops that have been genetically modified through the introduction of foreign gene material __________ regulated by the US government.

(a) is
(b) are
(c) was
(d) were

35. A teacher should never go into a class without knowing __________.

(a) the objective is for that hour
(b) the objective for what that hour is
(c) what the objective is for that hour
(d) what is the objective for that hour

36. The wounded bear __________ in the snow for several hours before it was discovered.

(a) lying
(b) has lain
(c) had lain
(d) has been lying

37. Two animals __________ highly intelligent are dolphins and whales.

(a) thought of to be
(b) thought to being
(c) that are thought of
(d) that are thought to be

38. __________ seemed to stand still, as the buzzer sounded and Carl threw the ball toward the basket.

(a) Time
(b) Times
(c) A time
(d) The times

39. The death of a 13-year-old boy brings __________ killed by bird flu in Asia.

(a) the number six to those
(b) to six the number of those
(c) the number of those to six
(d) to six of the number those

40. The emphasis on solid colors as well as a slimmer look __________ the fashion of men's suits over the past summer.

(a) is changing
(b) are changing
(c) has changed
(d) have changed

Part III — Questions 41—45

Identify the option that contains an awkward expression or an error in grammar.

41. (a) A: I think I'm allergic to something.
(b) B: Really? What are you allergic to?
(c) A: I'm not sure, but maybe it's the air pollution.
(d) B: That could be it. It's quite badly these days.

42. (a) A: Have you seen the scissors?
(b) B: Yes, I use them yesterday.
(c) A: But they're not in their usual place.
(d) B: Sorry, I'll go find them for you.

43. (a) A: Do you see that man feeding the pigeons?
(b) B: You mean that guy which is sitting on the park bench?
(c) A: Yes. He's always there at lunchtime feeding the birds.
(d) B: Are you sure? I haven't noticed him there before.

44. (a) A: I'm really worried about my Portuguese class.
(b) B: Oh, you'll be fine, since you can speak a little Spanish.
(c) A: You think knowing Spanish will help me understand Portuguese?
(d) B: Sure. It's easier to learn Portuguese already if you know Spanish.

45. (a) A: I don't have my share of the rent for this week.
(b) B: Not again! So, I suppose you want me to pay all of it?
(c) A: If you could. I promise I'll pay you back next week.
(d) B: Well, all right. I guess I will. But this is a last time.

Part IV   **Questions 46—50**

Identify the option that contains an awkward expression or an error in grammar.

46. (a) Have you ever wondered why it is easier to learn things when we are interested in that subject? (b) According to new research, learning things and liking them are tied together. (c) Researchers say true learning occurs when we feel positive about what we are learning. (d) In fact, when learning occurs, the brain releases chemicals that actual cause us to feel good.

47. (a) While working as a journalist in the Congo, I was impressed by the people there. (b) The majority of the Congolese I met were tired of fighting. (c) All they wanted was to be left alone to live of peace. (d) Nevertheless, they endured the terrible war with great patience.

48. (a) Recent studies show that being happily married is good for your health. (b) Men over 65 who are happily married usually live longer than unhappily married husbands. (c) A strong marriage is also beneficial for diabetes sufferers, to lead to better management of their disease. (d) Moreover, happily married people are less likely to abuse alcohol and drugs.

49. (a) American colleges and universities in size are varied a great deal. (b) Some colleges have just a few hundred students, whereas state universities may serve more than 100,000. (c) At smaller schools, students generally get to know their classmates and professors better. (d) But larger schools offer a greater selection of courses and activities.

50. (a) If, like many people, you struggle with a poor body image, you need to try to readjust your thinking. (b) A poor body image would have devastating effects on you psychologically. (c) So, consider whether this so-called "problem" is really worth worrying about. (d) Ask yourself: should improving my body shape really be a priority in my life?

This is the end of the Grammar section. Do NOT move on to the next section until instructed to do so. You are NOT allowed to turn to any other section of the test.

VOCABULARY

DIRECTIONS

This part of the exam tests your vocabulary skills. You will have
15 minutes to complete the 50 questions. Be sure to follow the
directions given by the proctor.

Part I **Questions 1—25**

Choose the best answer for the blank.

---

1. A: I've been having a lot of trouble sleeping lately.

 B: That explains why you look so ___________.

 (a) flat
 (b) tired
 (c) fresh
 (d) awake

2. A: Hi, I'm calling for Sam Perkins.

 B: Just a second, I'll go ___________ him.

 (a) get
 (b) ask
 (c) take
 (d) answer

3. A: Would you like to go out for dinner this weekend?

 B: Thanks, but I already have ___________.

 (a) plans
 (b) goals
 (c) meals
 (d) duties

4. A: I think I'll just stay home today.

 B: Fine, if that's what you ___________, but I'm going to Dave's party anyway.

 (a) hear
 (b) have
 (c) want
 (d) allow

5. A: Hi, I'm Kate's friend, Beth.

 B: It's great to ___________ you, Beth. I'm Robert.

 (a) greet
 (b) meet
 (c) contact
 (d) introduce

6. A: Can we come with you to the county fair?

 B: Sure. I'd be glad to have you ___________ me.

 (a) join
 (b) show
 (c) leave
 (d) bring

7. A: Do you think these shoes go with my outfit?

 B: Yes, they ___________ your dress quite nicely.

 (a) accord
 (b) match
 (c) equal
 (d) blend

8. A: I thought I told you not to touch my CDs.

 B: Sorry, I just wanted to ___________ to a little music.

 (a) roll
 (b) feel
 (c) play
 (d) listen

9. A: Shall I ask James to help me?

B: Don't __________ him. He's working now.

(a) alarm
(b) worry
(c) disturb
(d) concern

10. A: Is there a gas station around here?

B: Yes, keep __________ down this road.

(a) trying
(b) finding
(c) making
(d) driving

11. A: Hello, this is Martin's __________ Store. Can I help you?

B: Yes, I need some 3/4-inch screws for a building project. Do you have any?

(a) Grocery
(b) Fashion
(c) Hardware
(d) Electronics

12. A: I'm glad you became our manager.

B: Thanks for your __________.

(a) advice
(b) opinion
(c) support
(d) inference

13. A: Are you going to make it to the theater on time?

B: Yes, you can __________.

(a) lean on me
(b) lead me on
(c) take me on
(d) count on me

14. A: I need you to finish the report today.

B: Can't it __________ until Monday?

(a) last
(b) hold
(c) wait
(d) stay

15. A: What kind of insurance would you like on your rental car?

B: Just the minimum __________, please.

(a) measure
(b) coverage
(c) treatment
(d) possibility

16. A: I'd like to __________ my reservation.

B: Certainly. Your name and flight number, please?

(a) affirm
(b) assert
(c) certify
(d) confirm

17. A: This show is boring. Can you change the channel?

B: I would, but I can't seem to find the __________ anywhere.

(a) switch
(b) remote
(c) adapter
(d) converter

18. A: Stan and Margie always sit together at lunch.

    B: I know. I __________ they're dating.

(a) bet
(b) assure
(c) suggest
(d) recommend

19. A: Are we out of printing paper again?

    B: We are, but I just placed a(n) __________ for more.

(a) ad
(b) bid
(c) order
(d) supply

20. A: How did the presentation go?

    B: It didn't __________ as planned.

(a) turn out
(b) find out
(c) make up
(d) work up

21. A: I wish I could buy you that diamond necklace on display.

    B: Yeah, but let's be __________, honey. You can't afford it.

(a) realistic
(b) genuine
(c) justifiable
(d) thoughtful

22. A: I've had enough. I'm going to quit my job today.

    B: Really? Well, I think you're making a __________ decision that you might regret.

(a) swift
(b) hasty
(c) flashy
(d) prompt

23. A: I'm really pleased with your work on the project.

    B: Thanks. I appreciate the __________.

(a) inspiration
(b) consultation
(c) admonishment
(d) encouragement

24. A: This cell phone has a lot of cool features, don't you think?

    B: But it also cost you a(n) __________, remember?

(a) heart of gold
(b) arm and a leg
(c) piece of your mind
(d) chip on your shoulder

25. A: I found the lecture extremely boring.

    B: So I __________. I saw you yawning.

(a) agreed
(b) assessed
(c) gathered
(d) predicted

26. In a saucepan, add milk and butter, and stir until they are thoroughly __________.

(a) served
(b) heated
(c) mixed
(d) filled

27. After last week's robberies, many families in the neighborhood no longer feel __________.

(a) safe
(b) sure
(c) bold
(d) clean

28. With any purchase of $100 or more at our store, you will __________ a ten percent discount.

(a) return
(b) charge
(c) deduct
(d) receive

29. Police are investigating sightings of an __________ object in the sky, which has been confirmed as neither a civilian nor military aircraft.

(a) invisible
(b) imaginary
(c) unequalled
(d) unidentified

30. Psychology research has shown that blue has a calming effect, __________ our blood pressure and slowing our heartbeat.

(a) uplifting
(b) reducing
(c) removing
(d) expanding

31. Many Americans are not aware that African-Americans still face mistreatment in our __________.

(a) public
(b) society
(c) humanity
(d) civilization

32. With his book *In Cold Blood*, Truman Capote invented a new literary __________, journalism written with the language and structure of literature.

(a) trait
(b) genre
(c) example
(d) scenario

33. Paul's father wanted him to become a pianist, so in 1925 he __________ in the Royal College of Music to pursue that career.

(a) listed
(b) landed
(c) applied
(d) enrolled

34. Since everyone wanted water, there was a high __________ for more wells to be dug.

    (a) passion
    (b) request
    (c) demand
    (d) question

35. To tighten the screw, turn the screwdriver __________ until the screw stops rotating.

    (a) leftward
    (b) sideways
    (c) clockwise
    (d) backwards

36. When Einstein first __________ his theory of relativity in 1905, only a few physicists could understand it.

    (a) detected
    (b) publicized
    (c) remodeled
    (d) recognized

37. A middle-aged doctor was taken __________ yesterday and is now being held for ransom at an undisclosed location.

    (a) victim
    (b) refuge
    (c) convict
    (d) hostage

38. To receive a low annual percentage rate, your credit card account must be in good __________.

    (a) place
    (b) standing
    (c) acceptance
    (d) arrangement

39. People who use drugs begin to crave them all the time, and unfortunately many become __________.

    (a) addicts
    (b) fanatics
    (c) followers
    (d) adherents

40. The clothes we choose to wear reveal what group or professional circle we wish to be __________ with.

    (a) associated
    (b) acquainted
    (c) coordinated
    (d) collaborated

41. The writer's descriptions of his childhood give a clear __________ into what it was like to grow up in Siberia in the 1950s.

    (a) insight
    (b) outlook
    (c) broadcast
    (d) viewpoint

42. The leader was a(n) __________ figure, revered as a saint by some and despised as a dictator by others.

    (a) intangible
    (b) irresistible
    (c) controversial
    (d) argumentative

43. In light of the recent scandals, politicians' financial dealings should be open to public __________.

    (a) censure
    (b) scrutiny
    (c) reproach
    (d) estimation

44. Our company runs the risk of appearing
    unprofessional if employees are given
    free ___________ over what they wear to
    work.

    (a) rein
    (b) desire
    (c) policy
    (d) option

45. Green Park contains nearly 300 native
    plant species and ___________ fish and
    other aquatic animals found nowhere
    else.

    (a) lodges
    (b) harbors
    (c) confines
    (d) inhabits

46. In Egyptian mummification, the
    tightness of the bandaging helped to
    ___________ the shape of the body.

    (a) treat
    (b) form
    (c) maintain
    (d) assemble

47. Fleming's discovery of penicillin is
    one of the most important medical
    ___________ of the 20th century.

    (a) signposts
    (b) postmarks
    (c) timetables
    (d) milestones

48. After watching the romance *Spring in
    Paris*, Delia became ___________ with
    its handsome main actor Danny Jones.

    (a) raved
    (b) vexed
    (c) appalled
    (d) infatuated

49. As a(n) ___________ prize, runners-up
    will receive a new stainless steel toaster.

    (a) substitute
    (b) alternative
    (c) consolation
    (d) replacement

50. Political boundaries can act as barriers
    to the spread of ideas or knowledge,
    thereby ___________ cultural diffusion.

    (a) guarding
    (b) retarding
    (c) sheltering
    (d) screening

This is the end of the Vocabulary section. Do NOT move on to the Reading
Comprehension section until instructed to do so. You are NOT allowed to turn
to any other section of the test.

READING COMPREHENSION

DIRECTIONS

This part of the exam tests your ability to comprehend reading passages. You will have 45 minutes to complete the 40 questions. Be sure to follow the directions given by the proctor.

Part I Questions 1—16

Read the passage. Then choose the option that best completes the passage.

1. When people look for a job, they often search job centers or recruitment agencies, or they ask friends and family. But they would be better off searching online where more jobs can be found. In fact, 57% of recruiters use the Internet to advertise their openings. It is also a convenient way to search for a job because it can be done from home. So, if you are ___________________________, you should probably try going online first.

   (a) looking for a job
   (b) hiring a new employee
   (c) shopping for cheap products
   (d) searching for a new way to advertise

2. My wife and I had friends over for a barbecue and swimming party recently. Since many of us had children, we took turns eating so that an adult would always be watching the children as they swam. But ___________________________ when it was my turn to watch the kids. As my friend and I sat and ate next to the pool, my son was floating on a kick board. We both looked away for a moment, and when we looked back, he was nowhere to be seen! Then we saw him sinking under the water, and I dived in and rescued him. We were so lucky that day.

   (a) we ran out of food
   (b) a scary thing happened
   (c) my son did not want to swim
   (d) I already had something to eat

3. Food and nutrition specialists always have plenty of advice about what you should and should not eat. But there are really only two important rules for healthy eating. First, eat a good variety of different sorts of food. The best way to do this is to choose a wide assortment of foods from the five main food groups and include them regularly in your diet. The second important thing to remember is, try not to eat too much. If you follow these two rules ___________________________.

   (a) you will build more muscle
   (b) your food bill will be lowered
   (c) you will have a healthy, balanced diet
   (d) your mealtimes will be more interesting

4. Do you feel that you are overwhelmed with work at the office? Well, it might be that you just need to become more organized. If you have your work and your workspace well-organized, you might find that everything will become more manageable. The first step is to ensure that you have all the things that you use most often—pens, notepad, telephone, etc.—within arm's reach on your desk. Also, organize paperwork into folders and place these on your desk in order of priority. If you take these simple steps, you might find that ______________________________.

(a) you will be able to cope with your work better
(b) your job will be less boring than it used to be
(c) you will get more respect from your colleagues
(d) your working environment will feel more like home

5. What makes a marriage happy? Some people say that love and trust are important. Others say that flexibility and friendship are most essential. However, a large number of people say that ______________________________ is the key. This is because if two people can tell each other what they are thinking and feeling, they will have a better understanding of each other and will be better able to work out the problems. Honest and regular communication in a marriage relationship helps each spouse feel happy and satisfied.

(a) having a high income
(b) communicating openly
(c) spending time together
(d) arguing as little as possible

6. Since 1919 when the US Congress set aside the land known today as Grand Canyon National Park, we have been working hard to preserve its beauty. As a recognized World Heritage Site, it needs to be preserved and protected for future generations. Please help us safeguard this special place. We all need to work together to ______________________________.

(a) stop tourists from visiting it
(b) treat it with care and respect
(c) ask Congress to pass the law
(d) make our city more beautiful

7. Throughout musical history, it has often taken decades before the work of innovative composers has been accepted by mainstream audiences or has received international recognition. Even Johann Sebastian Bach, who has been a cultural icon of the Baroque music genre for more than two centuries, was little known for most of his life. And Beethoven, now a household name around the globe, was not at first recognized as a musical genius. Some of his works were not widely performed in concert programs until well into the 20th century. So, clearly, ________________________ is not a prerequisite for an enduring musical legacy.

(a) popularity during one's lifetime
(b) perfection in style and technique
(c) mastering the classical music genre
(d) pleasing those who criticize your music

8.

Dear Barbara,

Jeff and I are really excited that ________________________. It's hard to believe we'll be there in just a few days! Thanks for offering to pick us up. I just got the tickets today. We'll be flying in on Union Airlines flight 302, arriving at LA airport on May 10th at 5:32 pm. Oh, and while we're there, we'd like to visit my grandmother for a day. She lives in Ventura, which is not too far from you. Well, that's all for now. See you soon!

Your friend,
Jenny

(a) we are coming to visit you
(b) we can go on this trip together
(c) you have decided to come and see us
(d) you live near my grandmother's house

9. The fact that certain people acquire new languages faster than others could be related to neurological differences. In a recent study, those who were quickest to hear subtle differences in sounds in a foreign language were found to have the greatest amount of white tissue in a brain region responsible for sound processing. Brain scans of study participants revealed that the fastest learners had, on average, 70% more white matter in the left hemisphere than the slowest learners. So, it is now believed that _______________________________.

(a) the human brain needs to be more carefully studied
(b) language is an ability that is based on one's mental capacity
(c) fast language learners have brains that reach maturity quicker
(d) more white matter in the brain indicates quicker language acquisition

10. In 1542, Portuguese mariners navigating to Macao were pushed up the shore by powerful winds to a Japanese island near the port of Kyushu. They became the first European visitors to Japan, and they brought along the first firearms the Japanese had ever witnessed. Subsequently, in 1549 Catholic missionaries from Portugal set foot in Japan, and not long afterwards, another Portuguese merchant vessel sailing to China was also stranded not far from Kyushu. As a result of these three consecutive landings, Portugal _______________________________.

(a) severed its relations with neighboring Spain
(b) became revered for its expertise in sailing
(c) gave Japan its first impression of Europeans
(d) officially adopted Japanese religious beliefs

11. Was it a coincidence that Picasso developed Cubism at about the same time that Einstein published his theory of relativity? Physicist Arthur Miller thinks there was a direct link between the two. Miller has always been interested in art, Cubism and Picasso in particular. He also believed that if he combined his knowledge of physics with his love for art, he might be able to uncover the link. So, he began investigating _______________________________.

(a) to what extent Picasso had influenced Einstein
(b) whether Einstein's love for art affected his studies
(c) the roots of Cubism in connection with relativity theory
(d) how much Picasso's style of painting relied on other artists

12. The origin of the Nile was for years one of Africa's most enduring enigmas. The Greek geographer Ptolemy held that the river began in an undefined area of inner Africa which he called the Mountains of the Moon. After several hundred years of speculation, the actual sources of the Nile were unveiled in the 1870s to be mainly in Lakes Victoria, Edward and Albert. Regarding the Mountains of the Moon, they are chiefly identified now with the Ruwenzori mountain range. Ptolemy _______________________________, however, for the thawing snows of the Ruwenzori added to the lakes that eventually flow into the Nile.

(a) made an error in his estimations
(b) may not have been entirely wrong
(c) was not speaking of the same river
(d) identified the wrong mountain range

13. This internal study is a response to demands that the current deficiencies in the Canadian government's auditing processes be addressed. Thus, this preliminary report entails a full evaluation of current auditing practices, with the aim of increasing transparency and accountability and strengthening data security protocols within government. In reviewing the government's current practices, our review committee has come up with 102 recommendations which, if implemented, will _______________________________.

(a) permit Canadian citizens to pay less tax in the future
(b) improve the government's national security initiatives
(c) reduce government spending on superfluous inquiries
(d) address the current shortcomings of our auditing system

14. Blood flow is imperative to keeping a steady body temperature of approximately 37 degrees Celsius. Heat production and heat loss in numerous areas of the human body are counterbalanced naturally through blood circulation. When an individual gets overheated, the vessels open wide and an additional amount of blood flows to the skin. Heat then dissipates through the skin, effectively pushing the body temperature down. On the other hand, when an individual is cold, the vessels contract, diverting blood from the skin to prevent heat loss. All of this is essentially a process of _______________________________.

(a) distributing heat via the bloodstream
(b) cleansing the bloodstream of impurities
(c) perspiring when hot and shivering when cold
(d) changing the rate at which the heart pumps blood

15. Writing is an ancient form of communication that has been recorded on different mediums over the centuries. It was first recorded on stone, then on animal skins, and after that on paper. Of course, nowadays writing is often done not on paper but on a computer screen. We have come a long way in terms of the technology used in writing. _______________________, remarkably, the content of our writing has not changed. We still express the same emotions, desires and basic storylines.

(a) So
(b) Yet
(c) Then
(d) Because

16. Following Korea's financial crisis, it took four years for the soundness of most financial institutions to be restored. This restoration was accomplished through far-reaching structural reforms, which to most people made it appear that Korea as a whole had returned to the economic stability of pre-crisis years. _______________________, because the focus of structural reform was on normalizing distressed financial institutions and restoring their intermediary functions in the market, certain aspects of reform lagged behind.

(a) In sum
(b) Moreover
(c) For instance
(d) Nevertheless

17. Shakespeare's play titled *Antony and Cleopatra* is about the love between Antony, the
leader of the Roman Empire, and Cleopatra, the Queen of Egypt. Although Antony and
Cleopatra were famous world leaders, Shakespeare shows us that these lovers also had
their faults and personal problems. When we read or see the play, they are shown as just
normal human beings struggling with feelings of jealousy, love, shame and insecurity.
Through Shakespeare's portrayal of them, Antony and Cleopatra seem just like us,
despite their greatness as historical figures.

Q: How does Shakespeare mainly portray Antony and Cleopatra?
(a) As deeply in love
(b) As ordinary people
(c) As overly emotional
(d) As great historical figures

18. Historically speaking, Albania has been one of the least-industrialized European
countries. Approximately 50% of its people still work in agriculture, although the chiefly
mountainous terrain greatly limits the amount of land that is fit for farming. The main
food crops in this nation are wheat, corn and potatoes, while the major commercial
crops include cotton, tobacco, rice and fruits. Traditionally, sheep have been the most
significant form of livestock, but chickens, goats and cattle are also raised nowadays.

Q: What is the passage mainly about?
(a) Albanian cultural history
(b) The geography of Albania
(c) The history of Albanian farms
(d) Albania's agricultural lifestyle

19. In the past century, life expectancy has increased by 30 years. This means that you now
have many years to look forward to after you retire. Long Life, Inc. can help you plan
ahead for these years. We provide financial services that will take care of your annuities,
life insurance, long-term care insurance and healthcare risk management for the future.
With the wide variety of services that we offer, your future is guaranteed.

Q: What is the main focus of the advertisement?
(a) Long Life's statistics on life expectancy
(b) The need to stay healthy
(c) The financial burden of retirement
(d) Ways Long Life, Inc. can assist in future planning

20.

To Whom It May Concern:

Since joining our sales department in July 1998, Joe Douglas has proved an extremely reliable and valuable asset. Joe always shows a professional attitude toward work and is well-liked by colleagues and clients. He is capable of working both independently and as part of a team. I am confident that Joe will make a valuable addition to any corporation he joins and would recommend him very strongly without hesitation. Please feel free to call me should you need further information.

Regards,
Jaime Carson

Q: What is the purpose of the letter?
(a) To praise Mr. Douglas's sales record
(b) To request that Mr. Douglas be promoted
(c) To recommend Mr. Douglas for employment
(d) To ask Mr. Douglas to resign from his position

21. Records indicate that over 67 million pounds sterling has been overpaid for social welfare in the Irish Republic in the past couple of years. The Freedom of Information Act records indicate that the overpayment was mostly due to fraud. The issue at hand is one that has been emphasized in the past, both in state and in public social forums. However, to date, attempts to close the loopholes that let the welfare system be manipulated have not been successful.

Q: What is the main idea of the passage?
(a) The Irish government has failed to notice any welfare fraud.
(b) Irish society regards welfare fraud as a serious problem.
(c) Social welfare fraud continues to be a problem in Ireland.
(d) Ireland's welfare system is failing to meet its people's needs.

22. Mercury is highly toxic and can be harmful to humans if they eat contaminated fish. So, how do fish come to have mercury in them? Unfortunately, mercury is a by-product of many industrial processes, and it ends up in waterways. In the United States, coal-fired power plants alone pump about 50 tons of it into the air each year. That mercury then rains out of the sky into oceans, lakes, rivers and streams, where it becomes concentrated in the flesh of aquatic creatures. Even a small amount of mercury in a large lake can make all the fish in it unsafe to eat.

Q: What is the main topic of the passage?
(a) The process by which fish are contaminated by mercury
(b) The way mercury is transferred from aquatic life to humans
(c) The harmful effects of mercury pollution on aquatic creatures
(d) The industries responsible for causing mercury pollution in waterways

23. Singer David Crosby was arrested at about 1 am on Saturday in Times Square. The charges included illegal possession of a firearm and drugs. Crosby had checked out of the Doubleday Suites Hotel on Broadway after his performance at William Paterson University's Shea Center. Police reported Crosby had left behind a suitcase, which was found by a hotel worker. The worker went through the luggage, searching for identification, but instead discovered a handgun and drugs.

Q: Who first found Crosby's gun and drugs?
(a) A police officer
(b) A famous singer
(c) A hotel employee
(d) A university center worker

24. If you need a place to stay while you are looking for a permanent residence in South Florida, we have the right apartment for you. Our apartments are half the price of a hotel and twice as comfortable. Clover Corporate Housing offers weekly and monthly rentals of one-, two- and three-bedroom apartments, fully furnished and equipped. With beautiful interior designs and high-quality furnishings, Clover offers a unique temporary living experience that feels like home. If you are moving to South Florida, we invite you to be our guest at Clover.

Q: Which of the following is correct according to the advertisement?
(a) Furniture is not provided at Clover apartments.
(b) The Clover apartments come in two different sizes.
(c) Hotels are more expensive than Clover apartments.
(d) Clover Corporate Housing offers apartments for sale.

25.

Hi Mom,

I hope you are doing well. I have had so many new experiences during my stay here in Seoul. The other day in Jongno, I came across an auto-toilet. You just insert a coin and the door opens. Then, when you exit, the washroom starts to clean itself by spraying the whole booth with disinfectant. A toilet that keeps itself clean—great idea, isn't it? These are a lot cleaner than some public toilets here. Anyway, I'll be staying here for a few more weeks before coming home. I'll be sure to take lots of pictures (attached is one of the auto-toilet). See you soon!

Love,
Dan

Q: According to the email, which of the following is a benefit of the auto-toilet?
(a) It is portable and can be set up in any location.
(b) It disinfects itself after someone has used it.
(c) It gives change in coins for paper money.
(d) It costs very little to keep it clean.

26. The Hopi are unique among Native American tribes because women exercise much more power in Hopi society than men. This female dominance is expressed in their social customs. For example, at birth, Hopi children become members of their mothers' clans rather than their fathers'. In addition, ownership of property, such as land and houses, passes from mother to daughter instead of from father to son, as it does in other Native American tribes. However, women do not have all the power in this culture. Societal authority still rests in the hands of men, but that authority is passed on to men by their mothers.

Q: Which of the following is correct according to the passage?
(a) Hopi children are members of their fathers' clan.
(b) Hopi culture has no concept of societal authority.
(c) Hopi daughters inherit property from their mothers.
(d) Hopi men inherit societal authority from their fathers.

27. Our study has found that female doctors spend more time—about ten percent more—with patients than male doctors do. Also, they are more apt to talk with patients about lifestyle issues, such as work and relationships, and provide more reassurance and positive feedback. In reporting these findings, we wish to make clear that we are not suggesting there is evidence that female doctors provide better medical treatment than male doctors. Nor are we concluding that individual health will be better depending on whether you see a male or female doctor.

Q: According to the study, how do female doctors compare with male doctors?
(a) They provide better medical treatment.
(b) They are more likely to improve patients' health.
(c) They tend to respond more optimistically to patients.
(d) They spend more time discussing alternative treatments.

28. Eating specific foods can have a positive impact on your emotional health. For example, for depression and anxiety, doctors now recommend foods with omega-three fats, B vitamins and whole grains. Whole grains and foods with omega-three fats, magnesium and vitamin E have also been used in the treatment of other mental disorders. Some foods that are good for emotional health are salmon, a good source of omega-three, leafy greens, which contain vitamin B, and rye crackers, which are a nutritious whole grain snack.

Q: Which of the following is correct according to the passage?
(a) Rye crackers have less nutrition than salmon.
(b) Vitamin B can be obtained from leafy vegetables.
(c) Losing weight helps to improve emotional health.
(d) Doctors recommend eating a low-fat diet for depression.

29. Machu Picchu, a complex of ruins on a mountaintop in the vicinity of Cuzco, Peru, is one of the most gorgeous and mysterious ancient locales in the world. Legend has it that the area of Machu Picchu was revered as a holy place long before the Incas started constructing gigantic stone structures there in the early 1400s. Regardless of its origins, the Inca transformed the area into a small but extraordinary city. Not visible from below, surrounded by enough agricultural terraces to feed its people and watered by natural springs, Machu Picchu was indeed a great Inca city.

Q: Which of the following is correct about Machu Picchu according to the passage?
(a) It did not have its own source of water.
(b) It was built long before the Incas arrived.
(c) It became a sacred place in the early 1400s.
(d) It cannot be seen from below the mountaintop.

30. The Curtain Bluff Hotel cordially invites you to stay as our guest and enjoy our luxurious, yet quaint accommodations. Our newly renovated facility has 70 sea-view deluxe rooms and suites on the surf side of the magnificent Curtain Bluff. All of our deluxe rooms have received a complete makeover: they now feature homely quilts, plush cushions and room decor in seascape shades of blue, turquoise and green. As our guest, you will also enjoy our elegant wood sitting areas, picturesque walkways and spacious green granite and marble bathrooms. So, come and relax in a room overlooking the sea at Curtain Bluff Hotel.

Q: Which of the following is correct about the hotel?
(a) It will soon renovate its restaurant.
(b) It has elegant sitting areas located in the woods.
(c) Its rooms overlook the magnificent forest.
(d) Its large bathrooms are made of marble and granite.

31. There are a number of differences between stage musicals and their filmed adaptations. One of the most obvious is that live performances, unlike those on film, are never the same from night to night, and they involve a more direct relationship with the audience. In addition, the number of songs in stage musicals is generally much higher than in films, and these songs might fit differently into the overall structure. Film is also a more naturalistic medium, and therefore more disruptive when a character breaks into song in a film—which is why so many of the great film musicals are set in the theater.

Q: Which of the following is correct according to the passage?
(a) Characters seem less disruptive when they sing in films.
(b) Live performances are a more naturalistic medium than films.
(c) Many film makers have adopted theater settings for their musicals.
(d) More songs are introduced when stage musicals are adapted to film.

32. One of the central concerns of Chinese leaders throughout Chinese history has been state-building. Indeed, Chinese leaders down through the years often pursued the dream of a modern nation-state as a solution to the various crises that afflicted their country. In contrast to this preoccupation with state-building, the development of civil society, or social organizations and institutions, was given much less attention. This striking asymmetry of state and society decisively shaped the course of modern China.

Q: Which of the following is correct according to the passage?
(a) Chinese state and society developed in harmony until recently.
(b) The dream of state-building was pursued to help China become powerful.
(c) The China of today emerged from a state and society that were imbalanced.
(d) Chinese leaders were preoccupied with civil society at the expense of the state.

33. Would you like to do something worthwhile with your money? Then, come and check out Primero Bank Investment Services, Inc. We will help you invest for the long term in stocks, bonds or any of over 1,000 mutual funds. We can also introduce you to online trading. Our broad range of services covers everything from discount brokerage to professional investment guidance and planning. Call 1-800-321-5454 or visit us at www. primerobank.com.

Q: Which person would most likely use this company's services?
(a) Someone who needs to borrow money
(b) Someone who wishes to work at a bank
(c) Someone who wants to save for retirement
(d) Someone who wants to make a quick profit

34. After the solar eclipse of 1919 proved that light from faraway constellations is curved by the Sun's gravity, the Nobel Prize Committee started receiving many nominations for Albert Einstein for his work on the theory of relativity. However, the Committee chose to grant the award that year to Charles-Edouard Guillaume for having found a nickel-steel alloy that stayed fairly unaffected by changes in its surroundings. Although many observers overseas found Guillaume an odd choice, the fact was that few, if any, committee members had been convinced enough by research into the 1919 solar eclipse to change their view of Einstein's work.

Q: What can be inferred from the passage?
(a) The solar eclipse of 1919 failed to confirm Einstein's theory of relativity.
(b) The scientific world welcomed the Academy's choice of Guillaume over Einstein.
(c) The Nobel Prize Committee overestimated the significance of Guillaume's discovery.
(d) The Nobel Prize Committee allowed personal bias to influence their decision-making.

35. Singapore's economic infrastructure is about to undergo some dramatic changes, with the island's government pushing for a shift away from electronics, chemicals and other labor-intensive manufacturing activities. But what is the reason for this economic reshuffle? "In a word, China," says Singapore's deputy prime minister Lee Hsien Loong. China has virtually monopolized what used to be Singapore's primary markets, and rather than competing against such an economic giant, the island's government has decided to support specialization in less competitive sectors. "If we don't," Lee says, "our economy will become irrelevant on the global stage."

Q: What can be inferred about Singapore from the news article?
(a) Its economy depends too much upon Chinese imports.
(b) It will foster industries in which China is not dominant.
(c) Its government believes that the economic future is grim.
(d) It will begin to invest heavily in electronics and chemicals.

36. Some psychologists and psychiatrists believe that humor is a vital part of maintaining mental health. However, the humor that has the most value is not the kind we see on television or the kind contained in a quick joke. Though these may be delightful, they are superficial and temporary. The humor that is of most value is a more enduring kind of humor than these. It is a kind of humor that goes beyond jokes and laughter, and psychologists say we ought to cultivate this type as part of our general attitude to life. They say this type of humor is crucial in coping with the difficulties and complexities of modern living.

Q: What will the passage most likely discuss next?
(a) The value of comedy shows and humorous stories
(b) Ways to create your own kind of superficial humor
(c) Current psychological theories on the use of humor
(d) Examples of the kind of humor helpful in managing life's problems

37. Traditional Turkish village life obeyed Islamic customs and was extremely systematic and harmonious. There existed substantial differences in fortune, social hierarchy and rank among villagers, but long-standing or growing gaps among social classes did not actually exist. This was in part because most inhabitants were agriculturalists with enough access to privately owned territory and village commons. Besides, even though property was inherited from generation to generation, the repeated subdivision of property in every generation left the standing of a village's individual families unchanged. As wealthier landowners tended to have bigger families, more numerous inheritors mitigated against excessive property distributions.

Q: What can be inferred about traditional Turkish village life from the passage?
(a) Wealth inequalities were rarely inherited down the generations.
(b) Widespread poverty made differences in social status negligible.
(c) Islamic law forbade distinctions in social status on account of wealth.
(d) Farming success was more highly valued than wealth, status and rank.

38. At Maxy's Department Stores you can now buy the renowned SkyLife air cushion bed made by China's Wehai Rubber Products Co. (a) The bed is portable and can even be used as a couch. (b) Many companies these days are using China as a production base. (c) It is made of rubber and cotton and is available as a single or a double bed. (d) Each model comes with two manual pumps for inflation and a repair kit.

39. The basic types of family organizations in human communities are nuclear families, extended families and corporate descent groups. (a) In various societies these days, the understanding of "family" involves single parenthood, step-parenting, stay-at-home fathers and grandparents bringing up children. (b) Nuclear families comprise a husband, a wife and their children residing together and sharing a common household. (c) Extended families are bigger networks of related nuclear families that function as a unit. (d) Corporate descent groups are especially large extended family groupings found in numerous pre-industrial societies.

40. Many people wonder nowadays if newspapers will survive. (a) This is because most major newspapers around the world are now available on the Internet. (b) But the fact is that most people still like to read a morning paper while having breakfast. (c) It is a convenient and enjoyable part of their daily routine. (d) People sometimes have to subscribe to newspapers to read them online.

This is the end of the Reading Comprehension section. Please remain seated until the proctor has instructed otherwise. You are NOT allowed to turn to any other section of the test.

Listening Comprehension

Grammar

Vocabulary

Reading Comprehension

LISTENING COMPREHENSION

Part I ## Questions 1—15

You will now hear fifteen conversation fragments, each made up of a single spoken statement followed by four spoken responses. Choose the most appropriate response to the statement.

Part II ## Questions 16—30

You will now hear fifteen conversation fragments, each made up of three spoken statements followed by four spoken responses. Choose the most appropriate response to complete the conversation.

Part III **Questions 31—45**

You will now hear fifteen complete conversations. For each item, you will hear a conversation and its corresponding question, both of which will be read twice. Then you will hear four options which will be read only once. Choose the option that best answers the question.

Part IV **Questions 46—60**

You will now hear fifteen spoken monologues. For each item, you will hear a monologue and its corresponding question, both of which will be read twice. Then you will hear four options which will be read only once. Choose the option that best answers the question.

GRAMMAR

DIRECTIONS

This part of the exam tests your grammar skills. You will have 25 minutes to complete the 50 questions. Be sure to follow the directions given by the proctor.

Part I   **Questions 1—20**

Choose the best answer for the blank.

1. A: That spaghetti you cooked was really good.

B: Thanks. You can have some ___________ if you'd like.

(a) more
(b) other
(c) further
(d) another

2. A: Do we turn at this traffic light or the next one?

B: I'm not certain ___________ one would be better.

(a) which
(b) whose
(c) whatever
(d) whichever

3. A: I have a terrible headache.

B: ___________ you, dear? I'll get you an aspirin, then.

(a) Will
(b) Can
(c) Are
(d) Do

4. A: The sign says you can't smoke here.

B: Oh, ___________.

(a) I not noticed that
(b) I noticed that not
(c) notice that I didn't
(d) I didn't notice that

5. A: Did you spend much time in Athens?

B: Not really. ___________ there for about a week.

(a) I had been
(b) I've been
(c) I was
(d) I'm

6. A: Shall we keep waiting in line to get a table?

B: No, 30 minutes ___________ enough. Let's just go.

(a) are to be
(b) is to be
(c) are
(d) is

7. A: Here's your birthday gift. I hope you like it.

B: Thank you ___________ much.

(a) so
(b) too
(c) ever
(d) really

8. A: You're not going to believe this. Caroline is now dating Gary!

B: Come on, ___________!

(a) must be kidding
(b) kidding must be
(c) you must be kidding
(d) you kidding it must be

9. A: How did the thief get away?

   B: He simply ___________ over the fence.

   (a) jumps
   (b) jumped
   (c) has jumped
   (d) was jumping

10. A: Would you mind if I asked you a favor?

    B: No, ___________.

    (a) I wouldn't mind at all
    (b) not if I would mind it
    (c) at all I wouldn't mind
    (d) not at all I would mind it

11. A: Do you think we're going to face staff shortages again?

    B: Well, I certainly ___________.

    (a) don't hope it
    (b) hope so not
    (c) hope it not
    (d) hope not

12. A: Did you buy a new bike like you said you would?

    B: No, I just ___________.

    (a) got it repaired my old one
    (b) got repaired it my old one
    (c) my old one got repaired
    (d) got my old one repaired

13. A: I hear the opera *La Traviata* is worth seeing.

    B: Yeah, and we can easily go there after work since it ___________ nearby.

    (a) shows
    (b) was showing
    (c) is being shown
    (d) has been shown

14. A: Did you know kiwis can't fly?

    B: Yes, and ___________.

    (a) ostriches can't so
    (b) ostriches can't do
    (c) ostriches can neither
    (d) neither can ostriches

15. A: How did the swim match go?

    B: Really well. Julia, ___________ the best swimmer in our team, came in first place.

    (a) to be
    (b) being
    (c) she was
    (d) having been

16. A: What is this national park most famous for?

    B: Well, you can ___________.

    (a) here see some remarkable red rocks
    (b) remarkable red rocks see some here
    (c) here some remarkable red rocks see
    (d) see some remarkable red rocks here

17. A: What're you doing for Christmas?

    B: I ___________ yet.

    (a) haven't decided
    (b) won't be deciding
    (c) won't have decided
    (d) haven't been deciding

18. A: I've gained some weight since I took the medicine.

    B: Then, I'd advise ___________.

    (a) more you exercise
    (b) exercise doing more
    (c) you to exercise more
    (d) more exercising to do

19. A: Can you put these books in your bag?

    B: Sorry, but I don't have __________ for them.

  (a) room
  (b) a room
  (c) each room
  (d) another room

20. A: I never liked studying medicine in college.

    B: Then, __________ to become a doctor in the first place.

  (a) explain me why you decided
  (b) why you decided explain me
  (c) explain to me why you decided
  (d) why did you decide explain to me

Part II   **Questions 21—40**

Choose the best answer for the blank.

---

21. Walking through the park, the man began __________ about his worries at the office.

  (a) forget
  (b) forgot
  (c) to forget
  (d) forgotten

22. Some scientists estimate that as __________ as 10 million people around the world may already have the AIDS virus.

  (a) less
  (b) more
  (c) many
  (d) much

23. Spoilage as a result of bacterial action in food can be prevented by keeping the food __________.

  (a) extremely at temperatures low
  (b) extremely at low temperatures
  (c) at low temperatures extremely
  (d) at extremely low temperatures

24. Any books about technology run the risk of __________ outdated soon after they are published because technology is constantly changing.

  (a) become
  (b) became
  (c) becoming
  (d) to become

25. Bringing in outside food and drink __________ always prohibited in this theater.

  (a) is
  (b) are
  (c) is being
  (d) are to be

26. The young man accepted the job he __________ at a local bank.

  (a) offers
  (b) offered
  (c) is offered
  (d) was offered

27. The company had extensive database records on the __________ habits of thousands of people.

(a) purchases
(b) purchased
(c) purchasing
(d) to be purchasing

28. __________ an area of desert has sustained environmental damage, it recovers slowly, if at all.

(a) Now
(b) Once
(c) While
(d) Although

29. The Kyoto Protocol calls upon the United States to decrease greenhouse gas emissions to 7% below __________.

(a) 1990 level
(b) a 1990 level
(c) the 1990 level
(d) each 1990 level

30. Liaoning is a Chinese province __________ many remarkable fossils belonging to feathered dinosaurs have been found.

(a) in that
(b) for what
(c) in which
(d) of whom

31. For years, the use of animals for experiments __________ opposed on moral and philosophical grounds by many people.

(a) is
(b) are
(c) has been
(d) have been

32. Any person with blood pressure greater than 120/80 mmHg __________ high blood pressure.

(a) considered is for
(b) has to be considered
(c) is considered to have
(d) is considered to being

33. Coffee spread from Africa to Arabia where it was first used as a medicine __________ it became a beverage.

(a) after
(b) since
(c) unless
(d) before

34. The vacationers were making the most of __________ little of the summer was left.

(a) that
(b) what
(c) which
(d) whichever

35. The popular ice rink in front of Seoul City Hall will remain open __________ the end of the month.

(a) by
(b) until
(c) within
(d) toward

36. The boy was a gifted athlete, but __________ that most impressed his coach.

(a) work ethic it was
(b) it was his work ethic
(c) work ethic of his was
(d) ethic of his work was

37. This machine is faster than any other model, __________ over 5,000 stitches per minute.

(a) sews
(b) to sew
(c) it sews
(d) sewing

38. If the man had not consulted the doctor sooner, he __________ his life from a serious illness.

(a) can lose
(b) could lose
(c) could have lost
(d) could be losing

39. Sara loves going to the beach for many reasons, __________ to collect seashells.

(a) of which the least not is
(b) not the least of which is
(c) the least not which is
(d) which is not the least

40. The wife thought her husband __________ too hard in recent weeks and needed a break.

(a) works
(b) has worked
(c) will have worked
(d) had been working

Identify the option that contains an awkward expression or an error in grammar.

41. (a) A: Could you please send me an application packet?
    (b) B: Do you need the financial aid packet as well?
    (c) A: I'd appreciate it very well if you could send me both.
    (d) B: Certainly. They should arrive within the next two days.

42. (a) A: Let's go and see a movie tonight.
    (b) B: Tonight? I'm sorry, but I'm busy tonight.
    (c) A: Really? What should you be doing?
    (d) B: I'm going to have dinner with my parents.

43. (a) A: I'll need to see your driver's license and registration.
    (b) B: Yes, Officer, but what seems to be the problems?
    (c) A: You were driving way over the speed limit.
    (d) B: I'm very sorry. I'll be more careful.

44. (a) A: What's wrong with Betty? She looks rather stressed today.
    (b) B: She's a bit overwhelmed by all the work Mr. Jacobs has given her.
    (c) A: Why doesn't she just tell him that she can't handle it all?
    (d) B: She tried to, but he still demanded that she does it.

45. (a) A: Anna, do you want me to email you the photos at the party last week?
    (b) B: Thanks, that'd be great. How did they turn out?
    (c) A: Unfortunately, they didn't turn out that well. They're a bit dark.
    (d) B: I'm sure they are fine. I can't wait to see them.

Part IV   Questions 46—50

Identify the option that contains an awkward expression or an error in grammar.

46. (a) The amount of sleep an individual needs varies considerably from one stage of life to another. (b) An average infant sleeps up to 18 hours a day. (c) By age 4, sleeping time is reduced to about 9 hours. (d) By adolescence, it is further reduced to 7 hours, after which declines to about 6 hours.

47. (a) To develop critical reading skills, find an interesting article in a newspaper or magazine. (b) Make sure it is one that has at least three paragraphs. (c) Read the article carefully and pay close attention to the main idea. (d) Then, write the main idea down, summarize it in one sentence.

48. (a) Global Choice is a non-profit organization dedicating to helping the poorest people on earth. (b) We represent more than 50 international charities that all work towards this common goal. (c) Each year, Global Choice and its member charities improve the lives of millions of people. (d) Our funding and economic programs are now in place in every developing country.

49. (a) Flexibility is limited as you age because the connective tissue that coats muscles becomes stiff. (b) However, stretching can prevent this stiffening and can allow you to become more flexible. (c) It is perhaps least rigorous way to combat an inevitable decrease in flexibility. (d) It is also something you can do anywhere, at home or at the office, without the need for any equipment.

50. (a) There are few places in Southeast Asia more remote than the forested Nakai Plateau of southern Laos. (b) Over the decades, however, history seems to choose it as the center of intense activity. (c) During the Vietnam War, it was alive with the movement of Vietnamese troops heading down the Ho Chi Minh Trail. (d) Today, it echoes with the sound of dynamite going off for the construction of the Nam Theun Dam.

This is the end of the Grammar section. Do NOT move on to the next section until instructed to do so. You are NOT allowed to turn to any other section of the test.

VOCABULARY

DIRECTIONS

This part of the exam tests your vocabulary skills. You will have 15 minutes to complete the 50 questions. Be sure to follow the directions given by the proctor.

Part I Questions 1—25

Choose the best answer for the blank.

1. A: What does your company do to protect the environment?

B: For one thing, we use envelopes made of ___________ paper.

(a) genuine
(b) original
(c) recycled
(d) previous

2. A: Can I leave through this door?

B: No, you need to use the other ___________ .

(a) gap
(b) exit
(c) step
(d) alley

3. A: Do you have any seat preference?

B: Oh, yes. I'd like an ___________ seat on this flight.

(a) outer
(b) edge
(c) open
(d) aisle

4. A: How did you end up with so many old coins?

B: I've been ___________ them since childhood.

(a) following
(b) collecting
(c) arranging
(d) presenting

5. A: Paul! Fancy meeting you here.

B: It's quite a(n) ___________ to see you, too.

(a) honor
(b) interest
(c) emotion
(d) surprise

6. A: Mom, can I have an ice cream now? Can I, please?

B: Stop ___________ me about that. You can have one later.

(a) fooling
(b) picking
(c) bothering
(d) demanding

7. A: Have a great vacation.

B: Thanks. ___________ yours as well.

(a) Pack
(b) Enjoy
(c) Spend
(d) Create

8. A: What's the delivery ___________ ?

B: It's free if your groceries come to more than 30,000 won.

(a) money
(b) charge
(c) credit
(d) sum

9. A: Ace Rentals. How can I help you?

    B: Please put me through to your complaints __________ .

    (a) station
    (b) position
    (c) foundation
    (d) department

10. A: How do you make your face look so fresh?

    B: I __________ moisturizer every night.

    (a) set
    (b) wear
    (c) paint
    (d) apply

11. A: I have a sore throat.

    B: Then, take something to __________ it.

    (a) save
    (b) strip
    (c) rescue
    (d) relieve

12. A: I didn't do well on the English exam.

    B: Me, neither. I guess it's a __________ subject for both of us.

    (a) rigid
    (b) strict
    (c) tough
    (d) hardy

13. A: Hello. I'd like to stay at the hotel for one more night.

    B: Let me check if there is a __________ .

    (a) range
    (b) setting
    (c) position
    (d) vacancy

14. A: You're not thinking of changing your job, are you?

    B: Relax. I don't __________ to do that, at least not for the time being.

    (a) plan
    (b) guess
    (c) manage
    (d) suppose

15. A: Where's the laundry detergent?

    B: I'm afraid we __________ it.

    (a) put in for
    (b) ran out of
    (c) kept up with
    (d) looked down on

16. A: Is Dave the kind of person who can keep a secret?

    B: Oh yes, he can be __________ .

    (a) trusted
    (b) granted
    (c) restated
    (d) believed

17. A: I'm sorry I stepped on your foot. The bus is very crowded.

    B: That's OK. No __________ done.

    (a) pity
    (b) harm
    (c) excuse
    (d) accident

18. A: Where did you get the information for your newspaper article?

    B: I'm sorry, I can't __________ my sources.

    (a) alter
    (b) trace
    (c) disclose
    (d) regulate

19. A: Do you want to meet at nine
o'clock?

B: That _________ for me.

(a) does
(b) starts
(c) works
(d) prepares

20. A: Have you heard any more news
about layoffs at the company?

B: No, but I'm _________.

(a) turning over a new leaf
(b) making mincemeat of it
(c) keeping my ear to the ground
(d) looking a gift horse in the mouth

21. A: There must have been 20,000 people
at that rock concert last night.

B: That's a(n) _________. I'd say
there were maybe just 10,000.

(a) deflation
(b) elevation
(c) exaggeration
(d) discrimination

22. A: Is it true you kicked a student out of
your class today?

B: Yes, his behavior was _________.

(a) baffled
(b) arguable
(c) perplexed
(d) disruptive

23. A: I just heard our boss has resigned.

B: Really? I wonder whom they will
_________ as the new manager.

(a) allot
(b) induce
(c) replace
(d) appoint

24. A: I'd better go and close the window.

B: Yes, there is a _________ in here.

(a) gush
(b) draft
(c) blow
(d) current

25. A: Did you watch the football game last
night?

B: Yeah. I was _________ the Lions,
but they lost.

(a) taking up
(b) rooting for
(c) bailing out
(d) hanging onto

Part II Questions 26—50

Choose the best answer for the blank.

26. The debate __________ for four hours without any break.

(a) continued
(b) remained
(c) appeared
(d) spread

27. Please write your __________ name in the space provided.

(a) full
(b) total
(c) ideal
(d) perfect

28. It took the rest of the winter for the old lady to __________ her health.

(a) reserve
(b) regain
(c) repair
(d) retain

29. The film director's scripts were rarely written out in advance, and he encouraged his actors to __________ much of their dialogue.

(a) update
(b) supervise
(c) improvise
(d) neutralize

30. The student had to make his hobbies a __________ priority until his exams were over.

(a) slim
(b) low
(c) thin
(d) soft

31. The National Park Pass is __________ for one year.

(a) valid
(b) formal
(c) authentic
(d) detectable

32. Breast milk contains immunity-boosting substances that help a baby __________ infection.

(a) resist
(b) forgo
(c) waive
(d) deprive

33. Many linguists believe that language is an innate ability __________ to humans.

(a) specific
(b) superior
(c) transferred
(d) imprisoned

34. Visitors who are not family members are not __________ in the hospital after 9 pm.

(a) cleared
(b) allowed
(c) required
(d) accessed

35. The problem with Senator Brown is that he often __________ instead of sticking to the point for which he has taken the floor.

(a) varies
(b) curves
(c) pretends
(d) digresses

36. Marilyn Monroe died in 1962 from what some say was an accidental drug __________.

(a) stimulus
(b) overdose
(c) congestion
(d) discomfort

37. A request for a refund may be __________ if an item has been used or damaged.

(a) denied
(b) dilated
(c) pleaded
(d) upgraded

38. The families that __________ to the New World from Europe were full of hope for a new life.

(a) enrolled
(b) objected
(c) migrated
(d) broadened

39. As a result of a variety of human activities, the natural __________ of jaguars in North America has been lost.

(a) terrain
(b) habitat
(c) herbage
(d) rectitude

40. Besides earning millions of dollars in prize money, the golf champion makes a fortune by __________ many sports products.

(a) exposing
(b) endorsing
(c) plundering
(d) proclaiming

41. A collection of rare books is on __________ at the city library.

(a) exhibition
(b) inspection
(c) examination
(d) presentation

42. The new health care program is intended to cover part-time workers who are not otherwise __________ for employee health plans.

(a) hosted
(b) eligible
(c) obligated
(d) legitimate

43. The Pleiades is a group of stars or a star __________ that can be seen with the naked eye.

(a) gathering
(b) tribunal
(c) cluster
(d) envoy

44. African countries have __________ behind East Asian countries in terms of economic growth.

(a) lagged
(b) loitered
(c) delayed
(d) adjourned

45. The police officer ___________ the suspect to make sure that he was not carrying a concealed weapon.

(a) slaked
(b) frisked
(c) gouged
(d) dredged

46. Many people try to ___________ Canadian immigration laws by staging fake weddings in order to gain citizenship.

(a) skirt
(b) rend
(c) cajole
(d) allure

47. The young artist's ___________ use of color and skillful brushstrokes clearly show that he is a gifted painter.

(a) azure
(b) adroit
(c) gawky
(d) gauche

48. The oil crisis, ___________ by the closure of the Suez Canal, reached its height in 1979.

(a) exfoliated
(b) duplicated
(c) occasioned
(d) provisioned

49. To prevent genocide and other crimes against humanity, countries should initiate military action only as a last ___________.

(a) resort
(b) channel
(c) doctrine
(d) precaution

50. Some people buy designer label clothes solely for their ___________ value, but the sense of superiority they might gain is superficial.

(a) snob
(b) ductile
(c) chintzy
(d) unctuous

This is the end of the Vocabulary section. Do NOT move on to the Reading Comprehension section until instructed to do so. You are NOT allowed to turn to any other section of the test.

READING COMPREHENSION

DIRECTIONS

This part of the exam tests your ability to comprehend reading passages. You will have 45 minutes to complete the 40 questions. Be sure to follow the directions given by the proctor.

Part I   Questions 1—16

Read the passage. Then choose the option that best completes the passage.

1. Living in many different places over a lifetime is more common now than it ever
was. People move from city to city more freely, and even from country to country,
following their dreams or looking for better lifestyles. Better job offers can also make
people more willing to move from place to place. In short, like never before, people are
________________________ .

(a) not living in one area for long
(b) working in jobs they do not like
(c) renting more expensive apartments
(d) becoming more and more centralized

2. Last month a friend of mine was walking to her car when suddenly someone
attacked her and stole her purse. She wasn't seriously hurt but very shocked and
frightened. This incident made me think about my own safety, and I decided to
________________________ . Now, I'm a lot more confident when I go out at
night because I learned several basic ways I could protect myself.

(a) hold my purse tighter
(b) run over and help her out
(c) write a complaint about it
(d) take a class in self-defense

3. You no longer need to ask your neighbor to water your plants when you go away on
vacation. First, fill a big container with water. Then, set the container on the floor and
place a group of plants around it. Prepare a cotton rope and cut one end into pieces,
making sure each strand is long enough to reach all the plants from the water container.
Bury the strands in the dirt of each pot of plants to be watered and place the other end of
the rope in the water. The cotton will ________________________ .

(a) regulate the soil content of each plant
(b) absorb more water if the rope is very thick
(c) continuously transfer water into each plant
(d) adjust the level of water flow into your plants

4. While millions of young fans worldwide enjoy reading Harry Potter books, some parents have expressed worries about content in the books on death. It is, however, a concern that has been dismissed by Dr. Heather Sexton, an expert on childhood grief and mourning. She says the portrayal of death in such books provides a great educational opportunity. She explains that the books can teach children about ___________________________.

(a) the bad things to avoid in life
(b) the concept and nature of death
(c) the difference between right and wrong
(d) the benefits of reading outside of school

5. Researchers have found that girls rather than boys from working-class or poor families ___________________________. This may be due to the fact that many girls from these backgrounds want to work in health professions while the boys opt instead for trades. There is also a theory that a certificate from a high-tech company's training program may be worth more than a college degree, and it is the boys who are more likely to skip college to pursue positions in high-tech fields.

(a) are much more likely to go to college
(b) will end up working in the hospital industry
(c) are likely to marry into a middle-class family
(d) will drop out of college before they are twenty

6. About 30-40% of food grown for human consumption ends up in the garbage, of which 25% could quite safely have been eaten. Part of the reason for this waste is that people have come to expect fruit and vegetables to look uniformly perfect and farmers and consumers have, therefore, discarded imperfect produce. So, ___________________________.

(a) good-looking produce tastes much better
(b) edible food has actually been thrown out
(c) out-of-date products should be discarded
(d) vegetables that are old have to be cooked well

7. Many parents are allowing their grown children to return home after college, or perhaps after becoming unemployed, rather than encouraging them to find a place of their own. By bankrolling and housing their adult children, parents are minimizing their own lives and the potential for their futures. What these parents really need to do is to prepare for retirement. They also need time to adjust to life in a post-parenting marriage. In short, they should ________________________________.

(a) establish a comfortable and stable home life
(b) try not to be such a burden on their children
(c) be more accepting of their children's lifestyles
(d) focus on their own lives and not their children's

8. Many have pondered the question of what separates human beings from the rest of the animal kingdom. It is not the ability to think because every higher animal also has some degree of consciousness. The use of tools is not unique either, as apes, birds and even insects manipulate tools. Nor is the art of communication a unique quality. All animals communicate somehow, some in exceedingly sophisticated ways, but the ability to read and write is unique. This is what ________________________________.

(a) many creatures have been doing all along
(b) we are now able to teach to chimpanzees
(c) sets humanity apart from other species
(d) everyone should try to improve

9.

Dear Customer Service,

I purchased a mobile phone from your company at a store several days ago. The price I paid was 300,000 won, which seemed reasonable to me until I learned a couple of days later that I could've bought the same phone for 30% less at a different store. It turns out that there is no fixed price, and so you need to browse for the best price. Of course, I have the option of returning my phone and getting a cheaper one with my current warranty. Still, I believe this kind of pricing system makes your company look extremely inconsiderate toward its customers and

________________________________.

A dissatisfied customer,
Daniel Parkinson

(a) new models should not be sold at a discount
(b) you should allow them to return their phones
(c) the price should not be changed
(d) should thus be put to a stop

10. The four aspects of language ability—reading, writing, speaking and listening—
were researched separately by experts in New Zealand to ____________________.
According to their findings, the correlation between students' achievements in the two
receptive modes, reading and listening, was equally high. In other words, students
who performed well in reading showed a tendency to perform well in listening as well.
However, the correlation between writing and the two aforementioned receptive modes
was moderate, while the correlation between speaking and writing was low and the
correlation between speaking and the two receptive modes was even lower.

(a) design an intensive language program
(b) decide which aspect is easiest to assess
(c) seek ways to improve each skill uniformly
(d) investigate the relationships among these aspects

11. By the mid-thirties, each major American movie studio had developed its own unique
style. This was discernable by the ____________________. Emphasis
ranged from the lavish, star-oriented films produced at MGM to the unadorned,
workaday products from Columbia Pictures. The good, clean family productions at
Paramount stood in sharp contrast to Warner Brothers' sensationalized, tough character-
driven pictures.

(a) amounts paid to their actors
(b) logos representing each studio
(c) characteristics of their offerings
(d) number of Oscars each had won

12. In 1953, a chemical researcher made a surprise discovery while developing a rubber material that would resist deterioration from jet aircraft fuels. After accidentally spilling an experimental chemical on her tennis shoes, she tried to wash it off but failed to do so. As the weeks passed, she noticed that the part of her shoes where the chemical had spilled remained clean while the rest of her shoes had collected dirt and grime. The researcher was amazed at the contrast and realized that the chemical was ideal for ____________________.

(a) mending shoes
(b) gluing the rubber
(c) waterproofing shoes
(d) protecting against stains

13. The findings of our report refute the idea that there has to be a trade-off between immigration and economic progress. This report shows that cultural diversity and economic development are positively linked. After all, some of the world's richest and most developed countries are historically multiethnic, such as the US, Switzerland, Canada and Belgium. We found no evidence that ____________________.

(a) cultural diversity slows development
(b) development is independent of diversity
(c) immigration may lead to more ethnic conflicts
(d) more immigrants will bring economic stability

14. The point may be reached at which ____________________. No one is certain whether it will happen or not, but the likelihood that it will is increasing. Over the past 40 years, advances in agricultural techniques offset what could have been mass global starvation as the world's population doubled. Plant hybrids, pesticides and herbicides enabled farmers to produce more food per acre. However, at the present rate of population growth, advances such as these will not be enough to help satisfy the demand for agricultural products in the near future.

(a) food demand will outstrip food production
(b) Earth's natural resources will be exhausted
(c) agricultural techniques can no longer be used
(d) malnourished children will be a thing of the past

15. New Life Center is a shelter for victims of domestic violence. Women can access the shelter by calling our 24-hour, seven-day-a-week crisis hotline. We offer immediate intervention, safety planning, information and referral for anyone experiencing concerns about domestic violence. Our mission is above all to provide a safe and trustworthy environment. ________________________________, we guarantee complete confidentiality when dealing with clients and client records.

(a) In brief
(b) By contrast
(c) For this reason
(d) In the meantime

16. Throughout the 19th century, the concept of popular sovereignty found broad endorsement in the West. Many written constitutions and elected assemblies were thereby put in place, often before the actual attainment of independence. Even in two monarchies in the Western hemisphere, Mexico and Brazil, the emperors tried to make their rule legitimate by accepting constitutional limits on their thrones and by creating representative assemblies. ________________________________, widespread support for constitutional order and for representative government failed to stop agonizing factional conflicts, regionalism and military rebellions from occurring.

(a) Likewise
(b) In addition
(c) Nevertheless
(d) Consequently

Read the passage and the question. Then choose the option that best answers the question.

---

17. Many commercial cleaning products contain harsh chemicals and can also be expensive. Fortunately, they are not necessary. In fact, you can do common cleaning tasks with what you probably already have in the kitchen. Two effective low-cost alternatives are baking soda and vinegar. All you need to do is sprinkle a little baking soda on a sponge that has been dampened with vinegar. Now use the sponge to clean sinks, countertops and appliances safely and effectively.

Q: What is the passage mainly about?
(a) Using alternative home cleaners
(b) Buying better brands of cleaners
(c) Keeping a kitchen neat and clean
(d) Cleaning your home with chemicals

18. Stars come in a variety of colors, and these different colors can tell scientists a lot about the characteristics of stars. Some stars appear white, whereas others are blue-white, blue, yellow, orange or red. Contrary to what you might expect, the bluish stars are the hotter ones while the reddish ones are cooler. These bluish stars are also brighter and tend to be larger and denser.

Q: What is the passage mainly about?
(a) The basic kinds of star colors
(b) What star colors reveal about stars
(c) What the colors of the largest stars are
(d) The brightness, size and density of stars

19. We are delighted to inform you that Mr. Dan Keough has been appointed as the new Business Development Manager of Tindale Engineering Services. Mr. Keough has well over 10 years of experience in the civil engineering industry as well as valuable expertise working with Achyton, one of the leading national civil engineering contractors. We are positive that his breadth of experience and skills will serve him well as he assists Tindale to grow and prosper in the years to come.

Q: What is the announcement mainly about?
(a) The appointment of a new manager
(b) The achievements of a new manager
(c) Qualifications needed to become a manager
(d) Development strategies proposed by a manager

20. Nearly 1,000 years ago in the Gila National Forest of New Mexico, once the region of the Mimbres culture, people sat making tools, pots and bead jewelry. Today, the ground is pocked and scarred from looters who have illegally dug up and stolen the relics of these people's civilization. Although the federal government and many states prohibit the unauthorized removal of artifacts from public lands, "pot hunters" illegally raid thousands of archaeological sites each year. The problem has grown to such an extent that authorities now admit that it is a crime wave sweeping the United States.

Q: What is the news report mainly about?
(a) The US government's protection of ancient sites
(b) The plundering of ancient artifacts across the US
(c) The search for thieves of ancient cultural artifacts
(d) The kinds of relics taken from archaeological sites

21. According to popular wisdom, work is a burden most people bear out of necessity. Yet, when Britons were asked in a survey whether they would retire if they could, 80% said no. Many reasons can account for that, one of them being that human beings are genetically programmed to be productive. Indeed, our species would not have survived if people did not have a drive to advance their circumstances.

Q: What is the main idea of the passage?
(a) Human beings find work to be a burden.
(b) People are less productive when they retire.
(c) Humans have an innate desire to be productive.
(d) Working past retirement is the goal of most people.

22. In a recent experiment, a natural steroid mixture was tested on marathoners, who are inclined to suffer immune suppression due to the activation of several endocrinological changes that eventually result in decreased immunity. The result was that the marathon runners had less post-event inflammation, fewer hematological side effects and sustained adrenocortical status in comparison with their baseline values. The research thus indicated that the mixture enabled the elimination of the immunological shifts that generally accompany endurance training.

Q: What is the topic of the passage?
(a) Reasons for decreased immune systems in athletes
(b) Ways to improve the performance of marathon runners
(c) The benefit of natural steroids on marathon runners' immune systems
(d) The ineffectiveness of natural steroids on improving the immune system

23. See nature's most ferocious and unique creatures at Wilderness Land! Internationally recognized for its exotic animals, Wilderness Land is a 110-acre theme park and nature conservatory located at the head of the Florida Everglades. Come and see an amazing array of reptiles, lizards, turtles, giant frogs and exotic birds. Have a fun-filled day with the entire family. Admission for adults is $14.95, seniors $12.95, children ages 4-12 pay only $9.95 and children 3 and under get in free.

Q: Which of the following is correct about Wilderness Land according to the passage?
(a) Wilderness Land is famous for its unique animals.
(b) The park exclusively features reptiles and amphibians.
(c) Adults and seniors pay the same admission price.
(d) The park is free for all children under 12 years old.

24. I spotted a pair of nesting eagles recently when hiking through Willard Bay State Park, hoping to get some great shots of different birds. Of course, I knew that approaching too near would cause undue stress on the pair, and it was probably illegal anyway. But, as luck would have it, on this day I was testing out a new telephoto lens. So, I could stay where I was, about 100 meters away, and began taking photos of them. Some of the shots I took that day turned out to be the best I've ever taken.

Q: Which of the following is correct according to the passage?
(a) The writer had just bought a new camera.
(b) The writer photographed two eagles in a nest.
(c) The writer saw eagles when he was out hunting.
(d) The writer was lucky to photograph a baby eagle.

25. Our ClearView window shutters are made out of Durawood, a solid engineered wood composite. Because of the superior density of Durawood, ClearView shutters are less likely to break or warp. Our shutters are more environmentally friendly, too. Old-growth lumber is not used, and all of our shutters are made with non-toxic soy-based adhesives. Buy ClearView, and you'll have the satisfaction of owning superior shutters and of having helped the environment.

Q: Which of the following is correct according to the advertisement?
(a) Durawood is a plastic that looks like wood.
(b) ClearView shutters are flexible and bend easily.
(c) Durawood is made from old-growth forest trees.
(d) ClearView shutters are made with non-toxic materials.

26.

Dear Cathy,

How are you doing? I've been swamped with work and the kids. Both Macy and Lisbeth started new schools in the fall. Anyway, I was wondering whether you and David were doing anything on the weekend of November 10 and 11. Ben and I are going hiking in the Green Mountains, and we were wondering if you two would like to join us again. It would be like old times. Let me know what you think.

Bye for now,
Janet

Q: Which of the following is correct according to the email?
(a) Janet has to work on November 10.
(b) Janet and Cathy recently met each other.
(c) David and Cathy have not gone hiking before.
(d) Ben and Janet are going to the Green Mountains.

27. Were you aware that the US Postal Service can help you manage your business more efficiently? Our new Confirm Mail feature allows you to track your mail electronically as it moves through postal processing. You can use Confirm Mail to find out when customers receive orders and bills as well as when they mail out payments. These and a range of other features can help you better manage your business at minimal cost.

Q: What does Confirm Mail do for business mailers?
(a) It provides information about sent mail.
(b) It offers more security for processing mail.
(c) It ensures that customers receive mail faster.
(d) It allows businesses to pay for mailing online.

28. Hinduism, the primary indigenous religion of South Asia, presently has 800 million followers worldwide, making it the third largest religion in the world. It is also one of the oldest. In fact, followers of Hinduism call it the "eternal religion" because they believe it is the world's oldest living religion. Its earliest scripture, the Veda, dates to approximately 1500 BC. However, some features, such as goddess worship and perhaps yoga, might go back further to the Indus Valley civilization, around 2500 BC.

Q: Which of the following is correct according to the passage?
(a) Goddess worship and yoga are separate from Hinduism.
(b) Hinduism is believed to be the world's largest religion.
(c) The Veda scripture created goddess worship and yoga.
(d) Yoga tradition possibly dates back to before the Veda.

29. Inuits are an inter-related group of peoples found in Alaska, Canada and Greenland. They are thought to have migrated to North America from Siberia many thousands of years ago. They have been commonly referred to as "Eskimos" but prefer to call themselves Inuits. In fact, the use of "Eskimos" to refer to them is often considered offensive, especially in Canada. Inuits still live in small, isolated communities and share a strong cultural identity.

Q: Which of the following is correct according to the passage?
(a) Inuits prefer to be called Eskimos.
(b) Inuits and Eskimos are different ethnic groups.
(c) Inuits lived in Siberia before arriving in Canada.
(d) Inuits live exclusively in the arctic areas of Alaska.

30. The wine world has not been the same since the so-called "Judgment of Paris," a wine tasting event held in Paris in 1976. It sent shockwaves through the wine world when nine French wine experts concluded that wines from California were as good as, or better than, the best wines from French vineyards. The reaction from the French was disbelief followed by accusations that the competition was rigged. In 2006, a second wine tasting event was held in London to mark the anniversary of the "Judgment of Paris." Billed as an epic rematch, the outcome was yet another defeat for France.

Q: Which of the following is correct according to the passage?
(a) The French were delighted by the first "Judgment of Paris."
(b) The first wine tasting event was ignored by the wine world.
(c) The "Judgment of Paris" commemoration also took place in Paris.
(d) The wines judged superior to French wines in 1976 were Californian.

31. According to recent studies, many parents who turn out to be poor caregivers are those who had themselves been unloved, neglected or abused as children. Such parents often start out with the best intentions, vowing never to do to their children what was done to them, but often they are not emotionally equipped to cope with the realities of rearing a child. So, when their children are irritable, fussy or inattentive, these emotionally insecure adults may react like their parents did by withdrawing their affection, sometimes to the point of neglecting or abusing their children.

Q: Which of the following is correct about the parents who are insensitive caregivers?
(a) They do not attempt to treat their children kindly.
(b) Many of them experienced neglect in their childhood.
(c) They grew up in stable households with loving parents.
(d) They are unaware of how they were treated as children.

32. A volunteer at the Carmel Zoo is expected to be available on a regular basis and over a long period of time, such as months or even years. Volunteers are needed on weekends to collect entrance money, direct traffic, give tours, help clean enclosures and aid with other maintenance. Those volunteers who can assist during the week will be more involved with the care of our animals. The zoo will provide volunteers with training and guidance; however, they must provide their own transportation and meals.

Q: Which of the following is correct according to the passage?
(a) The volunteers can help out at their convenience.
(b) The zoo prefers that volunteers work for a short period.
(c) The zoo does not offer transportation or food to volunteers.
(d) The volunteers' main weekend task is to take care of animals.

33. Casanova's memoirs, written when he was an old man, include accounts of his adventurous life and vast and learned commentaries on philosophy, science, religion and love. The impression one gets from them is of a man predisposed to adventure, who continually ruined his prospects because of an irrepressible love for disreputable company. He was also a man who in his old age did not regret any past follies but rather the inability to commit more.

Q: What can be inferred about Casanova from the passage?
(a) He was both a risk taker and a scholar.
(b) He exaggerated many of the tales about his life.
(c) He advocated science over religion in his writings.
(d) He was bitter in his old age for his former mistakes.

34.

Dear Editor:

I am writing to express my indignation at the libelous statements made against myself and my office in the *King Valley Gazette*. The King Valley Office of Tourism has never released erroneous information. This would be counterproductive to our mission, which is to develop tourism in the King Valley region. Your journalist confused the facts. The only complaint against us has been for withholding information, not for giving out misinformation. The truth is that some local restaurants and hotels are angry at us for not promoting them, but our office is not their free advertising service. That is what your paper should have reported.

Sincerely,
Alfred Singleton
Managing Director

Q: What can be inferred from the letter?
(a) The editor is against Alfred Singleton's character.
(b) The King Valley Office of Tourism has just opened.
(c) Mr. Singleton has been blamed for discouraging tourism.
(d) An article was published criticizing the Office of Tourism.

35. *Blood Meridian* comes at the reader like a slap in the face, an insult that challenges us to tolerate a vision of the Old West mired in brutality and violence. While this makes Cormac McCarthy's sixth novel hard to finish, it is even more difficult to ignore. Any given page of this work reveals the author's originality, a passionate voice distributed equally to both ugliness and lyricism. Over the past two decades, the brutality of his works may have turned some readers off, but the power of his writing has earned him high critical acclaim.

Q: What can be inferred about McCarthy?
(a) He is known for works that are commonplace.
(b) His works are not known for their broad appeal.
(c) He depicts history from an idealized point of view.
(d) His earlier books are less brutal than *Blood Meridian*.

36. Advertise with MegaAd and experience the benefits of web-based advertising. We use keyword targeting to present highly visible and relevant text-based ads that promote your business to consumers who use major search engines. Ads using MegaAd have yielded click-through rates 5 times higher than average online ads, which demonstrates how effective our service is. If you run an online business, you can't afford not to use MegaAd. Call our information hotline today at 1-888-8-MEGAAD. Full service is available for large advertisers or agencies looking to spend $10,000 per month.

Q: What can be inferred about MegaAd's advertising service?
(a) It displays ads based on keyword searches.
(b) Text-based ads are an extra advertising option.
(c) Its advertising service is targeted toward smaller clients.
(d) Full service is available through many advertising agencies.

37. In literary studies, the connotation of a word refers to the associations, images or impressions carried by that word, as opposed to its literal meaning. For example, the word "mother" means literally "a female parent," but it often connotes warmth, love, sympathy, security and nurturing. Connotations may result from personal experience; they may be shared by people as a group—perhaps with the same professional, national, linguistic or racial background; or they may be common to everyone.

Q: What can be inferred from the passage?
(a) Connotative meanings can be group-specific.
(b) Connotations are being removed from most languages.
(c) Most people are concerned only with a word's literal meaning.
(d) A knowledge of word origins is essential for understanding connotations.

Part III   **Questions 38 – 40**

Read the passage. Then identify the option that does NOT belong.

38. Contrary to common myth, the majority of bats are highly beneficial to mankind. (a) If you happen to come across a bat, you should not panic. (b) For instance, tropical bats are imperative to the propagation of plant life. (c) They disperse seeds for a wide range of economically beneficial fruits, such as bananas and mangoes. (d) In addition, bats also consume a significant number of insects, including such pests as mosquitoes.

39. Impressionism was an art movement that came to prominence in the latter half of the 19th century. (a) The movement is usually associated with French painters like Manet, Monet and Renoir. (b) However, the emergence of Impressionism in the visual arts influenced similar movement in literature. (c) Originally, the Impressionist composers had two favorite mediums, the orchestra and the piano. (d) Writers influenced by Impressionism, for example, focused on the impressions and emotions of their characters.

40. Ancient stone tools were discovered on a hilltop in Minnesota by archaeologists inspecting a road construction site. (a) What gives these tools such significance is their apparent age, as they are thought to have come from the last Ice Age. (b) Much of Minnesota was covered by glaciers, while woolly mammoths, mastodons and giant beavers roamed the continent. (c) Of course, much more analysis of the tools is due before their accurate ages are broadly accepted by scientists. (d) However, if the above-mentioned estimates hold true, it means mankind inhabited Minnesota over 5,000 years earlier than archaeologists had previously believed.

This is the end of the Reading Comprehension section. Please remain seated until the proctor has instructed otherwise. You are NOT allowed to turn to any other section of the test.

서울대 최신기출 1
Listening Comprehension **Scripts**

1

M   Your hair looks good.

W   ___________________________

(a) My hairdresser's nice.
(b) I'm glad you think so.
(c) Yes, I need a trim.
(d) OK, I'll brush it.

2

W   Juniper Industries. How may I direct your call?

M   ___________________________

(a) You have the wrong number.
(b) Extension 4596, please.
(c) It's customer service.
(d) I'm calling overseas.

3

M   Welcome to Korea. Do you have any produce or alcohol to declare?

W   ___________________________

(a) No, I'm a tourist.
(b) I don't drink often.
(c) Just two bottles of wine.
(d) That's right, just these bags.

4

W   I'm thinking of studying forestry.

M   ___________________________

(a) My work is important.
(b) The exam's finally over.
(c) It depends on the school.
(d) That's an interesting field.

5

M   Kathy, why do you want to go to the mall?

W   ___________________________

(a) I need some new clothes.
(b) I hate window shopping.
(c) I've seen enough of it.
(d) I took the subway.

6

W   Let's study for the test together.

M   ___________________________

(a) I'm sure you'll pass.
(b) That would be helpful.
(c) You did well on the test.
(d) We've had too many exams.

7

M   How about a trip to the beach today?

W   ___________________________

(a) I'm done with packing.
(b) The water's very deep.
(c) Hope you have a good time.
(d) I'm afraid I already have plans.

8

W   What was your final grade in Physics 100?

M   ___________________________

(a) I'm at a different level.
(b) I knew it ended that way.
(c) I don't have enough points.
(d) I'm too embarrassed to say.

9

M   Hi, I think we've already met. Paula, right?

W   ___________________________

(a) Yeah, I heard the same thing.
(b) Actually, I only know a few here.
(c) Maybe you're right. I'll go check.
(d) Yes, we were introduced at Mark's party.

10

W Change the channel. I can't stand sitcoms.

M _______________

(a) But I'm watching it.
(b) I think it's that channel.
(c) Yes, a commercial is on.
(d) OK, I'll watch the sitcom.

11

M Maybe we should refurbish our apartment.

W _______________

(a) I'd prefer a furnished one.
(b) Yes, we had the locks changed.
(c) Sure, the furniture comes with it.
(d) Maybe it can wait for a year or two.

12

W Not getting that job was such a letdown.

M _______________

(a) I've sent résumés everywhere.
(b) I'm sure something will turn up.
(c) I've always wanted to work downtown.
(d) I hope the unemployment rate has gone down.

13

M You didn't do so well this term, Helen.

W _______________

(a) Well, we can't all be rich and famous.
(b) People will say anything for attention.
(c) That's how I managed to get on top of it.
(d) Sorry, sir. I guess I've kind of let things slide.

14

W I've been having sneezing fits all week.

M _______________

(a) You should've finished last week.
(b) Maybe it's something in the air.
(c) That doesn't sound correct.
(d) It's a medical diagnosis.

15

M Honey, I could use a hand changing this light.

W _______________

(a) Sure, I'll pick up another one.
(b) Just let me finish feeding the dog.
(c) I'm afraid it's always been that way.
(d) Maybe you should ask for some help.

16

W Hello. Could I see the manager, please?

M I'm sorry. She's not in right now.

W I see. So, when do you expect her back?

M _______________

(a) I don't expect much.
(b) It takes five minutes.
(c) Around three o'clock.
(d) She'll return them soon.

17

M Hi, Ms. O'Conor. What seems to be the problem?

W Hi, Dr. Park. I've been having trouble sleeping.

M OK, have you been taking any medication?

W _______________

(a) I'm so relieved to hear that, doctor.
(b) No, that's not the right prescription.
(c) I try to wake up at six every morning.
(d) No, I was hoping you could prescribe something.

18

W Hey, what's Mike O'Brien doing these days?

M Oh, I heard he moved to Boston.

W Oh, really. Why?

M _______________

(a) He found a job there, I think.
(b) It was a good move for him.
(c) He hasn't called since then.
(d) Well, it wasn't all that bad.

19

M Are you going anywhere during the long break?

W No, not this year. How about you?

M I'm thinking about going to Africa.

W ______________________________

(a) Sounds like quite an adventure.

(b) I thought you liked living here.

(c) I seldom take a break at work.

(d) Don't leave me so soon.

20

W Mark, you have an excellent singing voice.

M Thanks, I used to sing in the school choir.

W You could be famous with a voice like that.

M ______________________________

(a) Well, I wouldn't go that far.

(b) Thanks for not mentioning it.

(c) Let me see if I can make it out.

(d) Then I'd rather participate in it.

21

M Man, you wouldn't believe the day I've had.

W Why? Did something happen at work?

M Everything I did today seemed to go wrong.

W ______________________________

(a) Don't worry. I'll do that.

(b) I didn't notice anything wrong.

(c) Hopefully tomorrow will be better.

(d) I can't say whether or not it happened.

22

W Good morning. I have a 9 am appointment with Dr. Duncan.

M Oh I'm sorry, but he hasn't arrived yet.

W Oh, really? Why is that?

M ______________________________

(a) He left work early today.

(b) Because he arrived so late.

(c) Because he should sit down and relax.

(d) He's probably stuck in morning traffic.

23

M Excuse me, I'm looking for the Alpha Theater.

W The Alpha Theater? You're heading the wrong way.

M Really? It's not up this way?

W ______________________________

(a) It's not difficult to find.

(b) It's way more than that.

(c) It's not where I thought it was.

(d) It's several blocks in the other direction.

24

W Hello, Prestige Menswear, how may I help you?

M I'm calling to see if my suit's ready. It's James Burrows.

W One moment. I'll go and check.

M ______________________________

(a) I'll come back.

(b) All right. I'll hold.

(c) The sleeves need shortening.

(d) Sorry, I forgot to bring the receipt.

25

M Would you like to watch a DVD tonight?

W It depends on the time. I'm working late.

M Oh, how about 8: 30?

W ______________________________

(a) Yes, I'll be watching it.

(b) Great! Let's go together.

(c) That shouldn't be a problem.

(d) I think the movie will be over by then.

26

W Hi, are you here for the interview?

M For the admin position? Yeah, you too?

W Yep, but I don't feel that confident about it.

M ______________________________

(a) It's better to enjoy it.

(b) You're not the only one.

(c) The interviews are almost over.

(d) But you've been waiting for long.

27

M What did you think of the new ad campaign?
W Honestly, I'll be surprised if it boosts sales.
M What makes you think the public won't go for it?
W _______________

(a) It's not particularly attention grabbing.
(b) It's just idle speculation on your part.
(c) The public wasn't well informed.
(d) They'll make me go for it.

28

W It looks like those weights might be too heavy.
M But I want to build up my biceps.
W OK, but you're overdoing it. You could hurt yourself.
M _______________

(a) Maybe you can correct my form.
(b) My enthusiasm got the better of me.
(c) I can't work out any slower than this.
(d) There's no need to warn you about it.

29

M Some of us are heading to Mexico this winter. Interested?
W I don't know. How many people are going?
M Eight have committed so far. You'd be the ninth.
W _______________

(a) I'll let you know in a few days.
(b) I'm feeling a little under the weather.
(c) Let me know when you make a decision.
(d) I'd be happy to invite them along as well.

30

W I'm thinking of buying some stock this week.
M If I were you, I'd hold off on that.
W Why's that? Do you know something I don't?
M _______________

(a) I've always invested heavily in them.
(b) I know that you'll be acquiring stock.
(c) The markets are looking pretty grim.
(d) There's never been a better climate for it.

31

W Waiter! This fish is terrible!
M What's wrong with it, ma'am?
W It's undercooked. And, it's cold.
M Oh, I'm terribly sorry. I'll bring you another one.
W But I waited ages for this one to arrive.
M My apologies, ma'am. I'll be right back.

Q: What is the woman mainly doing in the conversation?
(a) She is learning how to cook fish.
(b) She is ordering fish at a restaurant.
(c) She is asking for one more fish dish.
(d) She is complaining about undercooked fish.

32

M Are you free Saturday night, Stacy?
W I don't have anything planned. Why?
M Well, I thought you might like to join me and my friends.
W What are you thinking of doing?
M We haven't decided yet, but we might go to a dance club.
W Sounds great. I'd love to go.

Q: What is the man mainly doing in the conversation?
(a) He is inviting the woman out.
(b) He is helping a friend plan a date.
(c) He is asking if the woman can dance.
(d) He is explaining what he did Saturday.

33

M I'm pretty excited about moving abroad.

W I can imagine. Have you decided what to take?

M I was just going to ship everything I have.

W I'd sell as many things as I could and ship as little as possible.

M Well, yeah. I guess that makes more sense.

W Besides, you could always buy new stuff over there.

Q: What is mainly happening in the conversation?

(a) The man is being advised on what to take overseas.

(b) The woman is suggesting the man not go abroad.

(c) The woman is telling stories about living abroad.

(d) The man is asking about how to save money.

34

W So, what brought you to the US?

M I wanted to get another degree in my major.

W And why did you pick this university?

M Because the computer science program here is excellent.

W So, computer science programs aren't that great in your country?

M Well, they are definitely not as good as here.

Q: What is the conversation mainly about?

(a) The man's desire to change his major.

(b) The man's opinion of American universities.

(c) The reason the man likes computer science.

(d) The reason the man came to study in the US.

35

M Hello, Nancy. Please sit down.

W Hello, Dr. Trent. So, are my results in?

M Yes, your pregnancy test results are right here.

W And? Should I be celebrating?

M Yes. The test came back positive. Congratulations! You're pregnant.

W Oh, thank you! What great news!

Q: What is the conversation mainly about?

(a) The doctor is arranging an appointment.

(b) The woman is talking about her pregnancy.

(c) The doctor is sharing pregnancy test results.

(d) The woman is finding it hard to get pregnant.

36

M What time does your plane leave?

W It takes off at ten in the morning.

M So, you'll get to New York at about 12?

W That's right. Then I go straight to a meeting with a supplier.

M Will you get to do any sightseeing?

W No, I'm booked on the seven o'clock flight back.

Q: What is the main topic of the conversation?

(a) People the woman will see in New York.

(b) The reason for the woman's trip to New York.

(c) The woman's meeting with a New York supplier.

(d) The woman's business trip to New York by plane.

37

W I wish my mother hadn't come over for dinner last night.

M I thought you liked having your mother over.

W No, cooking for her is so stressful.

M I guess it might be, knowing your mother.

W Right. She always criticizes my cooking.

M Well, the older people get, the harder it is to please them.

Q: What is the woman mainly talking about in the conversation?

(a) Her dislike of having to cook dinner.

(b) How she does not know how to cook well.

(c) Her regret at having cooked for her mother.

(d) How her mother hates cooking for her family.

38

M Angie, do you know where the monthly report is?

W I think I saw it over there on the conference table just a minute ago.

M Well, it isn't there now.

W That's strange. Maybe someone took it.

M Oh, wait, here it is, by the photocopier.

W Good. I knew it couldn't have gone too far.

Q: Which is correct about the monthly report according to the conversation?
(a) The woman is looking for it.
(b) The man took it to photocopy.
(c) The woman put it on her desk.
(d) The man found it by the copier.

39

M I like this radio station you're listening to.

W Yeah, me too. It's a college station.

M I thought so. The DJ seems like an amateur.

W Yeah. But the music is usually good.

M So, what is it? FM 90.5?

W Yes! Good guess.

Q: Which is correct according to the conversation?
(a) The man likes the woman's radio.
(b) The man was unaware the DJ was an amateur.
(c) The woman does not like the music that much.
(d) The woman is listening to radio station FM 90.5.

40

M Maggie, I thought you were going to fly to Hawaii yesterday.

W Yeah, but I missed my flight, so I came back to work.

M You missed your flight? What happened?

W It's embarrassing. I left my passport at home.

M And you didn't have time to go back and get it?

W No, I only realized it when I was checking in.

Q: Which is correct according to the conversation?
(a) The man planned to go to Hawaii.
(b) The woman did not get on her flight.
(c) The man brought the woman her passport.
(d) The woman lost her passport at the airport.

41

M Judy, did you put the swimming gear in the car?

W Yeah, I packed our snorkels and flippers.

M What about my goggles, the ones you gave me for Christmas?

W Oh yeah, I put those in, too.

M What else should we take? Oh, I know—sunblock.

W Of course! We can't forget that.

Q: Which is correct according to the conversation?
(a) The woman packed the goggles.
(b) The woman received the goggles as a gift.
(c) The woman forgot to purchase sunblock.
(d) The woman does not feel they need sunblock.

42

W Have you sent off all your grad school applications?

M Yeah. I applied to ten schools, so it was quite expensive.

W Well, I think it'll be worth it. You should get in somewhere.

M I hope so. The waiting is pretty stressful, though.

W Yes, that's the nerve-racking part.

M Anyway, I should hear something by next month.

Q: Which is correct about the man according to the conversation?
(a) He just got into grad school.
(b) He applied to five different grad schools.
(c) He recently had one application rejected.
(d) He expects application results by next month.

43

M I've got lots of clothes but not enough closet space.

W Well, I have a lot of clothes too, but I don't have that problem.

M Really? How is that possible?

W I use a special hanger that makes lots of room.

M Hey, I think I saw a commercial on TV about it.

W That's exactly where I found it.

M That might work for me, too.

Q: What will the man most likely do to solve his problem?
(a) Install a bigger closet.
(b) Purchase a special hanger.
(c) Get rid of his outdated clothes.
(d) Arrange his clothes based on length.

44

M Did you go to that new mall I told you about?

W Yeah, but I didn't like it that much.

M Why not? I thought you'd love the spaciousness.

W No, it was too big and I ended up walking too much.

M But it's got tons of stores.

W Right. I liked that part.

Q: What can be inferred from the conversation?
(a) The woman does not like to walk a lot.
(b) The man prefers exercising to shopping.
(c) The man knows exactly what the woman likes.
(d) The woman does not enjoy shopping with the man.

45

W Welcome to the Bridge Hotel. How can I help you?

M Yes, I need a room for the night, please.

W Certainly, sir. We have a vacant suite at $250 a night.

M Hmm... a suite. Do you have anything smaller?

W Well, we do have a single smoking room left at $85.

M I can live with the smell for $85.

Q: What can be inferred about the man from the conversation?
(a) He is more concerned about price than comfort.
(b) He finally succeeded in quitting smoking.
(c) He has stayed at the Bridge Hotel before.
(d) He was hoping a smoking room was vacant.

46

Two children and their mother are undergoing vaccinations for rabies after they took in a stray cat infected with the disease. The Baltimore family allowed the cat into their house during a torrential rainstorm last week. However, they soon became alarmed at its behavior and took it to a veterinarian. This is the second such incident in the area this month.

Q: What is the main idea of the news report?
(a) A stray cat with rabies was found.
(b) A second family in Baltimore has rabies.
(c) A cat with rabies was taken to a veterinarian.
(d) A family was vaccinated after taking in a rabid cat.

47

Another native American language I would like to talk about is the Navajo language. It is a language of extreme complexity. Its syntax and tonal qualities make it unintelligible to anyone without extensive training in it. It is spoken on Navajo lands in the US, and US military leaders used it as a code language in World War II.

Q: What is the speaker mainly talking about?
(a) Where the Navajo language is spoken.
(b) The complex syntax of the Navajo language.
(c) Some characteristics of the Navajo language.
(d) Why the Navajo language was used in WW II.

48

I'd like to begin today by discussing ball lightning. This is a little-understood form of lightning that takes the shape of a sphere. It's most often reported during thunderstorms, and it is believed to last longer than ordinary bolts of lightning. Reports of ball lightning describe it as anywhere from a few centimeters to several meters in diameter. It can move in any direction and even hover.

Q: What is the lecture mainly about?
(a) Physical aspects of ball lightning.
(b) Mysteries surrounding ball lightning.
(c) Ball lightning's various strange shapes.
(d) Ball lightning's effects on the environment.

49

I've talked about many changes early European immigrants faced when arriving in America, but one you might not be aware of is that many had their names changed by immigration officers. Overworked immigration officials often wrote down names the way they sounded, misspelling them or shortening syllables in long last names. But in keeping with their new life, immigrants often adopted such changes.

Q: What is the main idea of the talk?
(a) How strange the names of early immigrants were.
(b) How officials sometimes altered immigrants' names.
(c) How European immigrants Americanized their names.
(d) How Americans prefer names that are uncomplicated.

50

Visit Fisher's Office Supplies for all your back-to-school needs. We guarantee the lowest prices in town. And if you find any advertisements for an item at a lower price than ours, bring in the ad and we'll beat the price by 10%. Not only that, our stock selection is second-to-none. If it's not at Fisher's, you won't find it anywhere!

Q: What is the advertisement mainly about?
(a) Fisher's low prices and selection.
(b) The products available at Fisher's.
(c) Fisher's big sale for a limited time.
(d) Ways to get a special discount at Fisher's.

51

The introduction of a minute of silence at the beginning of the day in our schools concerns me deeply. Some claim this doesn't promote religion. However, I see it as an attempt to bring prayer back into public schools, and I oppose this. Official school prayer time was eliminated years ago. We simply don't need it when students can pray at home or outside of class hours.

Q: What is the talk mainly about?
(a) Teaching students various religious values.
(b) Saving students from the burden of prayer.
(c) Rejecting the minute of silence in schools.
(d) Explaining why students should not pray.

52

Rebel Helicopters offers you the unforgettable experience of seeing the Grand Canyon from the air. We also provide a personalized multi-camera DVD recording of the flight using interior and exterior cameras and a state-of-the art audio system. You can capture all the commentary, action and beautiful scenery, then share your experience with friends and family. Book a flight with Rebel Helicopters today!

Q: What is the advertisement mainly about?

(a) A helicopter fitted with an audio-visual system.

(b) A tour company that exclusively uses helicopters.

(c) A helicopter tour that features a recorded keepsake.

(d) A new helicopter tour company at the Grand Canyon.

53

Thank you all for coming to my talk on donations and tax benefits. Before you leave, I'd like to impart some final wisdom on giving wisely to charities: research before you give. Find out which charity has a mission and goals that best suit your priorities. Then, check exactly how your money will be used. Even though donations are deductible, you want to rest assured that your money is going to a good cause.

Q: What should a person do before giving to a charity according to the talk?

(a) Examine the resulting tax benefits.

(b) Find out how much money can be given.

(c) Research each charity's main objectives.

(d) Insist on how the money should be spent.

54

Hello. You've reached Bill's Plumbing. Our regular business hours are from 9:00 am to 6:00 pm weekdays. We're closed on weekends and holidays. If you would like to leave a message, please do so at the beep. In case of an emergency, please call our 24-hour hotline at 528-5187 for immediate service, and we will call you back right away. Thank you for calling Bill's Plumbing.

Q: Which is correct about Bill's Plumbing according to the message?

(a) They are open every day from 9:00 am to 6:00 pm.

(b) There is a special phone number for emergencies.

(c) They respond to all messages immediately.

(d) They do not call back on weekends.

55

Attention everyone. I'm pleased to announce that author Bharati Mukherjee will be delivering a lecture at 11 am on Wednesday, February 18, at Graham Chapel. Her lecture is titled "Beyond Multiculturalism: The Making of a New American Identity through Fiction." Mukherjee is best known for her novel *Jasmine*, and she has been a professor of English since 1990 at University of California, Berkeley. She will also participate in an informal discussion from 12:15 to 1:30 pm in the Women's Lounge of the Jenkins Building.

Q: Which is correct about Mukherjee according to the announcement?

(a) She will deliver her lecture in the Women's Lounge.

(b) She is most noted for her book *Beyond Multiculturalism*.

(c) She has been working at the University of California since 1990.

(d) She will conduct an informal discussion at 1:30 pm at Graham Chapel.

56

Class, in our lecture today on the ancient Phoenicians, we'll discuss one of the culture's most famous products, Tyrian, or royal, purple. The color was first produced in the Phoenician city of Tyre, in what is modern day Lebanon. It was an expensive commodity because it had to be painstakingly extracted from a small gland found in a particular sea snail. As a result, it was limited to royalty.

Q: Which is correct according to the lecture?

(a) Royal purple was imported by the Lebanese.

(b) Royal purple was taken from sea snail shells.

(c) Dye extraction was a relatively easy procedure.

(d) Tyrian purple was reserved for an exclusive group.

57

And now for the weather. The ridge of high pressure we've had across the UK all week will likely continue our cold spell. This ridge is sandwiched between two areas of low pressure, a system which at this time of year results in fog and frost. So, we can expect a frosty night and a cold and overcast day tomorrow. There will be some sunshine in the northwest, but the region will likely get rain later in the day.

Q: Which is correct according to the weather forecast?
(a) It will get milder over the next few days.
(b) Conditions are going to be frosty overnight.
(c) The northwest will be sunny all day tomorrow.
(d) Tomorrow most of the UK will experience rain.

58

Today's talk focuses on children's literature. If you're looking for a good children's book, it's usually safe to buy an award-winner, perhaps one that the American Library Association (ALA) has given their prestigious Newbery or Caldecott award to. However, such books are not the only ones to look for. After all, the enduring classic *Charlotte's Web* didn't win a Newbery award! Today we'll give you some recommendations that we feel are similarly deserving of the highest praise.

Q: What can be inferred from the talk?
(a) Non-awarded books often stand the test of time.
(b) The Newbery and Caldecott awards are overrated.
(c) The ALA tends to be biased towards certain authors.
(d) Some non-awarded books are as good as awarded ones.

59

I'd like to discuss the unsupported claim that minority children from underprivileged families are facing discrimination within the public education system. This is a groundless accusation. As a school administrator, I am well aware that the Education Department is doing everything at its disposal to ensure that minority students enjoy access to quality education. Just look at our country's Kids First program and literacy campaigns. People are criticizing the Department for a wider social problem for which it is not responsible.

Q: Which of the statements would the speaker most likely agree with?
(a) More support is needed in minority education.
(b) The public education system has many failings.
(c) Minority students do not perform as well as other students.
(d) Underprivileged students are not denied quality education.

60

In this part of the lecture I want to discuss the link between changes to the magnetic field and volcanic eruptions. This link went unnoticed until what is called the mantle plume theory was developed, which suggests that plumes of magma, or great masses of hot rock coming to the Earth's surface, can interrupt Earth's magnetic field. To see whether magnetic field changes have coincided with volcanic activity driven by mantle plumes, scientists searched for evidence in the geologic record. Their efforts were not in vain.

Q: What will the speaker likely discuss next?
(a) Times when magnetic fields were more stable.
(b) Predictions of future massive volcanic eruptions.
(c) Periods of volcanic activity and magnetic anomalies.
(d) Evidence supporting the existence of mantle plumes.

서울대 최신기출 2

Listening Comprehension Scripts

1

M Hi, may I speak to Mary, please?

W _______________________

(a) This is she.
(b) Sure, I'll hold.
(c) Please wait for the beep.
(d) I'll give her the message.

2

W May I borrow your pen for a moment?

M _______________________

(a) You didn't have one.
(b) I'd rather use a pencil.
(c) Certainly, here you are.
(d) No, don't worry about it.

3

M Excuse me. Don't I know you from somewhere?

W _______________________

(a) That's quite all right.
(b) Yes, I think we've met.
(c) No, I'm not well-known.
(d) I'm pleased to meet you.

4

W Don't fret over the exam. You can retake it.

M _______________________

(a) It was a surprise test.
(b) That's good to know.
(c) I need to grade it.
(d) I'll take that one.

5

M Would you like to go bowling tonight?

W _______________________

(a) I'll have to pass this time.
(b) No, I've never been there.
(c) Yes, I've made other plans.
(d) I thought you were doing that.

6

W Sorry I'm late, but traffic was backed up.

M _______________________

(a) The traffic wasn't my fault.
(b) That's OK. I was late myself.
(c) You should have driven here.
(d) We'll meet another time, then.

7

M We ought to change today's meeting schedule.

W _______________________

(a) I started it on schedule.
(b) It might be too late for that.
(c) Mention that at the meeting.
(d) That could happen to anyone.

8

W Did you finish doing inventory?

M _______________________

(a) No, it'll take another day.
(b) We have a busy week ahead.
(c) I'm afraid we're out of stock.
(d) Yes, I'll get started right away.

9

M Emily keeps trying to make me jealous.

W _______________________

(a) I'll inform her of your plans.
(b) She's always making excuses.
(c) You know, she's quite attractive.
(d) In that case, I'd stay away from her.

10

W You're looking so fit and healthy, Tim!

M _______________________

(a) Yeah, I should start working out.
(b) I have been trying to get in shape.
(c) It's about time you took me seriously.
(d) That's disappointing after all I've done.

11

M Are you allergic to any medications?

W _______________________

(a) None that I'm aware of.
(b) I've been sneezing a lot.
(c) I take aspirin occasionally.
(d) They're good for my health.

12

W Let's pay a visit to Grandma Saturday.

M _______________________

(a) But it'll cost her a fortune.
(b) Great idea. It's been a while.
(c) OK. See you when you return.
(d) She'll be thrilled to hear from you.

13

M I think I deserve a huge bonus this year.

W _______________________

(a) Brace yourself for big changes next year.
(b) I was pretty surprised when I heard.
(c) Just be satisfied with what you get.
(d) No one mentioned anything to me.

14

W Is it dangerous to exercise in the park at night?

M _______________________

(a) You might find it awkward.
(b) The main thing is to keep at it.
(c) It should help to walk regularly.
(d) Not if you stick to well-lit areas.

15

M Listen, can we talk about a rather delicate matter?

W _______________________

(a) I'd rather not. It's pretty trivial.
(b) Thanks. I appreciate your input.
(c) Sure. No one can eavesdrop here.
(d) Bad idea. Let's keep it between us.

16

W How did the conference go?

M I don't even want to talk about it.

W Was it really that bad?

M _______________________

(a) It was the worst ever.
(b) There's no other way.
(c) It'll be very informative.
(d) I'm not looking forward to it.

17

M Please open your suitcase, ma'am.

W But I have nothing to declare.

M I still have to check. It's airport policy.

W _______________________

(a) OK. But it's just clothes.
(b) I'm here for a conference.
(c) It's an expensive suitcase.
(d) Well, I'm on my way home.

18

W Can you watch my laptop for a minute?

M Sure. Where are you going?

W I'm just going to the bathroom.

M _______________________

(a) Thanks. I won't be long.
(b) You need a newer model.
(c) OK. I'll keep an eye on it.
(d) The battery might be dead.

19

M Excuse me. Is there a post office nearby?

W I think there's one farther along.

M Oh? About how far?

W __________________________

(a) It's open until five.

(b) Maybe a block away.

(c) You can park in front.

(d) I thought it was farther.

20

W I wish this movie would end.

M It's only been half an hour.

W I know, but it's pretty boring.

M __________________________

(a) All right. It's up to you.

(b) Let me know in an hour, then.

(c) We don't have to see that one.

(d) Wow. You can be really critical.

21

M I didn't care for that opera.

W Really? I enjoyed it a lot.

M The soprano didn't quite hit all the high notes.

W __________________________

(a) It's my first opera.

(b) Sure, I prefer classical music.

(c) Maybe, but she's got talent.

(d) I should've worked on them more.

22

W What should we do this weekend?

M Nothing much. I'd prefer to relax.

W I thought we could go shopping.

M __________________________

(a) You were quite clever.

(b) OK, but not for too long.

(c) I hope you got a good deal.

(d) Why not? Shopping bores me.

23

M I lost my umbrella today.

W That's the second one this winter.

M Yeah, I left it on the bus again.

W __________________________

(a) It wasn't the same bus.

(b) You're so absent-minded.

(c) I'll check beneath the seat.

(d) But the forecast was incorrect.

24

W That novel you lent me was so violent.

M It's superbly written, though.

W But the subject matter turned me off.

M __________________________

(a) Really? I honestly cannot see the appeal.

(b) I guess it's not to everyone's taste.

(c) I was quite impressed by it, too.

(d) Yes, I figured you would agree.

25

M I just discovered a crack in our bathtub.

W Oh, we'd better get it repaired right away.

M You think we should replace the tub?

W __________________________

(a) No, we can buy a repair kit.

(b) I think the color is OK.

(c) I think you did a good job.

(d) Yes, we replaced it last month.

26

W Your acting was excellent in tonight's performance.

M Actually, I forgot two of my lines.

W You're kidding! I didn't notice.

M __________________________

(a) I'm sure I can take care of that.

(b) Incidentally, I didn't notice, either.

(c) You should come and see the play.

(d) That's a relief. I thought it showed.

27

M How's it going with your taxes?
W These forms are incredibly complicated.
M It'd be easier to get a professional to do it.
W __________________

(a) Just follow three simple steps.
(b) I'll get an accountant next year.
(c) You must've studied with a tutor.
(d) Maybe when I receive the refund.

28

W Losing your grandfather to cancer must be devastating.
M Well, we knew it would happen sooner or later.
W How is your grandmother taking it?
M __________________

(a) She's always very down-to-earth.
(b) Not too bad. She's hanging in there.
(c) It seems like she's taking it for granted.
(d) OK. She feels quite at home these days.

29

M Hey, Cindy. Nice to see you're back at work.
W Thanks. Those 8 weeks went by fast.
M Is that the limit for maternity leave?
W __________________

(a) Actually, I was hoping to stay longer.
(b) I'll have it specified in your contract.
(c) Well, any more would be unpaid.
(d) Yeah, quicker than I anticipated.

30

W Why is that contract still on your desk? It should've been mailed!
M Since when is that my responsibility?
W It's written right there, on the folder.
M __________________

(a) Oh, I didn't even notice that.
(b) If that's the case, put it on my desk.
(c) Don't worry. The folder's right here.
(d) Thank goodness. You had me worried.

31

M Alicia's birthday is coming up.
W Yeah, I know. We should get her a gift.
M I don't know. She's really difficult to shop for.
W Then let's take her somewhere instead.
M Like where? What do you have in mind?
W Well, we could surprise her with a ski trip.

Q: What are the man and woman mainly discussing?
(a) A friend's love of skiing.
(b) Plans for a shopping trip.
(c) What birthday gift to give.
(d) How they will pay for a ski trip.

32

W Hello, may I speak with Mr. Carson?
M I'm sorry. Mr. Carson is away on business.
W Oh. Is there a number where I can reach him?
M He usually doesn't like to give it out.
W It should be OK. I'm his sister-in-law.
M Oh, in that case, it's 561-887-9040.

Q: What is the woman mainly doing in the conversation?
(a) Confirming an appointment.
(b) Trying to contact Mr. Carson.
(c) Explaining who Mr. Carson is.
(d) Taking a message over the phone.

33

M Ruth, how did your poetry reading go?
W Terrible. It was a disaster.
M Was it really that bad? What happened?
W I was so nervous, I fumbled my words.
M Oh, I'm sure it wasn't that bad.
W It was, especially at the beginning.

Q: What are the man and woman mainly discussing?
(a) A new poem the woman wrote.
(b) A critic's review of the woman's poetry.
(c) The woman's dislike of giving presentations.
(d) The woman's performance at a poetry reading.

34

M Did you ask the Andersons to dinner this Saturday?

W Yes, but they have tickets to a baseball game.

M That's too bad. Did they say when they'll be free?

W They're free Sunday, but they're out of town all next week.

M Well, we have to go to Andy's recital on Sunday, remember?

W You're right. I guess dinner will have to wait.

Q: What are the man and woman mainly doing?

(a) Trying to schedule a dinner party.

(b) Preparing to attend a baseball game.

(c) Going over the next week's schedule.

(d) Discussing their plans for the evening.

35

W Mr. Reese, I've got the results of your checkup.

M So, how am I doing, doctor?

W Well, your cholesterol is rather high.

M Oh, that's no good. What do you recommend?

W You'll need to make some dietary changes, for a start.

M Sure. Whatever they are, I can do them.

Q: What is the conversation mainly about?

(a) Diet suggestions for the man.

(b) A cholesterol test and its results.

(c) The man's worries about his failing health.

(d) The man's health problem and how to solve it.

36

M I hear you're buying a used car.

W Trying to, but I'm not sure what.

M Well, maybe I can help. My cousin owns a dealership.

W Really? Could he give me a good deal?

M Probably. I'll set up a meeting, if you want.

W Thanks, that'd be great.

Q: What is the man mainly doing in the conversation?

(a) Offering to introduce a dealer to the woman.

(b) Giving advice to the woman about new cars.

(c) Trying to convince the woman to buy a car.

(d) Describing his cousin to the woman.

37

W Do you keep a record of your expenses?

M I don't like to bother with that.

W Then how do you know how much you spend?

M I use different credit cards for different things.

W So you have a card for groceries and another for clothes?

M Right, and I just check their statements.

Q: What is the conversation mainly about?

(a) Keeping track of spending.

(b) Cutting down on expenses.

(c) Using too many credit cards.

(d) Buying food and clothes on credit.

38

M Excuse me, how long is this flight today?

W It'll be roughly 10 hours.

M So, we'll be landing in Amsterdam in the morning?

W That's correct, sir.

M And how many meals are we getting?

W Two full meals, including a breakfast.

Q: Which is correct about the man according to the conversation?

(a) His plane is departing from Amsterdam.

(b) His flight arrives at 10 in the evening.

(c) He is going to be served three meals.

(d) He will get breakfast on the flight.

39

M Maria, have you seen Josh recently?

W I ran into him yesterday. Why?

M I was wondering if he's finished his thesis.

W He said he did and that he'll be graduating soon.

M Oh, that's great news. I should congratulate him.

W Yeah, you should give him a call.

Q: Which is correct according to the
conversation?
(a) The woman has not seen Josh lately.
(b) Josh has not yet completed his thesis.
(c) Josh has recently graduated.
(d) The woman suggests phoning Josh.

40

M Jane? Is that you? I thought you quit your
job and went to Italy.
W Well, I did, but I had to come back.
M Was it different from what you'd expected?
W It was great, but I went through all my
savings really fast.
M Oh, no. So what are you going to do?
W I guess I'll look for a new job here and start
all over.

Q: Which is correct about the woman according
to the conversation?
(a) She was recently fired from her job.
(b) She did not enjoy living in Italy.
(c) She ran out of money in Italy.
(d) She recently got a new job.

41

W Sorry I couldn't make the meeting today.
M That's OK. We just discussed changes to the
office computer network.
W Great. It's time for some change.
M So, why couldn't you come to the meeting, if
I may ask?
W I had to meet my lawyer over some legal
troubles. It's kind of stressful.
M Well, if you ever want to get some lunch and
talk, I'm here.

Q: Which is correct according to the
conversation?
(a) The woman was late to the meeting.
(b) The meeting was about rearranging the
office.
(c) The woman had to see her lawyer over legal
matters.
(d) The man wants to ask the woman's advice
over lunch.

42

M Well, what did you think of the exhibit?
W Oh, it was quite good, except there were too
many photos to see in one visit.
M I liked it too, but I wish some of the photos
had been blown up.
W The landscapes did seem a bit on the small
side.
M The wildlife photos were exceptional, though.

Q: Which is correct according to the
conversation?
(a) The woman thinks there were too few
pictures at the exhibit.
(b) The man would have liked some photos to
be smaller.
(c) The woman thinks the landscape photos
were too big.
(d) The man was impressed by the wildlife
photos.

43

M Excuse me. Do you know where the
university Administration Building is?
W It's a little difficult to explain, but I can show
you.
M Really? Are you going that way?
W Yeah, I'm heading that way to give a lecture.
M Great. I guess I asked the right person.
W Right, you were in luck.

Q: What can be inferred from the conversation?
(a) The man and woman are close friends.
(b) The woman is a university instructor.
(c) The man often gets lost on campus.
(d) The woman is living on campus.

44

W   Before exploring your career options, tell me, when are you most happy?

M   Hmm. Probably when I'm doing something that engages my imagination.

W   Are you able to do that in your current job?

M   No, I'm happier at home spending time on hobbies.

W   So, your job is tolerable but not so stimulating?

M   Yeah, I have to find fulfillment outside of work.

Q: What can be inferred about the man from the conversation?
(a)   He usually feels lonely when not at work.
(b)   He spends a lot of money on his hobbies.
(c)   He would prefer a more challenging job.
(d)   He complains endlessly about his work.

45

M   Has anyone rented your other apartment yet?

W   Unfortunately, no, and I'm starting to worry.

M   Why? Is it costing you money?

W   Yeah, I'm still paying off a mortgage on it.

M   Oh, I see. You need the rent to cover your debt.

W   That's right. I'm slowly going broke.

Q: What can be inferred from the conversation?
(a)   The man is also paying a mortgage.
(b)   The woman is anxious to find a tenant.
(c)   The man will rent the woman's apartment.
(d)   The woman will borrow money from the man.

46

Welcome. This meeting is about recent market research indicating that consumer preferences are split 50-50 between us and our largest competitor. We need to change this situation. I suggest we develop an advertising campaign that shows our competitor cannot offer the same kinds of high-quality products we can. In other words, I want their products made less attractive to the public, so that ours look better.

Q: What is the main idea of the talk?
(a)   The company should hire more professionals.
(b)   Market research needs to be conducted soon.
(c)   Today's competition is the strongest in years.
(d)   The company should advertise against rival products.

47

When traveling, never let strangers talk you into carrying their baggage. A woman appearing innocent might approach you at an airport and say that she has more luggage than is allowed. Someone else might tell you he is too weak to carry his belongings and thus requires your assistance. These are common schemes used by drug smugglers. Countless foreigners are held prisoners in jail in Asian countries because they tried to aid a stranger. Play smart. Do not become the next victim.

Q: What is the main point of the advertisement?
(a)   Never carry the bags of others while traveling.
(b)   Most criminals are skillful at fooling strangers.
(c)   Many foreigners have been arrested for drugs in Asia.
(d)   Always keep a close eye on your luggage at the airport.

48

Earlier I told you that German immigrants adopted American customs after two or three generations. Well, this extended to some of them adopting new names during World War I. When war broke out, Americans began expressing anti-German feelings. It got so bad that many Germans decided to Americanize their names to avoid trouble. For instance, the name "Koenig" was directly translated as "King."

Q: What is the main topic of the talk?
(a)   Why German-Americans changed their names.
(b)   What some German names mean in English.
(c)   Famous German names in American history.
(d)   Americans who descended from Germans.

49

Some teachers here may already have recognized one of the biggest drawbacks of large classes because grading essays is so time-consuming, teachers reduce or even eliminate writing assignments in large classes: Well, it is possible to incorporate meaningful writing assignments into your course without being swamped by papers to grade. Flexibility is the key. Set different due dates for different students or assign shorter essays.

Q: What is the talk mainly about?
(a) Getting students' attention in a lecture.
(b) Including student writing in large classes.
(c) Grading students properly in large classes.
(d) Organizing a curriculum for a writing course.

50

I am giving this talk to urge all Canadians to change their lifestyles. As you know, an ecological footprint is the amount of land it takes to support each person's consumption of natural resources—to grow their food, extract petroleum they use, et cetera. There are only about 2.2 hectares of productive land for each person on Earth, yet the average Canadian's ecological footprint is 7.8 hectares! We are being too extravagant with Earth's resources.

Q: What is the main idea of the talk?
(a) The amount of productive land on earth is shrinking.
(b) The fragile ecosystems of Canada are under threat.
(c) Canada uses more resources than other countries.
(d) Canadians should reduce resource consumption.

51

Attention, class. Next week we'll be discussing Kurt Vonnegut's *Slaughterhouse Five*. This novel had a great impact upon its release in 1969 and continues to be widely read. Its theme of rejecting inevitability captured America's transformative mood, coming out as it did against the backdrop of war in Vietnam, racial unrest, and cultural and social upheaval. Even today, as we face another unpopular war and continuing racial tensions, the novel resonates with its readers.

Q: What is the main idea about *Slaughterhouse Five* in the talk?
(a) It accurately predicted 60s social upheavals.
(b) It is synonymous with radical political change.
(c) It has always won readers by its social relevance.
(d) It strongly criticized America's cultural transitions.

52

Picture that monthly envelope that normally comes with your electric bill, and then imagine that it does not contain a bill but rather a statement of credit. That is the Department of Energy's vision for homes and buildings of the future. By the year 2020, we wish to make this green vision a reality. Our goal is to have 120 percent energy-efficient buildings that demand so little energy—and generate so much of their own—that they give back to the grid.

Q: What does the Department of Energy hope to accomplish?
(a) Reduce electricity bills by as much as 50 percent.
(b) Achieve energy self-sufficiency in buildings and homes.
(c) Build new homes and buildings that use more energy.
(d) Create new billing statements for energy users.

53

According to a recently released report on immigration, more African immigrants have arrived in the United States voluntarily since 1990, than the total number who were transported as slaves before 1807, when international slave trading was outlawed. Legal immigrants from Africa now number about 50,000 annually, which is more than in any of the peak years of slave transportation. Moreover, since 1990, more Africans have immigrated to the US than in the preceding two centuries.

Q: Which is correct according to the news report?
(a) More slaves than immigrants have entered the US from Africa.
(b) International slave trading became illegal in 1907.
(c) About 50,000 immigrants now come from Africa every year.
(d) More Africans came to the US in the 1980s than since 1990.

54

Hello and thank you for calling the Goodman catalog ordering service. Please choose the appropriate option from the following menu. If you are ordering from the winter clothing catalog, please press 1. For all other clothing orders, press 2. For Goodman camping equipment and other outdoor supplies, press 3. Stay on the line if you would like to talk to one of our sales associates. Online orders can be made at goodman.com.

Q: Which is correct according to the message?
(a) Winter clothing can be ordered by pressing 2.
(b) Clothing orders can be placed by pressing 3.
(c) Outdoor supplies are currently unavailable for orders.
(d) Goodman catalog ordering service is also available online.

55

Ladies and gentlemen, I am honored to present this award of appreciation to Dr. Philip Lee for his efforts to increase access to life-saving drugs in this country. We are all committed to providing the best possible health care for our nation, but without Dr. Lee's dedication, standards would not be as good as they are today. This award also recognizes Dr. Lee's humanitarian efforts in Africa, helping to streamline the pharmaceutical system with considerable success.

Q: Which is correct about Dr. Lee according to the talk?
(a) He is being awarded for developing a new life-saving drug.
(b) Healthcare standards have fallen despite his dedication.
(c) He is being recognized for his work in the Middle East.
(d) He made medicine distribution more effective in Africa.

56

Let me begin today by refreshing your memory on human teeth development. Like most mammals, humans grow two sets of teeth throughout their lives. The first is comprised of 20 small teeth known as the deciduous or "baby" teeth. These start growing approximately two months after conception, and they begin to grow above the gum line when an infant is six or seven months old. By age six, a second set of 32 larger, permanent teeth begin to emerge, ultimately displacing the deciduous teeth.

Q: Which is correct according to the lecture?
(a) Having two sets of teeth is rare among mammals.
(b) Deciduous teeth start to develop in the mother's womb.
(c) People develop more deciduous than permanent teeth.
(d) Some people keep a few deciduous teeth all their lives.

57

Easter Island, located west of Chile, is best known for the giant stone heads called "moai" that dot its landscape. Almost 900 "moai" exist, and they average 13 feet tall and nearly 14 tons in weight. They were probably erected between 1400 and 1600 AD. Some researchers believe the moai represent important ancestors, such as chiefs; while others claim they may have acted as spiritual conduits between the people and their gods.

Q: Which is correct about moai according to the lecture?
(a) They are small stone sculptures in Chile.
(b) Over 1,000 of them exist on Easter Island.
(c) Researchers think they represent common people.
(d) They may have connected people with their gods.

58

I would like to touch upon one of the most pressing concerns in the field of agricultural biotechnology. Agribusiness giants are standardizing plant cultivation, causing some plant varieties with poor aesthetics or disagreeable taste to become unavailable. Some may even face extinction. Now, any loss of genetic diversity is bad news. Without genetic diversity plant species do not have the ability to adapt to changing environments, such as new pests and diseases, and new climatic conditions.

Q: What can be inferred from the lecture?
(a) A loss of some plant species may be beneficial.
(b) Agriculture as a business is on the decline worldwide.
(c) Most plant extinctions nowadays are caused by agribusinesses.
(d) Standardization may increase plants' vulnerability to climate change.

59

Attention, please. Following some recent complaints, airport security has decided to implement stricter rules on parking. All cars left unattended outside of airport terminal building entrances or exits will be subject to towing. Also, please make sure to load and unload passengers in the designated areas only. Loading or unloading outside the designated areas can result in a fine and/ or towing at the owner's expense.

Q: What can be inferred about the airport from the announcement?
(a) Several unattended cars have been stolen.
(b) Cars get towed away from it on a daily basis.
(c) Luggage trolleys are being left in the way of traffic.
(d) People have left cars parked near terminal entrances.

60

The next major issue I want to talk about is stalking, something that has risen sharply over the past two decades. The legal definition of stalking now is willful, malicious, repeated following and harassment. This was not an illegal activity in the United States until 1990, when the first anti-stalking law was passed. Before that, the most that police could do was arrest stalkers for a minor offense or suggest the victim obtain a restraining order.

Q: What can be inferred from the talk?
(a) Stalking primarily happens to celebrities.
(b) Many people do not realize stalking is illegal.
(c) Stalkers are more sophisticated than in the past.
(d) People were not charged with stalking before 1990.

서울대 최신기출 3

Listening Comprehension Scripts

1

M Christine! It's good to see you again.

W ___________________________

(a) I'm fine, thanks.
(b) Yes, it's been a while.
(c) OK, let me know when.
(d) I'll be seeing you soon.

2

W Hello, I'm calling to speak to Mr. Miller.

M ___________________________

(a) Let's go and ask him.
(b) Please come back by 4.
(c) Sorry, he's not in right now.
(d) But he didn't leave any message.

3

M Thank you for coming to the party.

W ___________________________

(a) Thank you for inviting me.
(b) I'll try to make it on time.
(c) I can bring some snacks.
(d) I can come earlier.

4

W Do you like to grow plants?

M ___________________________

(a) Well, I haven't seen that many.
(b) Yes, I'd rather plant mine in spring.
(c) Sure, I have a passion for gardening.
(d) Thanks, I could use a few extra seeds.

5

M Why are you upset with your landlord?

W ___________________________

(a) I've never met him before.
(b) He wants to put the rent up.
(c) We're moving out of his apartment.
(d) He's two months behind on his rent.

6

W Honey, don't forget to pick Danny up after work.

M ___________________________

(a) Don't worry. I won't.
(b) I haven't seen him all day.
(c) I'll remember to remind him.
(d) But he's more forgetful than me.

7

M Excuse me, but this coffee is not hot enough.

W ___________________________

(a) Sorry, I'll bring you another one.
(b) I've heard similar complaints.
(c) I wouldn't mind a cold drink.
(d) Well, I knew you'd like it.

8

W I wish I could lose weight somehow.

M ___________________________

(a) Tell me how you did it.
(b) It's less than you think.
(c) Just exercise and eat less.
(d) That much isn't necessary.

9

M Would you like some more wine?

W ___________________________

(a) Yes, I've had more than enough.
(b) I didn't have time to try every kind.
(c) I'd better not. I've already had too much.
(d) But I'm nearly finished with my first glass.

10

W Andrea seemed pretty upset about what I said.

M ___________________________

(a) She had no way of knowing that.
(b) I suggest you apologize to her.
(c) She says the strangest things.
(d) I'm not sure who said that.

11

M Annie? It's William calling. Are we still on for tonight?

W ___________________

(a) Well, I'm still waiting for it.
(b) Sure. We all had a great time.
(c) Probably. That was the forecast.
(d) Absolutely, if that's OK with you.

12

W Kathy looks kind of down today.

M ___________________

(a) We'll find that out soon enough.
(b) Something must have fallen off.
(c) I don't think it's the right occasion.
(d) Hopefully nothing bad has happened.

13

M Professor Lauren, is there a prerequisite for your course?

W ___________________

(a) You'll gain experience in the lab.
(b) I doubt I have a choice in the matter.
(c) You need to have taken Biology 101.
(d) I'm teaching two courses this semester.

14

W How dare Sara talk back to me like that!

M ___________________

(a) Talking to her wasn't easy at all.
(b) No need to get worked up about it.
(c) I know. It was a lengthy discussion.
(d) But she can usually speak up for herself.

15

M Julia, I was wondering if you could lend me $500.

W ___________________

(a) I'm afraid that's out of the question.
(b) I can't always be responsible for you.
(c) Go over your spending plan regularly.
(d) It's not too late to ask around for more.

16

W What are your plans for this summer?
M I'm thinking of going to New York.
W Really? What are you going to do there?

M ___________________

(a) I'll see you there.
(b) Probably by train.
(c) Shopping and sightseeing.
(d) I know it will be expensive.

17

M Oh, Jessica! Hi. I'm so glad I ran into you!
W Hi, Tony. What's up?
M Can I borrow your notes to study for tomorrow's exam?

W ___________________

(a) I'm glad to meet you, too.
(b) No problem. Here they are.
(c) I didn't take an exam today.
(d) Sure. I'll give you some hints.

18

W Hello. I'd like to make an appointment with Dr. Brown.
M I'm afraid he's on vacation until the 12th.
W Oh. Is there another doctor available, then?

M ___________________

(a) You do need to see a doctor.
(b) It's best to make an appointment.
(c) Dr. Thomas is free this afternoon.
(d) Dr. Brown is in Spain for two weeks.

19

M What's wrong with my MP3 player?

W Oh, sorry. I dropped it, and it stopped working.

M Why didn't you tell me earlier?

W _______________________

(a) I downloaded a song for you.
(b) I couldn't find it. That's why.
(c) I think mine is working fine.
(d) I was going to, but I forgot.

20

W Excuse me. Where can I find the bread, please?

M It's in aisle three, across from the dairy section.

W OK, but which way is aisle three?

M _______________________

(a) It's just over there to your right.
(b) I have no idea where the bread is.
(c) You left it on the shelf behind you.
(d) You're not asking the right question.

21

M Hey, Melanie. Congratulations.

W What for?

M You got all A's, didn't you?

W _______________________

(a) Actually, I have one B.
(b) I can't make any promises.
(c) I hope I do well in the final.
(d) Don't worry. You'll get all A's.

22

W David, have you started working out like you said you would?

M Yes, I joined that gym near the station last weekend.

W Hey, that's where I go.

M _______________________

(a) OK, but it won't be easy.
(b) I promise I'll exercise harder.
(c) I'm surprised you work there.
(d) Then, I might see you there sometime.

23

M Too bad our baseball team won't make the finals.

W I know. It's disappointing.

M I guess there's always next season.

W _______________________

(a) I thought it was in season now.
(b) But that's what we said last year.
(c) Tickets might be more expensive by then.
(d) Let's go to their finals match this weekend.

24

W Good afternoon. You must be Ben Duncan.

M Yes, hi. Was it you I spoke to on the phone about the job?

W That's right. I'm Susan Phillips.

M _______________________

(a) Nice to meet you. My name is Ben Duncan.
(b) I'm glad we can talk face to face.
(c) It sounded urgent on the phone.
(d) I'm happy I could be of help.

25

M Why don't we see that new Ridley Scott movie tonight?

W That sounds good. Will you come and pick me up?

M OK. It starts at 8. So, what if I come by at 7?

W _______________________

(a) All right. I'll be home by 8.
(b) I think I saw that movie before.
(c) OK, I'll pick up the movie on the way.
(d) Make it 6, so we'll have time for dinner.

26

W I'm going to break up with my boyfriend.

M Why? I thought you two were getting along well together.

W We were, but then he changed.

M _______________________

(a) I told you it would fix itself.
(b) He should've asked you out first.
(c) It wasn't what she recommended.
(d) Things like that happen in relationships.

27

M Here, have a piece of this cake I bought.
W No thanks, I'm watching my weight.
M Are you sure? It's delicious.
W ______________________

(a) There is one more piece.
(b) Please don't tempt me like that.
(c) I'll put aside an extra piece for later.
(d) I'll have another helping if you insist.

28

W We need more trees in our yard.
M More trees? What for?
W We need more privacy from our neighbors.
M ______________________

(a) Then, let's step into the shade.
(b) That might prove a bit costly.
(c) But the yard is tidy enough.
(d) You can't just repot them.

29

M Your big job interview is today, isn't it?
W Yeah, I'm heading out soon.
M Got any pre-interview jitters?
W ______________________

(a) It's crucial for the interview, though.
(b) It'll be conducted elsewhere today.
(c) I'll know more after the interview.
(d) Actually, I feel surprisingly calm.

30

W Do you remember Rachel Campbell from high school?
M Sure, what about her?
W She called me out of the blue the other day.
M ______________________

(a) I knew she was feeling down.
(b) I'll handle the call, if you like.
(c) Yeah, I said you'd give her a call.
(d) Wow, I wonder what she's been up to.

31

W I've got a computer problem. Can you help?
M Sure. What's wrong?
W I can't seem to get any Internet access.
M Let me have a look. Mmm... I see what you mean.
W What could it be?
M Nothing serious. Just a loose cable.

Q: What is the main topic of the conversation?
(a) An Internet connection problem.
(b) An interesting Internet site.
(c) A computer that is too old.
(d) A new computer program.

32

M Have you traveled a lot, Monica?
W Yes, I've been to 19 different countries.
M That many? Have you been to Italy, then?
W Yes, I've been there twice.
M What about Greece?
W Well, no, I haven't been there yet.

Q: What are the man and woman mainly talking about?
(a) Countries the woman has visited.
(b) Good countries for sightseeing.
(c) Plans for the next vacation.
(d) Difficulties with traveling.

33

M We should get a second car.
W I agree, but can we afford it?
M We can, if we take out a loan.
W What about the cost of insurance and gas?
M I think we could manage, if we got a small car.
W OK, then, let's look at some models.

Q: What are the man and woman mainly discussing?
(a) Whether they can buy a second car.
(b) How they will pay off a car loan.
(c) What model of car they will buy.
(d) Why they need a small car.

34

W   Ugh, deadlines are terrible.

M   There's no avoiding them for a journalist.

W   But if I had a couple more hours for this article, it'd be much better.

M   All journalists wish they could have more time.

W   Even you, with all of your experience?

M   Oh, sure. Deadlines give me a lot of stress.

Q: What is mainly being discussed?

(a) The deadline that the woman missed.

(b) The burden of meeting deadlines.

(c) The man's skills at journalism.

(d) The due date of an article.

35

M   Olivia, have you seen my car keys?

W   No dear, did you look on the kitchen counter?

M   Yeah, but they weren't there. They weren't on my dresser, either.

W   Why don't you check your pants pockets?

M   Good idea. But where are my pants?

W   I put them in the laundry basket.

M   OK, I'll check.

Q: What is mainly taking place in the conversation?

(a) The man is looking for his keys.

(b) The woman is gathering the laundry.

(c) The man is asking where his pants are.

(d) The woman is washing the man's pants.

36

M   Are you ready for your trip to Hawaii?

W   Yeah, everything's organized.

M   How will you get to the airport?

W   Oh, I guess I'll just take the subway or a bus.

M   Why don't I give you a ride to the airport?

W   Could you? That would be great!

Q: What is the conversation mainly about?

(a) Taking a flight to Hawaii.

(b) Getting out to the airport.

(c) Driving with a friend in Hawaii.

(d) Visiting someone at the airport.

37

M   Your new apartment looks really nice. Did it set you back much?

W   Yeah, I really had to stretch my finances to buy it.

M   Was it wise to spend so much?

W   Well, I've always wanted a fancy apartment.

M   Yeah, but it's going to be expensive to maintain.

W   I know. I'll just have to make some sacrifices.

Q: What is the conversation mainly about?

(a) The difficulty of getting finances to buy an apartment.

(b) The trouble the woman has with her new apartment.

(c) The high cost of the woman's new apartment.

(d) The woman's love of luxurious apartments.

38

W   Excuse me, sir. We're serving the in-flight lunch now.

M   Oh, uh, sorry, I dozed off.

W   Which would you like sir, the salmon or the pasta?

M   I'll have the pasta, please.

W   All right. Here you are. Would you like a drink with that?

M   I'll have tomato juice, please.

W   Certainly. One moment. There you go.

Q: Which is correct about the man in the conversation?

(a) He was sleeping before lunch.

(b) He wants another orange juice.

(c) He is disappointed with the lunch.

(d) He wants to have salmon for lunch.

39

W   Do you have any plans for winter vacation?

M   I'm going to Thailand for three weeks.

W   I've never been there. So, what are you going to do there?

M   I think I'll lie around on the beach all day.

W   That sounds great. I wish I could do that.

M   Well, start saving up.

Q: Which is correct according to the
   conversation?
(a) The man is going to be in Thailand for over a
    month.
(b) The man plans to spend his vacation at a
    beach.
(c) The woman has visited Thailand many times.
(d) The woman has been saving for a vacation.

40

M Did you get the new credit card you applied
   for?
W No, I didn't.
M Really? What happened?
W They turned me down because my credit
   history is too short.
M That's too bad. You might need to get
   someone to co-sign.
W Probably, but it's a hassle.

Q: Which is correct about the woman according
   to the conversation?
(a) Her credit card has to be paid off very soon.
(b) Her credit card application was rejected.
(c) She turned down a credit card offer.
(d) She has too much credit card debt.

41

M Why are there so many people on the
   platform?
W I don't know. The subway train is late for
   some reason.
M Maybe there was an accident up the line.
W Yeah, that's possible. I wish they'd tell us
   what's happening.
M I'd say it might be a long wait.
W Yeah. Let's go up and get a taxi.

Q: Which is correct according to the
   conversation?
(a) The man arrived late at the station.
(b) The woman saw an accident on a train.
(c) The man does not want to wait for a taxi.
(d) The woman is unsure why the train is late.

42

W Mr. Lee, your prescription is ready.
M Thank you. Now, how should I take these?
W Two tablets after each meal. It's on the label,
   right here.
M And how many days do I have to take them?
W You have enough for seven days, as your
   doctor recommended.
M OK, then. Thank you.

Q: Which is correct about Mr. Lee according to
   the conversation?
(a) He has to go see a doctor.
(b) He must take two tablets a day.
(c) He needs to take pills after meals.
(d) He got two weeks' worth of tablets.

43

M Hi, Amy. This is James calling.
W Oh, hi, James. How are you?
M Good. Say, did you get a cat? I can hear one
   in the background.
W That's my neighbor's. I'm looking after him
   for a few days.
M But aren't you allergic to cats?
W I used to be, but not so much these days.

Q: What can be inferred from the conversation?
(a) The man has never liked cats.
(b) The neighbor has several cats.
(c) The woman does not own a cat.
(d) The cat has kept the woman busy.

44

M Can I use your printer?

W You can, but how many pages are you going to print out?

M About 50.

W In that case, you'd better use the printer in the next room.

M You mean the one in Dr. Stanton's office?

W Yes, it's a laser printer, and it's much faster than this one.

M OK. Thanks.

Q: What can be inferred from the conversation?
(a) The woman does not have a laser printer.
(b) The printer in Dr. Stanton's office is new.
(c) The man usually uses his own printer.
(d) The man has just run out of paper.

45

M Sue, have you finished the finance report I asked for yet?

W Umm, I'm just about done with it.

M But I requested it two days ago.

W I know. I'm sorry. I've been swamped with Tim's orders.

M OK, well, when will you have it done?

W If nobody else bugs me, I'll get it to you in an hour.

Q: What can be inferred about the woman from the conversation?
(a) She has little experience doing reports.
(b) She usually finishes her work on time.
(c) She is not good at setting priorities.
(d) She gets work from several people.

46

Welcome aboard the USS Reginald. The Reginald is a Class VII Destroyer that was built in 1998 at its home port of Norfolk, Virginia. This ship is equipped with state-of-the-art weaponry and has the most advanced command and control combat management system available in the world today. Please feel free to have a look around the designated areas and to ask any questions you may have. Thank you.

Q: What is the speaker mainly doing in the announcement?
(a) Welcoming visitors to a warship.
(b) Giving orders to sailors on a ship.
(c) Describing exhibits in a war museum.
(d) Explaining the mission of a destroyer.

47

Let me stress to all of you that running a fundraiser has a lot in common with running a business. Both require the same time and talent to set goals and reach financial objectives. Both ventures need leadership and have the same goal of making money! So, approach your fundraising project as a business owner would, and you'll be more successful.

Q: What is the speaker's main point about fundraising?
(a) It should be run as if it were a business.
(b) Its goals are best met by making money.
(c) Special training is required to succeed at it.
(d) Volunteers for it should have business experience.

48

One thing first-year med students must remember is that fever itself is not an illness; it's a symptom of one. It occurs as a result of illness and is a defense mechanism that helps increase the production of antibodies to rid the body of toxins. It can work with antibiotic medications to shorten an illness and make it less contagious. In short, fever is a sign of the body attempting to ward off illness, so it is a good idea to let it run its course.

Q: What is the main idea of the lecture?
(a) Several benefits can come from a fever.
(b) It is dangerous to leave a fever untreated.
(c) Fever should not be treated as an illness.
(d) Fever makes an infection less contagious.

49

Today's lecture focuses on the heroines of Shakespeare's plays. Feminism and women's rights were not a part of his era, yet Shakespeare insightfully explores women's issues through his depiction of how heroines come up against a social structure largely determined by men. It might be argued that he is even cynical towards his society's values, for example, when one of his heroines has to disguise herself as a man so that men will listen to her views.

Q: What is the main point of the lecture?
(a) Shakespeare's forward thinking contributed to feminism.
(b) Shakespeare was cynical about the idea of women in power.
(c) Shakespeare's heroines succeed because of an inner strength.
(d) Shakespeare was critically aware of inequalities faced by women.

50

There was a great deal of change in the English language before Old English became Modern English. Some changes occurred in grammar, but the most dramatic changes occurred in vocabulary. You may be surprised to hear that only about 20% of Modern English vocabulary can be traced to the native words of Old English. Words added to English from foreign sources, such as Latin, Greek or Old Norse, make up about 80% of the total Modern English vocabulary.

Q: What is the main topic of the lecture?
(a) The reason why Old English has changed.
(b) The borrowed words used most in English.
(c) The development of vocabulary in Old English.
(d) The history behind Modern English vocabulary.

51

In political news, Democrats stated today that the President's tax cut will cause a shortfall for the social security system and that this is further proof of his lack of credibility. The Democrats labeled the President's tax plan as nothing more than political grandstanding, and are demanding he produce a tax alternative that will not endanger the nation's welfare system. In response, the President said that the Democrats have done their math wrong and that they are relying on erroneous figures.

Q: What is the main idea of the news report?
(a) The President is rejecting statements made by the Democrats.
(b) The Democrats are insisting that the President is incompetent.
(c) The President's tax plan is causing welfare recipients to suffer.
(d) The Democrats are criticizing the President over a proposed tax plan.

52

OK, let's get this meeting started. I wanted to speak to you all about the talks we will be having with Forex executives concerning the proposed merger, so that all employees will be aware of what's going on. Rest assured, in our negotiations, we'll do our best to see that none of you will lose your job. Your position may change after the merger—we can't really control that—but we will make it clear that downsizing is not an option.

Q: What is the speaker mainly doing in the talk?
(a) Convincing employees that their jobs will not change.
(b) Assuring employees that their employment is secure.
(c) Persuading executives to go ahead with the talks.
(d) Soliciting support for the company's merger.

53

The motto of the NY DJ Academy is simple: education and access. NY educates budding DJs and enthusiasts in deejaying by supplying them with the right equipment, providing them with the right curriculum and giving them access to world famous DJ instructors. At NY, we aim to unify, legitimize, validate and extend the role and importance of deejaying by teaching it as an art form, as a hobby and as a profession, and by educating the public of its merits.

Q: Which is correct about the NY DJ Academy?
(a) It trains people to become DJ instructors.
(b) It supplies equipment to the music industry.
(c) It instructs students on the art of deejaying.
(d) It hosts free promotional events for the public.

54

I'm here today to talk about diabetes. Diabetes occurs when the body no longer makes, or is unable to use, insulin, which is a type of hormone. Usually, insulin helps transfer glucose, or sugar, into cells to provide them with energy. However, when insulin is not present or is ineffective, the glucose cannot be absorbed by cells and blood sugar levels rise. That's when you have diabetes. If untreated, high blood sugar levels can cause damage to the eyes, nerves, kidneys and other vital organs.

Q: Which is correct according to the talk?
(a) Insulin prevents the absorption of glucose.
(b) Insulin causes our blood sugar levels to rise.
(c) Excessive blood sugar levels damage nerves.
(d) Diabetes can result from excessive hormones.

55

As I mentioned before, early humans did not have historical records or sciences to turn to for explanations of the world around them. Thus, they created myths to explain things that defied their understanding. The Old Testament's story of Babel, for example, was a myth that explained for them why different languages existed on earth. This tendency—creating fantastical stories for what is not understood—has existed in all human societies from primitive times onwards.

Q: Which is correct according to the lecture?
(a) A single language once existed among all humans.
(b) Ancient myths invariably have some basis of truth.
(c) Myth-making was a part of culture among early humans.
(d) Different ancient societies often invented similar myths.

56

Win a millionaire's vacation at the Paradise Island Resort in the Bahamas! By purchasing any item worth over $100 at any Big-Mart store, you automatically get the chance to win an all-expenses-paid vacation of a lifetime for two, valued at over $150,000. For 8 days and 7 nights, you will stay in the renowned 4,800-square-foot Presidential Suite, with a personal concierge, a limo and a 50-foot cabin cruiser all on standby. Enter the contest at any Big-Mart store now!

Q: Which is correct about the contest according to the advertisement?
(a) Two resort prizes can be won.
(b) It has a prize of living in luxury for 8 days.
(c) Shoppers are restricted to one entry each.
(d) Shoppers can win store items worth over $100.

57

Let's begin our Western Philosophy course by jumping back to the sixth century BC, when conceptual thought about the real nature of the universe and of human life emerged. This transition from superstition toward explanation is materialized in the old Greek thinkers, of whom the Pythagoreans were among the most important. They supported Pythagoras' view that all aspects of the universe followed arithmetic ratios and a regularity order, and they further maintained that the goal of humans was to live in harmony with that natural regularity.

Q: Which is correct according to the lecture?
(a) Ancient philosophy underpinned the tenets of superstitious thought.
(b) Pythagoreans were the first ancient Greeks to pursue abstract thinking.
(c) Philosophy emerged in ancient cultures around the world simultaneously.
(d) Some early philosophers saw reality in terms of mathematical relationships.

58

The first thing on the agenda at this board meeting is company travel expenses. Up until now, we have relied on employees to judge what is or isn't a legitimate travel expense—and I'm confident none has willfully wasted money on luxuries during business trips. However, a situation has arisen, where what an employee saw as reasonable expenditure was not regarded as such by the management. To avoid such disputes, we need clearer policies that set out what can and can't be reimbursed.

Q: What can be inferred about the company from the talk?
(a) Its employees receive a generous salary.
(b) It will put a stop to employee business trips.
(c) It lacks detailed guidelines on travel expenses.
(d) Its travel expense records will be examined again.

59

Everyone at this conference today needs to redouble their efforts against illiteracy. It is indeed urgent, when roughly 20% of adults—perhaps as many as 7 million people—do not even have functional literacy. Without basic reading ability, they cannot accomplish routine tasks like finding a plumber in the telephone directory. These people are getting left further and further behind, especially now with the world's increasing dependence on the Internet. The question is what should be done to educate them.

Q: What can be inferred from the speech?
(a) Studies in functional literacy have made many advances.
(b) Higher literacy is a by-product of the age of technology.
(c) Functional illiteracy inhibits the proper use of computers.
(d) Adult education is unlikely to counter functional illiteracy.

60

And now to local news. According to newly released statistics, nearly half the people who earn teaching degrees in this state do not end up teaching at local state schools. The statistics further show that, of the teachers who begin their careers in local schools, one third leave within four years. The reasons cited for quitting included lower-than-average pay and poor administrative support. The Office of Education has announced that measures to increase teacher retention will be considered in response to the findings.

Q: What can be inferred about the state's education system?
(a) It has fewer schools than surrounding states.
(b) It has failed to adopt career incentives for teachers.
(c) It will concentrate more spending on teacher training.
(d) It will begin recruiting new teachers from other states.

서울대 최신기출 4

Listening Comprehension Scripts

1

W Jason got admitted to medical school.

M ___________________________

(a) Good for him!
(b) He became a doctor.
(c) Yes, he admitted to it.
(d) I'm on medication, too.

2

M Hi, Jill! How have you been?

W ___________________________

(a) It's my pleasure.
(b) Have a nice day!
(c) Really well, thanks.
(d) I haven't been there.

3

W Why don't you buy a house while the housing market is still good?

M ___________________________

(a) But I have no money.
(b) I hope the result is good.
(c) You did? Congratulations!
(d) You should come to my house.

4

M Jasmine, is that you? You look so different.

W ___________________________

(a) I thought I had a chance.
(b) I don't have any change.
(c) I see things differently.
(d) I changed my hairstyle.

5

W Excuse me. Is there a taxi stand nearby?

M ___________________________

(a) You can take a bus.
(b) You shouldn't stand here.
(c) I thought you said it was near.
(d) Up ahead, near the subway station.

6

M Jane, are you still coming over at two?

W ___________________________

(a) I think it's better now.
(b) Sorry, but I can't make it.
(c) Certainly, just tell me when.
(d) I'm not sure I can stay that late.

7

W Professor Wong, when will I get my paper back?

M ___________________________

(a) The paper is past due.
(b) I've already received it.
(c) I'll finish grading next week.
(d) Please get it done by tomorrow.

8

M Take this pill. It'll relieve your migraine.

W ___________________________

(a) I'll get rid of mine.
(b) I haven't taken any.
(c) I hope it'll work fast.
(d) I'll hang around for a while.

9

W Hello, I'd like to open a checking account.

M ___________________________

(a) I'll get you the forms.
(b) Sorry, it's not for sale.
(c) Yes, it should be open.
(d) Thanks for your check.

10

M   Where do we pick up our suitcases?

W   ______________________________

(a) Put them in the overhead bin.
(b) Please take them to check-in.
(c) At baggage claim, further down.
(d) Don't worry. Just carry them on.

11

W   Robbie and I are going for drinks after work. Want to come along?

M   ______________________________

(a) Sure, help yourself.
(b) He's come along well.
(c) I'm afraid I'll have to pass.
(d) Actually, we get along fine.

12

M   What do you think of my short story?

W   ______________________________

(a) I'm unable to match the content.
(b) People like reading short stories.
(c) I imagined myself becoming a writer.
(d) The plot structure needs a little more work.

13

W   I think I'd better get a credit card for online shopping.

M   ______________________________

(a) It should arrive next week.
(b) You deserve a lot of credit.
(c) Maybe you left it at the store.
(d) Then, you might spend more money.

14

M   Once you graduate, you'll quickly find a good job.

W   ______________________________

(a) You'll be making decent money.
(b) I wish I shared your confidence.
(c) I barely earn enough to cover my rent.
(d) You'd better file for unemployment benefits.

15

W   I'm so overwhelmed with all the work I have to do.

M   ______________________________

(a) You should control yourself.
(b) You'll need to help me out here.
(c) I'm not sure why you want to quit.
(d) I guess you'll be working late again.

16

W   How was your trip to Hawaii?
M   We had a great time.
W   What was the weather like?
M   ______________________________

(a) It was a relaxing trip.
(b) It was nice and warm.
(c) We liked the food best.
(d) We preferred waterskiing.

17

M   Can I help you with dinner?
W   Sure. You can peel potatoes.
M   OK, where shall I do it?
W   ______________________________

(a) I appreciate it.
(b) Over by the sink.
(c) Anytime you want.
(d) Your advice is helpful.

18

W   It's unbearably hot today!
M   Yeah. Why don't we go to a beach this afternoon?
W   That's a good idea.
M   ______________________________

(a) It's the easy way.
(b) I hope you had fun.
(c) Let's go around 2:30.
(d) I once lived by the beach.

19

M Hello? Is Kim there?

W Oh, Ted, is that you? What's up?

M Well, I was in the neighborhood and was wondering if you're busy.

W ______________________________

(a) Sorry, I missed your call.
(b) Not at all. You should come by.
(c) Thanks for calling, see you later.
(d) I'm afraid I can't help you right now.

20

W Do you have any plans for the weekend?

M I'll probably go sailing Saturday.

W Didn't the weather forecast say it'd be bad that day?

M ______________________________

(a) You're welcome to come.
(b) I don't think it'll be severe.
(c) No problem. I'll let you know.
(d) But I can't wait until Saturday.

21

M I just realized it's Michelle's birthday tomorrow.

W It is? I haven't sent a card or anything.

M Why don't we send an e-card?

W ______________________________

(a) I hope she'll like our present.
(b) I forgot about Michelle's party.
(c) I don't know what gift to get her.
(d) I guess that's better than nothing.

22

W When is the charity concert being held?

M I think it's tomorrow night.

W What's it for, anyway?

M ______________________________

(a) To raise money for the poor.
(b) I have music practice.
(c) They said it'd be fun.
(d) It won't be for long.

23

M It's very cold in here.

W Yeah, there's a draft from somewhere.

M Maybe the sliding door isn't properly shut.

W ______________________________

(a) I don't think it'll turn up.
(b) That could be it. I'll check.
(c) We didn't change the door.
(d) It'll help you breathe better.

24

W Have you heard any news about the logo competition?

M My design made it to the final round.

W Wow, that's great! Congratulations!

M ______________________________

(a) Well, I haven't won yet.
(b) I should've designed a logo.
(c) I'd better design something now.
(d) Thanks, but I don't like competition.

25

M How long does it take to get to the campus from this bus stop?

W About 15 minutes.

M Does the shuttle service run often?

W ______________________________

(a) It leaves every ten minutes.
(b) I don't think they need servicing.
(c) It makes several stops along the way.
(d) The shuttle service is currently running.

26

W Honey, what time will you get home tonight?

M The usual, unless there's an emergency.

W Well, I'll be late. Can you help Sammy with his homework?

M ______________________________

(a) I'll do it before I get home.
(b) I'll have Sammy do it, instead.
(c) That's fine. I'll take him home.
(d) Don't worry. I'll take care of him.

27

M   Could you stop by the dry cleaners after work?

W   I guess so, but it's a bit inconvenient.

M   Are you kidding? It's on your way home.

W   ______________________________

(a) But it's on a congested road.
(b) Yes, but I'm leaving home later.
(c) Give me directions on cleaning it.
(d) I've already dropped off two suits.

28

W   Someone stole my briefcase this morning.

M   Oh no! Did you lose anything important?

W   It had all my documents for today's meeting.

M   ______________________________

(a) That's too bad. I hope you have extra copies.
(b) I'm not sure what today's meeting is about.
(c) Put them in a safe place when you're done.
(d) We can resume the meeting after lunch.

29

M   Haven't you chosen a camera yet?

W   They all look good. I don't know which one to buy.

M   Just go by the specifications.

W   ______________________________

(a) I know. My photos aren't too bad.
(b) They'll have to be drawn up later.
(c) The problem is I don't have a camera yet.
(d) You're right. Let's ask the clerk to explain them.

30

W   The workload at this company has increased dramatically.

M   I'll say. They're squeezing two months of work into one.

W   Why are they being so unreasonable?

M   ______________________________

(a) I'll have to hurry to finish.
(b) It takes a long time to complete it.
(c) Because last time we weren't ready.
(d) They want to get ahead of the competition.

31

M   Did you see Tim's thumb?

W   No. Why?

M   It's all black and blue.

W   Really? What happened?

M   He says that he hit it with a hammer.

W   Ouch, he should've been more careful.

Q: What is the conversation about?
(a) Tim hurting his thumb.
(b) Tim losing his hammer.
(c) Tim looking black and blue.
(d) Tim making a lot of mistakes.

32

W   That's a catchy song.

M   Not for me. I'm sick of current pop music trends.

W   You're not a fan?

M   No, the songs are so unsophisticated.

W   But they represent an aspect of our culture.

M   Yeah, but there's nothing original about them.

Q: What is mainly happening in the conversation?
(a) The man is composing a new song.
(b) The woman is teaching the man a song.
(c) The woman is enjoying listening to music.
(d) The man is criticizing mainstream pop music.

33

W   Did you hear about the train crash?

M   No. What train crash?

W   A train derailed this morning.

M   Oh, were there many casualties?

W   No fatalities but a lot of injuries.

M   Do they know how it happened?

W   They're still investigating.

Q: What is the main topic of the conversation?
(a) An update on a recent hit-and-run case.
(b) The injured people from a train accident.
(c) A railway accident that happened that day.
(d) The increasing number of transport accidents.

34

W I heard you're looking for an apartment.

M Yes, I'm looking for a one-bedroom apartment near the university.

W That's going to be pretty expensive.

M I know, but I'll try to find something inexpensive.

W If you get a place farther away, it'll be cheaper.

M Yeah. I might have to do that if I don't get lucky.

Q: What is the man trying to do?
(a) Move far from school.
(b) Rent out his apartment.
(c) Move into the woman's apartment.
(d) Rent a cheap place near the university.

35

W Where do you want to have lunch?

M Anywhere will do. What do you feel like?

W I wouldn't mind some noodles.

M In that case, let's go to a place I know down the street.

W Oh, does it have a good menu?

M Yes, there's plenty of choice. You'll like it.

Q: What is the main topic of the conversation?
(a) Where to go and have lunch.
(b) What to order at the restaurant.
(c) How to find the closest restaurant.
(d) Whether or not to have noodles for lunch.

36

M Hi, welcome to Seattle. What can I do for you?

W Can you suggest an affordable place to stay for the next few days?

M Sure. Just tell me your price range and location preference.

W Well, something downtown for around $80 a night.

M There aren't any downtown hotels in that price range, I'm afraid.

W Then, please check guesthouses.

Q: What is mainly happening in the conversation?
(a) The man is booking a room at a guesthouse.
(b) The man is checking into a downtown hotel.
(c) The woman is staying with the man at a hotel.
(d) The woman is seeking affordable accommodation.

37

M I've got to do something about my office.

W Why, what's wrong with it?

M The sun is so bright that I have to keep the blinds closed.

W So, what's the problem?

M Well, then I lose my view.

W Did you try shifting your desk to avoid the sun?

M I did, but that didn't help.

Q: What is the man's main concern?
(a) He wants a better view from his office.
(b) He needs help rearranging office furniture.
(c) He does not like working in an office all day.
(d) He cannot block sunlight while keeping the view.

38

W Let's get some coffee before the next session begins.

M Sure, but where? At the vending machine?

W No, there's a coffee shop downstairs.

M Do we have enough time?

W We've got 20 minutes.

M OK, then, let's go.

Q: Which is correct according to the conversation?
(a) The next session starts in 20 minutes.
(b) The coffee vending machine is not working.
(c) The man will give a talk at the next session.
(d) The woman wants to pay for the man's coffee.

39

W Excuse me, but you look familiar. Do you work at Smithklein?

M Actually, I do, in accounting. My name is Dave.

W I thought I recognized you. I'm Sara. I'm in sales.

M Yes, I think I've seen you at the cafeteria.

W Oh, I have lunch there everyday.

M Really? Maybe we can have lunch together one day.

Q: Which is correct according to the conversation?

(a) Dave works with Sara in accounting.

(b) Sara waited on Dave at the cafeteria.

(c) Dave and Sara work at the same company.

(d) Dave and Sara have lunch together every day.

40

W Have you heard anything about the promotion yet?

M Yes, they announced it today, but I didn't get it.

W Even after all your work on the Mayberry project?

M Yeah, a guy in my department with seniority ended up getting it.

W Well, I'm sure there'll be other opportunities.

M I guess so. I'll just have to wait and see.

Q: Which is correct about the man?

(a) He has seniority in his department.

(b) He worked on the Mayberry project.

(c) He was promoted to a senior position.

(d) He is waiting to hear about the promotion.

41

M Emily, do you want to come skiing with us next weekend?

W I'd love to. I haven't skied yet this year.

M Great. We'll be leaving on Friday after work.

W Is there anything you want me to bring?

M Not really. We've booked a lodge, and it has everything we need.

W Sounds great. Then, I'll see you Friday.

Q: Which is correct about the woman?

(a) She will take Friday off from work.

(b) She will meet the man at the lodge.

(c) She does not need to bring anything.

(d) She has not had any experience skiing.

42

M Miss Crawford, why has the stadium project been delayed?

W There's excessive water on-site.

M Didn't you complete groundwater studies?

W I did, but detected nothing. I'm investigating the source.

M Do you have a timeline or cost estimate?

W I'm sorry, sir, but I can't accurately ascertain anything yet.

Q: Which is correct according to the conversation?

(a) The stadium needs a new water source.

(b) The man was informed of future cost estimates.

(c) The project will proceed without further investigation.

(d) The woman cannot predict when the problem will be fixed.

43

M Hi Stacy, are you still in your suite?

W I'm waiting for Heather. She's running late.

M Well, I'm calling to remind you that the tour bus leaves the hotel in five minutes.

W I'll tell her to hurry, but you know what she's like.

M Tell her everyone else is on the bus already.

W OK, I'll go and hurry things up.

Q: What can be inferred from the conversation?

(a) The woman will leave Heather behind.

(b) The man will take the woman to the bus.

(c) The woman is not used to Heather being late.

(d) The man does not want the woman to miss a tour.

44

M   How come I don't see much of you on campus any more?

W   I'm taking most of my courses online this semester.

M   I don't think they offer anything like that in my department.

W   They're doing it as a pilot project for psychology majors.

M   So, how do you like it?

W   It's great because I can do everything at home.

Q: What can be inferred from the conversation?

(a) The man has a different major than the woman.

(b) The man will switch his major to psychology.

(c) The two people attend different universities.

(d) The woman misses her friends on campus.

45

W   Are you ready to order?

M   Not quite. I have a question about these spaghetti dishes.

W   What would you like to know?

M   It seems that they all have meat in them.

W   Yes, there is either bacon, beef or chicken.

M   Could I have the spaghetti without meat?

W   I'm not sure. I'll ask the chef.

Q: What can be inferred from the conversation?

(a) The chef updated the menu recently.

(b) The man will not have a vegetarian dish.

(c) The restaurant provides vegetarian meals only.

(d) The woman has not heard similar requests before.

46

On tonight's home-style program, we offer some simple methods to reduce your water bill. One method you can use is to take short showers rather than baths. In addition, you should always turn off the water while brushing your teeth. Finally, use your washer only when you have a full load of clothes to wash. Follow these suggestions, and you will drastically reduce your water bill.

Q: What is the speaker mainly talking about?

(a) Saving money on your water bill.

(b) Using water when cleaning your home.

(c) The benefits of showers over baths.

(d) Keeping the bathroom in good condition.

47

I want to start by extending my congratulations to everyone present on getting accepted at Bradberry University. I know that all of you are very much looking forward to your future campus life. I would therefore like to stress something that's clear but that the majority of students seem to forget: that the success of your life here depends on you. Our faculty will try hard to educate you, but it is your responsibility to do the work.

Q: What is the speaker's main point?

(a) Students will be treated like adults at university.

(b) Students should not give up on their career goals.

(c) Students are ultimately responsible for their own success.

(d) Students must consult professors whenever they need help.

48

The government has to make more efforts to help the disabled. There are simply too many homeless people among the disabled whose only means of support is panhandling in the streets or on the subways. However, the government is not showing enough concern about these people. Hopefully, our march through the downtown area today will get this issue the necessary attention it deserves.

Q: What is the speaker's main point?

(a) Homeless people should survive by begging.

(b) People with mental problems should not be ignored.

(c) Panhandling on the subway should be outlawed.

(d) The government should help the disabled homeless.

49

Come to AutoEasy's professional service, where the most modern equipment is used to comprehensively go over your car. Set up an appointment before your vehicle's warranty runs out, before you purchase a used car or before you go on an interstate trip. Our experienced technicians will inspect your car and provide you with a detailed log of its needs. Inquire about our special savings deal. To make an appointment, call 649-298-2755.

Q: What is the advertisement about?
(a) A savings plan on a car loan.
(b) An auto-body repair business.
(c) An inspection service for vehicles.
(d) A school for training auto technicians.

50

Getting a divorce before turning 30 has become so common that it has created a phenomenon known as the starter marriage. A starter marriage is one that only lasts for a couple of years and normally comes to an end before the couple has children. Indeed, some young couples stay married for a mere few months. Although the divorce rate leveled off in the 1990s, research shows that these marriages that end within the first five years are on the rise.

Q: What is the main point of the report?
(a) At least half of all marriages end in divorce.
(b) More people are marrying before they are 30.
(c) Divorce rates after the 1990s have increased.
(d) Starter marriages are becoming more common.

51

I often talk about how businesses need to reduce energy usage and emissions to prevent climate change, but individual homeowners can also play their part by reducing home energy consumption. However, in order for them to participate in energy reduction on a large scale, local governments should give incentives, such as lessening restrictions on integrated solar panels and wind turbines, to encourage homeowners to generate their own power.

Q: What is the main idea of the speech?
(a) It is the governments' responsibility to reduce energy waste.
(b) Minimizing climate change requires help from businesses.
(c) Individuals should be encouraged to pursue homeownership.
(d) Governments should encourage homeowners to reduce energy consumption.

52

We now turn to the third phase of language development, which starts at approximately 18 months of age. At this point in their lives, babies communicate through telegraphic sentences consisting mainly of nouns. For instance, an English-speaking child might say "Mommy, cup" instead of "Mommy, I want a cup." Vocabulary is still fairly undeveloped at this point, so babies will frequently resort to echolalia, or continual repetition of the identical word or phrase.

Q: What is the main topic of the lecture?
(a) The importance of repetition in advancing a child's speaking skills.
(b) Emotional maturity in children and its relationship with language.
(c) Typical problems with telegraphic communication for children.
(d) Aspects of the third stage of childhood language development.

53

Hello. I'm sorry I can't answer your call right now. If you're calling concerning the advertised apartment for rent, it's no longer available. However, we still have plenty of items for sale, including this answering machine you are listening to. If you would like to drop by to see what we have to offer, simply leave your number and I'll return your call to set up a time. Bye now.

Q: Which is correct according to the recorded message?
(a) The caller has to leave a name and address.
(b) The speaker is selling the answering machine.
(c) The apartment advertised for rent is still available.
(d) The things the speaker owned have already been sold.

54

The handcrafted objects on display at this next exhibit originate from the British slave trading ship Henrietta Marie, which sunk off Florida's Key West in 1701 after delivering a load of African slaves to the island of Jamaica. The ship set out from Africa with up to 300 captives who had been purchased with iron and copper bars by the British crew. After its human cargo was unloaded for a significant gain, the Henrietta Marie sailed out to meet its fate with the loss of every crew member aboard.

Q: Which is correct about the Henrietta Marie?
(a) It offloaded all of its slaves in Florida.
(b) It sank with 300 captive slaves on board.
(c) It was carrying iron and copper when it sank.
(d) It transported slaves from Africa to Jamaica.

55

A new study published by the National Center for Health Statistics suggests that marriage may actually benefit your health and longevity. The study, based on surveys of 127,000 single and married adults, shows that married people have less tendency to smoke, drink excessively or be physically inactive. Moreover, they are less likely than their single counterparts to have poor health, migraine headaches or stress symptoms.

Q: Which is correct about married people?
(a) Their health is usually better than that of singles.
(b) They tend to take up smoking after marriage.
(c) Their stress levels are higher than those of singles.
(d) They have more opportunities to drink than singles.

56

Let's look now at how airplanes are protected from lightning. The majority of aircraft skins are produced using aluminum, which conducts electricity. Some contemporary aircraft, however, are made of composite materials which include layers of conductive fibers that protect them from lightning currents. As airplanes are built to have no gaps in conductive tracks, a lightning current makes its way along the exterior of the craft and then leaves the plane at some extremity, such as the tail.

Q: Which is correct according to the lecture?
(a) Conductive paths are usually engineered without gaps.
(b) Some aircraft skins are designed not to conduct electricity.
(c) Few aircraft are constructed with aluminum exteriors.
(d) Lightning currents are bounced off the exteriors of aircraft.

57

The subject of today's lecture concerns one of the most important figures in French literature, Michel de Montaigne. He published intimate essays about his own mind, feelings and habits. During the Renaissance, he wrote about his failing memory, his ability to be emotionally detached, his disgust for man's pursuit of lasting fame and his attempts to detach himself from worldly things. But the true genius of Montaigne is that in describing himself, he described all people.

Q: Which is correct about Montaigne according to the lecture?
(a) His emotional detachment kept him from pursuing fame.
(b) His personal writings accurately portrayed human nature.
(c) He used self-criticism as a means of critiquing humanity.
(d) He ingeniously detailed common people's everyday lives.

58

Although many people know the names of a few constellations or perhaps even a group of constellations, they may have difficulty locating most of them in the sky. In the Northern Hemisphere, the constellation most commonly found is Polaris, which is some 50 light years from Earth and is situated on the edge of the constellation Ursa Minor. Despite the fact that its scientific name is Polaris, it is more typically referred to as the North Star.

Q: What is the speaker likely to discuss next?
(a) The exact location of the North Star.
(b) Stars in the Southern Hemisphere.
(c) The measurement of a light year.
(d) How the North Star got its name.

59

Tonight at eight on ABS, our nutritional experts will demonstrate how to go on a diet without giving up fast food. Believe it or not, there are healthy choices on virtually every fast food menu. We've analyzed the nutritional value of foods at five different fast food restaurants and produced our selection of their healthiest choices. Tune in to our special on diets tonight at eight on ABS.

Q: What is likely to be shown in the dieting special?
(a) How bad eating fast food can be for dieters.
(b) Which fast food restaurants serve the best food.
(c) What to eat and what to avoid in fast food restaurants.
(d) Why some fast food restaurants are better than others.

60

As I noted in my previous lecture, children learn the basic rules of social interaction from parents or caregivers. As they grow up, they go through other emotional, social and cognitive experiences that are more complicated and harder to deal with. In peer group relationships in particular, the social norms children obtained through their first interactions with adults are absent. As a result, young children frequently feel less comfortable and skilled associating with other children than they do with adults.

Q: What can be inferred about children from the lecture?
(a) They are usually insecure with unlearned social rules.
(b) Those with siblings adapt best to new social situations.
(c) Those who do not interact well with peers become depressed.
(d) Extroverted ones are more quickly accepted into groups.

서울대 최신기출 5

Listening Comprehension **Scripts**

1

W Hey, John, how's it going?
M _______________________

(a) Same here.
(b) I wish I could.
(c) Not bad, thanks.
(d) Nice to meet you.

2

W Could you take a look at this report?
M _______________________

(a) No, I can't find it.
(b) Sure, I can do that.
(c) It's been reported.
(d) Please don't look at me.

3

M This class assignment is so hard.
W _______________________

(a) I'm late again.
(b) OK, I'll try again.
(c) I know. It's not easy.
(d) Yes. He's in my class.

4

M Do you mind if I smoke?
W _______________________

(a) Of course not.
(b) Thanks for asking.
(c) I know, it's a bad habit.
(d) No thanks. I'm trying to quit.

5

W Shall we go see a movie this afternoon?
M _______________________

(a) I have two tickets.
(b) Sorry. I have to work.
(c) I already saw that one.
(d) Yes, I really enjoyed it.

6

M This is terrible. I can't find my wallet!
W _______________________

(a) I'll keep it for you.
(b) Well, I don't like it anyway.
(c) It's black with a silver stripe.
(d) Why don't you check the drawer?

7

M Are you still thinking of buying a car?
W _______________________

(a) No, I decided not to.
(b) I'm afraid I already sold it.
(c) Right. It's not the right model.
(d) Let me know if you need help.

8

M Francine, your term paper could've been
   a lot better.
W _______________________

(a) I'm not quite finished yet.
(b) I didn't know it was due today.
(c) Sorry. I'll try harder next time.
(d) My paper will be on Korean history.

9

W It's awfully cold in here.
M _______________________

(a) I'll turn on the heater.
(b) Are you sure it's not here?
(c) Check the medicine cabinet.
(d) It's not as awful as you think.

10

W Rob, what does your father do for a living?
M _______________________

(a) He works hard.
(b) He's self-employed.
(c) He's living in Seattle.
(d) He's washing the car.

11

M Your sister seems to have a very good memory.

W ___________________

(a) We should go visit her.
(b) She's very interested in you.
(c) It was certainly a memorable moment.
(d) Yes, she remembers almost everything.

12

M Do you understand what I'm saying?

W ___________________

(a) Of course. I know what you mean.
(b) You can say that again.
(c) Well, I totally disagree.
(d) Well, it's not enough.

13

W Is the conference room occupied at the moment?

M ___________________

(a) I don't think it has started yet.
(b) I believe you're right about that.
(c) We should wait for the right moment.
(d) Not for now, but it's reserved for later.

14

M Can you recommend anything on the menu?

W ___________________

(a) How about today's special?
(b) I'm impressed by your choice.
(c) I wouldn't mind eating out tonight.
(d) Your order will be ready soon, sir.

15

W Wow, you look handsome in that suit, Tim!

M ___________________

(a) I'd be glad to show you one day.
(b) Come on, you're just saying that.
(c) This tie will go well with that shirt.
(d) It's OK. I know what you're trying to say.

16

M Would you like something to eat?
W No, thanks. I'm not hungry.
M How about a nice cold drink?

W ___________________

(a) This drink is delicious.
(b) Not really. I'm starving.
(c) I made it especially for you.
(d) Thanks. That sounds wonderful.

17

M What are your plans for this summer?
W I'm going to New Zealand.
M All by yourself?

W ___________________

(a) I'm flying economy class.
(b) It sure is a beautiful place.
(c) No, with a couple of my friends.
(d) Well, the trip will be for seven weeks.

18

M How do you like this chair?
W Looks gorgeous. How much did it cost?
M The lady next door gave it to me.

W ___________________

(a) Please take a seat.
(b) Really? You're so lucky!
(c) I think you paid too much.
(d) That's OK. I already have one.

19

M   Why are you so late?

W   Sorry. I got locked out of my car.

M   You're kidding. Again?

W   __________________________

(a) That's a really good idea.

(b) You know how forgetful I am.

(c) The traffic was horrible this morning.

(d) I'll change the locks as soon as possible.

20

M   I'd like to rent a car for the weekend.

W   OK. What kind of vehicle would you like?

M   Well, do you have any mini-vans available?

W   __________________________

(a) Will you be paying by card?

(b) Please return it by Monday.

(c) I just bought one for myself.

(d) Sorry, they've all been rented out.

21

W   Hello. East-West Real Estate.

M   Hi. I'm calling about the one-bedroom apartment you advertised.

W   Yes. What would you like to know?

M   __________________________

(a) How much is the monthly rent?

(b) Please let me know if there's a vacancy.

(c) I'd like to know when I need to move out.

(d) I'm calling to find out how many bedrooms it has.

22

W   You seem to be really concerned about the environment.

M   I am. How did you know?

W   Because I noticed you recycle a lot.

M   __________________________

(a) I never knew that.

(b) I do as much as I can.

(c) Cycling keeps me fit.

(d) My garbage can is full.

23

M   You haven't changed your mind about going to Japan, have you?

W   No. Why?

M   Well, isn't it expensive?

W   __________________________

(a) I'm flying first class.

(b) I can lend you some money.

(c) Yeah, but I've been saving up.

(d) No, that's why I'm flying in tonight.

24

W   What a lovely picture! Is this your family?

M   Yes, that's me, my parents and my younger sister.

W   Your sister looks a lot like your mother.

M   __________________________

(a) People say that all the time.

(b) That's because they're twins.

(c) They get that from my father.

(d) She cares a lot about her looks.

25

M   Who are you going to vote for class president?

W   Melanie Benson.

M   Why don't you vote for Jimmy Doyle?

W   __________________________

(a) Jimmy's in my math class.

(b) I heard he's not trustworthy.

(c) Yes, I'm hoping he wins this year.

(d) It's too late now. I've already voted.

26

M   Hi. I'm on the 2:30 to Boston, but I can't find my boarding gate.

W   Oh, they just changed the gate number. It's D32 now.

M   Thanks. Oh, and is there anywhere for a bite to eat near there?

W   __________________________

(a) Sure. There's a snack bar next to the gate.

(b) No, no meals are served on flights to Boston.

(c) We're sorry, but the change was unavoidable.

(d) I haven't eaten a decent meal since yesterday.

27

M Good morning, Karen.

W Good morning, Ed. You're in late this morning.

M Well, I stayed out partying last night.

W _______________

(a) That's why I slept in today.
(b) I didn't know it was your birthday.
(c) Yes, it was quite a night, wasn't it?
(d) I guess it'll be a long day for you, then.

28

W I can't believe I got the promotion!

M Congratulations. I knew you'd get it.

W You knew about it?

M _______________

(a) At this stage, it's just a rumor.
(b) Why not? I think you deserve it!
(c) No, but you were the best candidate.
(d) Nobody did. We were counting on you.

29

W Oh, no. I was supposed to call Chris at 2!

M Why didn't you call him?

W I was so busy, it slipped my mind.

M _______________

(a) Then I'll call him at 2.
(b) You'd better call him now.
(c) Call me when you're free.
(d) Well, no news is good news.

30

M It's been a fun evening, but I have to leave.

W Yes, it's late. I'd better be going, too.

M Do you need a ride home?

W _______________

(a) I appreciate your saying so.
(b) Well, I can show you the way.
(c) Sure. Thanks again for dropping by.
(d) I was dreading a walk in the cold, thanks.

31

M Excuse me. Is the town library near here?

W Not really. It's about ten blocks away.

M That's too far to walk. Is there a bus I can take?

W Yes, you can take bus 56. It stops outside the library.

M Thanks a lot.

W You're welcome.

Q: What is the man trying to do?
(a) Find the bus stop.
(b) Take bus 56 to work.
(c) Get directions to the library.
(d) Return a book at the town library.

32

W How do you like your new office, Tom?

M Great. It has a lovely view of the courtyard.

W And is it big enough for you?

M Oh, yes. It's much bigger.

W I'm glad you find everything comfortable.

Q: What is the man mainly talking about?
(a) His responsibilities in his new job.
(b) What he likes about his new office.
(c) His desire to move into a new office.
(d) How the offices are of different sizes.

33

M Hello?

W Hi, is Mr. Parker home, please?

M Yes, speaking.

W Oh, I'm calling from your home security company.

M Oh, you must be calling about our alarm that went off.

W Yes, I am. Is everything all right?

M Everything's fine. The alarm was set off by accident.

W All right. Not a problem. Have a good day.

Q: What is the main reason for the phone call?
(a) To warn about an accident.
(b) To check on a security alarm.
(c) To promote a new alarm system.
(d) To inquire about security services.

34

W   Did you ever serve in the military, Mr. Collins?

M   Yes, I was a lieutenant in the Navy during the Vietnam War.

W   Really? What kind of ship were you on?

M   A supply ship. We delivered supplies from Sydney.

W   So, you were spared from combat?

M   Yes, thankfully, we weren't caught up in the fighting.

Q: What is the man mainly talking about?

(a) His supply ship in the Navy.

(b) His memorable visits to Sydney.

(c) His time in the Navy during a war.

(d) His experiences fighting in Vietnam.

35

W   Is this the maintenance office?

M   Yes, it is. How may I help you?

W   We're not getting any heat. My apartment is freezing.

M   Is the heater on?

W   Yes, but it isn't doing anything.

M   OK. I'll be right over.

Q: What is the woman's problem?

(a) She lost the key to her apartment.

(b) She is unable to heat her apartment.

(c) She has trouble picking out a heater.

(d) There is no one at the maintenance office.

36

M   I wish we could go back in time.

W   Why do you say that?

M   Because I'd like to relive our three years in Honolulu.

W   Those were the good old days.

M   I miss Waikiki Beach so much.

W   So do I. I especially miss Hanauma Bay.

Q: What are the speakers mainly talking about?

(a) Why Honolulu is such a great place.

(b) How they fondly remember Honolulu.

(c) Which beaches are the best in Honolulu.

(d) Where to live in Honolulu for the next three years.

37

M   So, has your father recuperated from the surgery yet?

W   Not yet. He's feeling better, though.

M   It'll probably be a while before he's back to normal.

W   Yeah. But he's getting there, one day at a time.

M   At least he had no complications.

W   Yes, that was fortunate.

Q: What is the main topic of the conversation?

(a) Potential complications from surgery.

(b) The failing health of the woman's father.

(c) The father's recovery from an operation.

(d) The schedules set for the father's surgery.

38

M   Hello?

W   Hello. I'd like to speak with Mr. Green.

M   This is he. May I ask who's calling?

W   This is Sheila Waters with the New Castle Eye Clinic.

M   Oh, are you calling about my new glasses?

W   Yes, you may pick them up at any time.

M   OK. Thank you.

Q: What does the woman want the man to do?

(a) Take a message.

(b) Talk with Mr. Green.

(c) Pick up his new glasses.

(d) Come in for an eye exam.

39

W   What are you doing?

M   I'm opening the windows.

W   Why? You're letting in the cold air.

M   But we need some fresh air in here.

W   Well, don't leave them open too long.

M   I'll close them in a few minutes.

Q: Which is correct about the man?

(a) He wants to go out for a walk.

(b) He is trying to fix the windows.

(c) He does not want to let in cold air.

(d) He thinks the room needs fresh air.

40

W   Where are you off to?

M   I have a train to catch to New York.

W   Oh, that's right. You've got that conference.

M   Yes, and it starts at 9.

W   You'd better hurry, then.

M   Right, I don't want to be late.

Q: Which is correct about the man?
(a) He is leaving at 9.
(b) He is going to New York.
(c) He is hurrying to get a taxi.
(d) He is late for his conference.

41

W   Oh, no. I left my passport in my hotel room!

M   Uh-oh, you're going to need that for today's tour.

W   We'd better go back.

M   But then we'll fall behind in our travel plans.

W   But I can't go on the tour without my passport.

M   Well, I guess we have no choice, then.

Q: Which is correct according to the conversation?
(a) The man left behind his travel plans.
(b) The woman has forgotten her passport.
(c) The man decided not to go back to the hotel room.
(d) The woman does not need her passport for the tour.

42

M   What are you doing?

W   Filling out a credit card application.

M   What for? Don't you already have several credit cards?

W   Yeah, but I've reached my credit limit on all of them.

M   That's a lot of debt. You shouldn't get another one, then.

W   Don't worry. I'll pay it off eventually.

Q: Why is the woman applying for a new credit card?
(a) She collects cards as a hobby.
(b) She wants to have more than one card.
(c) She likes the high credit limit the card offers.
(d) She has no credit remaining on her other cards.

43

M   Hello, officer, what's the problem?

W   Are you aware of the speed limit in this area?

M   It's 80 kilometers per hour, isn't it?

W   No, it's 60.

M   Oh, well, I...

W   And what speed were you traveling at?

M   I think it was around 60.

W   No, it was a lot faster than that.

Q: What will most likely happen next?
(a) The man will try to drive faster.
(b) The woman will stop the man's car.
(c) The man will receive a speeding ticket.
(d) The woman will apologize for her mistake.

44

W   When are you going to start your class assignment?

M   Soon. There's no need to rush.

W   But it's due in one week!

M   Relax. I'll get to it.

W   Relax? I think you're a little too relaxed!

M   I'd rather be relaxed than stressed out like you!

Q: What can be inferred from the conversation?
(a) The man has not started working on the assignment.
(b) The two people are working on the project together.
(c) The man does not know when the assignment is due.
(d) The woman is worried that the man will fail the course.

45

M Well, we're going to miss you around here.

W I'm going to miss being here.

M What's next? Any plans?

W I've got a few things in mind.

M At least you won't have deadlines to meet anymore.

W Right. After working for twenty years, I'm just going to relax.

M Well, it'll be hard to replace you.

W Thanks. But I'm sure they'll find someone.

Q: What can be inferred about the woman from the conversation?

(a) She is looking forward to being retired.

(b) She is being laid off from the company.

(c) She wants to stay on at the company.

(d) She plans to try a new career path.

46

Would you get in the water at a beach with big waves, sharp rocks and prowling sharks? That's what 24 daredevil surfers are going to do in this year's Maverick Beach Surf Contest on Wednesday. Catch the excitement of this world-famous competition, which is once again living up to its reputation as the most dangerous surf contest in the world. The danger begins at Maverick Beach on Wednesday at 10:00 am.

Q: What is the speaker mainly talking about?

(a) A beach known for big waves, rocks and sharks.

(b) The courage of surfers who take on huge waves.

(c) The dangers faced by surfers at Maverick Beach.

(d) A surfing competition to be held at Maverick Beach.

47

Scientists at Tory Institute announced today that they have discovered a tiny genetic mutation which enables some fruit flies to survive on a fraction of the sleep fruit flies usually need. Like human beings, fruit flies generally require around 6 to 12 hours of sleep every night, and they demonstrate signs of physical stress if they don't get it. However, the scientists reported that certain flies carry a mutation in one of their genes that lets them thrive on just three or four hours of sleep.

Q: What is the news report mainly about?

(a) How long fruit flies normally live.

(b) How fruit flies differ from humans.

(c) Why fruit flies need 6 to 12 hours of sleep.

(d) What effect a genetic mutation had on fruit flies.

48

Many of our customers have said they would like our cruise line to offer adult-only cruises. The reason, they say, is because of bad experiences with kids whose parents failed to control them. But I do not think that would be a wise direction for our company to head in. As you may remember, one of our former competitors, Pacific Cruise, organized an adult-only cruise some years ago, and it made the company go bankrupt. I don't think we should make the same mistake again.

Q: What is the speaker's main point about adult-only cruises?

(a) They made Pacific Cruise go bankrupt.

(b) They would not be successful if offered.

(c) They are requested by many customers.

(d) They will allow adults to be more relaxed.

49

In today's class we'll look at challenges faced by biologists studying African elephants. One particular challenge is monitoring the numbers of forest elephants. This is because the normal method of counting elephants by helicopter, as used on the African savanna, just doesn't work. But there are other solutions: one is to count dung piles; another is to listen for elephant vocalizations. These alternative methods allow biologists to identify the presence of elephants over large areas, without visual sightings.

Q: What is the main topic of the lecture?
(a) The difficulty of counting elephants.
(b) The communication between forest elephants.
(c) The technology used to analyze elephants.
(d) The survival of elephants in African forests.

50

On news of his death today, the nation's journalists have been reflecting on the life of fellow journalist Hunter S. Thompson. For three-plus decades, Thompson was an outspoken writer who broke the rules of journalism by injecting himself so thoroughly into his reports that he became the story, giving us "Thompson with the Hells Angels," "Thompson in Las Vegas," and so on. His brand of journalism was seen by many as a refreshing change from the kind of impersonal, dispassionate reporting that preceded him.

Q: What is the main purpose of the report about Hunter S. Thompson?
(a) To detail some of the highlights of his career.
(b) To criticize his negative effects on journalism.
(c) To explain how he influenced other journalists.
(d) To pay tribute to him and his style of journalism.

51

The invention of paper and printing only allowed information to be disseminated to limited numbers of people. It was a slow process by today's standards. Today, the Internet enables information to spread rapidly worldwide, and it can reach millions of people instantaneously. This is a profound capability that human beings have never had before. It is obviously a major advance in human communications.

Q: What is the main idea of the talk?
(a) The spread of information in the current age is unprecedented.
(b) The invention of computers was a major advance in history.
(c) The amount of information on the Internet is overwhelming.
(d) The Internet has reduced our reliance on paper.

52

Ladies and gentlemen, let me be clear. Freedom means the right to assemble, organize and debate openly. And it means citizens can openly disagree with the policies of their governments. It means they can peacefully express their ideas and opinions without worrying about being taken away from their loved ones and imprisoned, mistreated, or denied their freedom and dignity.

Q: What is the speaker mainly talking about?
(a) The basic human rights that freedom entails.
(b) The consequences of not fighting for freedom.
(c) The way the government abuses basic freedoms.
(d) The right to speak out against injustices in public.

53

Your call has been forwarded to an automated answering machine. If you would like to talk to a representative from the customer service department, please call back during normal work hours. In all other cases, please remain on the line and leave a voice message along with your name, phone number and a brief description of the problem you are having. If you are located outside the US, contact us toll free at 888-357-2762. Thank you for using Androtech. Have a great day.

Q: What are international callers instructed to do?
(a) Call during normal business hours.
(b) Leave a recorded message.
(c) Hang up and dial a different number.
(d) Wait for a customer service representative.

54

As a model, I always read the *Women in Rags* weekly magazine. It's the fashion industry's hottest news source. It covers everything in fashion: from business issues to fashion trends, from retail developments to market overviews. *Women in Rags* is the news source for anyone who is serious about fashion. Get the latest in modern fashion with *Women in Rags*, the fashion industry's authority on fashion.

Q: Which is correct about *Women in Rags*?
(a) It sells fashionable clothing for women.
(b) It reports fashion news on a monthly basis.
(c) It is mainly for models and model agencies.
(d) It is a key news source in the fashion
   industry.

55

Fitness experts in California have come up with a new workout method which enhances blood flow. The method uses a series of deep yoga stretches mixed with quick bursts of cardiovascular activity. For instance, after executing five minutes of leg stretches, people are encouraged to carry out two minutes of intense biking and then return to doing slow, deep leg stretches. The method is called Push Yoga and has been gaining popularity among image-conscious stars whose careers rely on appearing healthy and toned.

Q: According to the passage, what is one of the benefits of Push Yoga?
(a) It increases flexibility.
(b) It strengthens leg muscles.
(c) It stimulates hormone release.
(d) It improves blood circulation.

56

This lecture will discuss the exchanges of views in the historical evolution of Indian and Chinese medicine. Both Indian and Chinese medicine emerged independently, each being linked closely to its own native religious and cultural viewpoints. Their geographical separation, however, did not stop the interchange of ideas and acquisition of theories and practices from one system to the other or from other neighboring cultures. Even so, following the precise routes and confirming the exact dates of these interactions is very arduous.

Q: Which is correct according to the lecture?
(a) The exact routes for exchange have been
   discovered.
(b) Religion had close connections with Indian
   medicine.
(c) Chinese and Indian medicine did not
   influence each other.
(d) Little is known about the origins of Chinese
   medicine.

57

One term you'll often hear in this class is "urbanity." The notion of urbanity refers to a mode of social relations proper to urban life. It is often used to define the socio-cultural identity of city inhabitants as well as a type of social organization which is specific to urban society. Our class discussion of urbanity will thus encompass the economic, political, social and cultural impetuses of cities, as well as the major impact these forces have on city dwellers.

Q: Which is correct about the term "urbanity" according to the lecture?
(a) It describes how social relations are formed in rural areas.
(b) It refers to the social structure of a city environment.
(c) Its economic definition will be the main focus of the class.
(d) Its application to rural dwellers will be a discussion point.

58

First of all, welcome everyone to our annual end-of-the-year meeting. I'd like to thank all resellers who traveled from all over the world for your efforts in selling our Pander Business Communications' products this year. I'd also like to acknowledge this year's winner of Pander's reseller incentive scheme competition. The best-performing reseller was Scalable Networks based in Sussex, whose staff members were rewarded with vacation vouchers to any destination of their choice. Congratulations on a job well done!

Q: What can be inferred about Pander Business Communications?
(a) It has a network of resellers worldwide.
(b) It specializes in arranging special vacation tours.
(c) It rewards the customers who purchase the most.
(d) It is a newly launched company with a branch in Sussex.

59

Have you ever noticed how an enthusiastic salesperson in a department store can get you, the customer, more excited about merchandise? Or have you observed how an enthusiastic speaker can excite audiences? If you have enthusiasm, those around you will have it, too. All you have to do is think enthusiastically, and you'll be enthusiastic. Then, others will catch the enthusiasm.

Q: What is implied about enthusiasm?
(a) It is able to make the world better to live in.
(b) It is most helpful in sales and at conferences.
(c) It begins with an optimistic view of the future.
(d) It can be learned by anyone with a desire for it.

60

In observing the satire in Jonathan Swift's *Gulliver's Travels*, let's first look at the excerpt in which Swift's protagonist, Gulliver, portrays his native England's social institutions to the king of one of the exotic lands he visits. Gulliver, who is naturally accepting of and blindly favorable to his native society, endeavors to persuade the king of its advantages and importance. Yet, after hearing Gulliver's account, the king reaches the conclusion that the English must be the "most pernicious Race of little odious Vermin that Nature ever suffered to crawl upon the Surface of the Earth."

Q: What can be inferred from the lecture?
(a) The English do not realize how great their country is.
(b) Travelers must try harder to understand other cultures.
(c) Citizens should learn to regard their own society critically.
(d) People in high positions often have one-sided viewpoints.

서울대 최신기출 6
Listening Comprehension **Scripts**

1

M   Excuse me, where is the subway station?

W   _______________

(a) Well, I'm not going.
(b) It's farther up this road.
(c) The next one arrives at 2.
(d) The gas station is that way.

2

W   It's way past Kenny's bedtime, isn't it?

M   _______________

(a) It must be over.
(b) I don't know how.
(c) Yes, I'll tuck him in now.
(d) No, I think it's your turn.

3

M   Hello. Could I speak to Sue, please?

W   _______________

(a) Speaking.
(b) I'm on the phone.
(c) She hasn't called.
(d) You can call her now.

4

W   Pardon me, could you help me change my flight?

M   _______________

(a) Yes, but I'll need to see your ticket.
(b) No, it should still be on schedule.
(c) Well, I'm not sure where to go.
(d) Sure. It'll arrive on time.

5

M   I can help you move your things this Saturday.

W   _______________

(a) I'll hand them over.
(b) Really? That'd be great.
(c) Yes. I found that helpful.
(d) That's where I'm moving.

6

W   Have you seen Jennifer around?

M   _______________

(a) No, not recently.
(b) I'll go and tell her.
(c) Of course, she'll drop by.
(d) I haven't seen her do that.

7

M   Which do you like better, coffee or tea?

W   _______________

(a) I prefer coffee.
(b) I enjoy them a lot.
(c) I usually have it hot.
(d) I like my tea with cream.

8

W   You've spilled juice on my dress!

M   _______________

(a) Oh, I'm terribly sorry.
(b) Just have some of mine.
(c) You can bring me a drink.
(d) OK. I'll get something else.

9

M   I was worried you'd have trouble finding my place.

W   _______________

(a) I like your new place.
(b) No problem. You'll be fine.
(c) Not at all. I had a map to guide me.
(d) We did manage to find a new place.

10

W You made some careless mistakes in your report.

M ___________________________

(a) I'm almost ready.
(b) I know it's due today.
(c) Thanks, but don't bother.
(d) I'm sorry. It won't happen again.

11

M I'm so nervous about my interview this morning.

W ___________________________

(a) I'll be happy to take care of it for you.
(b) Take a deep breath and loosen up.
(c) Don't worry. I'll catch up later.
(d) I haven't asked about it yet.

12

W Let me introduce you to Derek when he arrives.

M ___________________________

(a) I was hoping you might.
(b) That's something I've never done.
(c) I'm surprised you've never met him.
(d) We aren't certain when he'll be back.

13

M Our home team is losing again. They're hopeless.

W ___________________________

(a) I can't believe it ended in a tie.
(b) They sure leave a lot to be desired.
(c) You're forever boasting about them.
(d) We have no right to demand more.

14

W Good morning, Mr. Lee. I'm calling to talk about our draft contract.

M ___________________________

(a) That hasn't been factored in yet.
(b) Coincidentally I'm going over it now.
(c) I'll certainly note down that concern.
(d) I traced around it to make an outline.

15

M The director gave us the green light on our proposal.

W ___________________________

(a) There will be other chances.
(b) We should've worked harder.
(c) Switch it on and see if it works.
(d) Let's get down to business, then.

16

W Good morning, sir. Can I help you?
M Yes, I'm trying to find some canned peaches.
W They're down this aisle.
M ___________________________

(a) I can't find the lid.
(b) They look quite ripe.
(c) Great. I'll have a look.
(d) Sorry, I forgot which one.

17

M I'd like to get something to eat.
W Me, too. Let's go to the café on the corner.
M But I don't have any cash.
W ___________________________

(a) I'm not really hungry.
(b) That's OK. I have enough.
(c) Just order some fast food.
(d) Sure, I'll have another coffee.

18

W Jim, can you come over to my house right away?
M Now? I'm sort of busy.
W But somebody broke in. The place is a mess.
M ___________________________

(a) Oh no! I'll be right over.
(b) Wait. I've got a spare key.
(c) I hope you can get it back.
(d) I can't help you if it's broken.

19

M Excuse me, is there a flower shop near here?
W You can find one right around the corner.
M Would it still be open?
W ___________________________

(a) Not anymore. It just moved.
(b) No, I don't think I can this time.
(c) Yes, the evenings can be dull around here.
(d) Most likely. Local stores usually stay open late.

20

W What time does the next train for New York leave?
M At 10:25 from platform 3.
W Are there any tickets left?
M __________________________

(a) Yes, you should go at least once.
(b) I'm sorry. I just sold the last one.
(c) Actually, it takes about three hours.
(d) No, the last train left 30 minutes ago.

21

M Do you know where the new art museum is?
W Yes. It's not far from my apartment.
M Really? So, it's on the west side?
W __________________________

(a) I'm thinking of going there.
(b) I know. It's a wonderful gallery.
(c) Right, just a few blocks from me.
(d) Well, I'm moving there next week.

22

W B.T. Business Systems. Can I help you?
M Yes, I'm calling about the PCs you advertised in the paper.
W Do you have any particular model in mind?
M __________________________

(a) I'm interested in the top-of-the-line model.
(b) I'm afraid that won't be necessary.
(c) That depends on the model.
(d) I'm looking for a new PC.

23

M How is the research going?
W Well, I've nearly finished my second experiment.
M How far are you from completing all of your experiments?
W __________________________

(a) I'm not even close.
(b) I appreciate your help.
(c) I need to change my topic.
(d) I'm trying to finish them all.

24

W Jack, what do you say to a date with a girl I know?
M Sure. Who is it?
W She's an old friend from college.
M __________________________

(a) Yes. I love going to college reunions.
(b) Right. I didn't like her attitude.
(c) All right. I'll give it a try.
(d) OK. I'll look for her.

25

M I'm going to sell my sports car.
W Why? I thought you loved that car.
M I do, but I need the money badly.
W __________________________

(a) Then you should get a nicer car.
(b) You'll never know until you try it.
(c) I hope you find other ways to raise cash.
(d) You'd be better off trying another type of sport.

26

W Did you have to get stitches for your cut finger?
M Yeah, quite a few, actually.
W Well, what did the doctor say about it?
M __________________________

(a) He said the nurse would return shortly.
(b) He said the hospital was relatively new.
(c) He said he had seen my symptoms before.
(d) He said I was lucky it hadn't been worse.

27

M I was so glad you could come to my wedding.
W Well, thanks for inviting me.
M I was afraid you might be too busy to make it.
W __________________________

(a) I would never have missed it.
(b) I'll try and do everything I can.
(c) The reception was really great.
(d) I'm afraid I have another appointment.

28

W　Did you hear about the new expressway?
M　Yes, they're putting it right through town.
W　You don't sound impressed.
M　_______________

(a) That's news to me.
(b) I'll start working on it right away.
(c) I'm not. It's going to cause problems.
(d) That's true. It does make a lot of sense.

29

M　Thanks for agreeing to see me, professor.
W　Come on in. How can I help you today?
M　I'd like some advice on whether to study architecture or not.
W　_______________

(a) I'm not sure when to broach that issue.
(b) Not yet, but I'll look at your designs tonight.
(c) Oh, let's cross that bridge when we come to it.
(d) Perhaps you could fill me in on your background first.

30

W　Dr. Jones, would it be possible to use you as a reference?
M　Sure. I'd be glad to help. How are your applications going?
W　The paperwork is a real hassle. It's stressing me out.
M　_______________

(a) You knew it would require a lot to pass.
(b) You really shouldn't get your hopes up.
(c) You'll see it's not what I meant.
(d) You'll feel better once it's all over.

31

M　Was school a lot different when you were a student?
W　Well, the teachers were stricter.
M　So, school was tougher than it is now?
W　In one sense, but now you have more homework to do.
M　And what else was different?
W　We weren't under as much pressure as students are now.

Q: What is the conversation mainly about?
(a) Past school life compared to the present.
(b) How students do less work nowadays.
(c) How the woman behaved at school.
(d) Schools that have strict teachers.

32

W　Look out!
M　Hey, where did that car come from?
W　You almost hit it!
M　Yeah, that was close.
W　Maybe you'd better slow down.
M　Yes. I'd better.

Q: What is the conversation mainly about?
(a) A careful driver.
(b) A report on a car crash.
(c) A potential car accident.
(d) A street too narrow for cars.

33

M　Are you ready to go onstage and sing?
W　I'm nervous. I've never sung in front of an audience before.
M　But you've been practicing for months.
W　I'm afraid I'll make a mistake.
M　Don't worry. I'm sure you'll be great.
W　Thanks, I appreciate that.

Q: What is the man trying to do in the conversation?
(a) Help the woman practice singing.
(b) Make the woman sing a new song.
(c) Tell the woman where the stage is.
(d) Comfort the woman before she sings.

34

M Would you like to come out for a drink tonight?

W OK, but I'll have to check with my friend.

M Why? Did you have something else planned?

W Yeah, we were planning to have dinner together.

M How about meeting up afterwards?

W Yes, that would work.

Q: What is the conversation mainly about?
(a) Deciding on a place to meet.
(b) Getting together for a drink.
(c) Canceling a dinner engagement.
(d) Making an appointment for dinner.

35

W How do you usually come to work?

M By subway. That's the only way to be on time.

W Don't you have a problem getting a seat?

M Luckily, no. It'd be hard to stand for an hour and a half.

W Wow, that's a long ride! So, what do you usually do during the ride?

M I take a nap because it's a long commute and I don't get enough sleep at night.

W But you could easily miss your stop like that.

M Fortunately, that hasn't happened to me yet.

Q: What is the main topic of the conversation?
(a) The man's feeling about a long commute.
(b) The man's commute to work by subway.
(c) How the man gets a seat on the subway.
(d) What type of transportation is best.

36

M So, what do you want to do tonight, dear?

W Why don't we go to the movies?

M That's an idea. We haven't done that in ages.

W We could call Tim and Erica and invite them.

M Sounds good. Let's do that.

W OK, I'll give them a call.

Q: What are the man and woman mainly discussing?
(a) Their love of movies.
(b) Their plans for the evening.
(c) The type of entertainment they like.
(d) The need to get in touch with Tim and Erica.

37

M Did you hear that our bonuses have been temporarily suspended?

W What? Did the board of directors give a reason?

M They say the economic downturn has made this a lean year.

W I'll bet the managers found money for their bonuses.

M Who knows? They did say they'd make it up to us, though.

W Are you kidding? They're just taking us for a ride.

Q: What is the conversation mainly about?
(a) Methods for maintaining financial stability.
(b) Unfair management practices in bonus payments.
(c) A strategy for overcoming an economic downturn.
(d) Frustrations over the company's poor performance.

38

W Why didn't you come to my party last night?

M I was on my way there, but the hospital called me.

W Really? What happened?

M I was paged to cover a shift in emergency.

W But you could've at least called to tell me.

M I know, and I feel bad about that.

Q: Why didn't the man go to the party?
(a) He had to go to work.
(b) He was not feeling well.
(c) He did not feel like going.
(d) He forgot which day it was on.

39

M What kind of dressing would you like with your salad?

W What do you have?

M Well, we have honey mustard and Italian.

W Are those low-fat dressings?

M I'm afraid not.

W Then, none for me. I'm watching my weight.

Q: What kind of dressing will the woman have?

(a) Honey mustard.

(b) Italian dressing.

(c) A low-fat variety.

(d) No dressing at all.

40

M Angie, what a surprise to see you here!

W Hi John, what are you doing in this area?

M I live in that building over there. What brought you here?

W I'm looking at apartments to buy in this complex.

M Oh, I see. Are you going through a real-estate agent?

W Yes, he should be here soon to show me around.

M OK, well, I hope you find something. It's a good area.

W Thanks. I hope so.

Q: Which is correct about the man according to the conversation?

(a) He is thinking of buying a new apartment.

(b) He is selling his apartment to the woman.

(c) He is working as a real-estate agent.

(d) He is living in a nearby building.

41

M I'd like acupuncture treatment again next Thursday, please.

W All right. Would the same time suit you?

M Um, after 2 might be better.

W I can book you in for 2:30 next Thursday.

M Actually, is there an opening at 3?

W Yes, that's possible. I'll book you in for then.

Q: When is the man getting acupuncture treatment next Thursday?

(a) At 2.

(b) At 3.

(c) At 2:30.

(d) After 3.

42

W Hi, Dad. I'm sorry to have kept you waiting.

M That's no problem. It's great to see you.

W You, too. I've missed you a lot.

M Where's Jack? Is he still out of town?

W No, but we couldn't find a babysitter so he stayed home.

M That's too bad. I haven't seen him for a long time.

W I know, but it's a school night so the kids can't stay up late.

M That's understandable. We'll catch up next time.

Q: Why couldn't Jack come?

(a) He was looking for a babysitter.

(b) He was out of town on business.

(c) He had to work late at the office.

(d) He had to take care of the children.

43

M Julia, can I ask for your advice about something?

W Sure, what is it?

M I want a nice gift to surprise my seven-year-old niece.

W Well, what kinds of things does she like?

M She likes books, but I don't know which books are at her level.

W A lot of children's books have recommended ages written on them.

M Oh good. I'll look around for some this afternoon.

Q: What will the man probably do in the afternoon?

(a) Go to a bookstore for children's books.

(b) Seek more advice from the woman.

(c) Ask his niece what gift she wants.

(d) Give his niece a birthday party.

44

W Did you know many common foods are genetically modified?

M I know, and I don't like it one bit.

W Well, I've eaten some of them, but I'm all right.

M Yes, but the effects may not be realized for years to come.

W I think that's highly unlikely.

M Regardless, genetically modified foods should be labeled as such.

W Oh sure, I agree with you there.

Q: What can be inferred from the conversation?

(a) The man might decide to become a vegetarian.

(b) The woman prefers genetically modified products.

(c) The man is suspicious of genetically modified foods.

(d) The woman thinks naturally grown foods are the healthiest.

45

M Mom's birthday is coming up. What shall we do for it?

W How about going to a nice restaurant?

M It's her 60th; we should do something more special.

W How about a Caribbean cruise? We can all go together.

M Sounds fabulous, but I don't think I can get time off.

W What if just Mom and Dad go, then?

M Of course! Mom would love that.

Q: What will the speakers most likely do for their mother's birthday?

(a) Organize a special night.

(b) Send their parents on a cruise.

(c) Go on a Caribbean tour as a family.

(d) Throw a surprise party at a restaurant.

46

The existence of unidentified flying objects, or UFOs, is a source of debate that splits people into those who believe in them and those who don't. I belong to the second group. There is no solid proof that UFOs exist, and sightings can generally be accounted for by weather disturbances or electrical and magnetic waves or frequencies in the air. Even meteors have often been mistaken for and reported as UFOs. There is simply no tangible evidence that supports their existence.

Q: What is the main idea of the talk?

(a) There is no factual evidence of UFO existence.

(b) People who believe in UFOs are irrational.

(c) The existence of UFOs is no longer debatable.

(d) Some people believe in UFOs and some do not.

47

Welcome to English 206, Introduction to Shakespeare. I know a lot of you have fears about Shakespeare's allegedly sophisticated English. However, I would like to ease some of your concerns. Let me tell you, for instance, that almost all of the vocabulary Shakespeare utilized is still used in our time. In addition, his language may seem weird from time to time, but don't worry, because you'll soon learn to love Shakespeare's imaginative genius with the English language as much as I do.

Q: What is the main point about Shakespeare according to the lecture?

(a) His plays require substantial efforts to understand.

(b) His writings are difficult because of the vocabulary.

(c) His language is not as complex as most people think.

(d) His use of English vastly differs from that of today.

48

On tonight's show, we're going to look at insulating your home. The best time to insulate your home is in the springtime. It's more affordable at that time because most contractors are not busy and so rates are often lower. Doing it then also allows you to save on your summer electricity bill because having your home insulated reduces the need for air-conditioning. Then, when winter rolls around, your new insulation will keep heat in, which lowers your heating bill as well.

Q: What is the main idea of the talk?
(a) Contractors are not busy during the spring months.
(b) Everyone should get home insulation if they can afford it.
(c) Early home installation has many benefits for the home owner.
(d) Insulation has been known to lower home electricity costs.

49

A question that has puzzled many who study human emotions is "What makes people happy?" Studies show that factors such as money, marital status, age, beauty and weather do not significantly influence the happiness of most people, although many of us think they do. It turns out that heredity and one's mental attitude are the true sources of unhappiness or happiness. Those people with a negative disposition are often unhappy no matter what their circumstances, and the converse is true of people inclined towards a positive outlook.

Q: What is the talk mainly about?
(a) Differences in the ways that people handle emotions.
(b) Common emotional conflicts people are subject to.
(c) Circumstances that lead to unhappy thoughts.
(d) Sources of positive and negative emotions.

50

The number of male news readers on TV has now reached an all-time low, with women accounting for 57% of TV news anchors nationwide. Recent reports have found that it starts at university. At the University of Winston this fall, for instance, women outnumbered men 227 to 125 in the journalism major, which includes broadcasting. Those numbers also explain why women are also outnumbering men as reporters, news producers and writers.

Q: What is the main idea of the talk?
(a) Fewer males are interested in studying journalism.
(b) More successful women are in the media spotlight nowadays.
(c) Fewer males and more women now work in the news industry.
(d) Female news readers have become more popular than male ones.

51

Now I'd like to talk about the art scene in Paris as the 20th century began. The diversity of art was enormous. Masters of the Impressionist style came to Paris, and together with them came Modernists, such as Pablo Picasso, who were starting to make a name for themselves with radical new art. No single style predominated at this time, but it was not long before Modernism dominated the scene.

Q: What is the main idea of the talk on turn-of-the-century Paris?
(a) Exponents of major art movements moved there.
(b) Everyone agreed that Pablo Picasso was a great artist.
(c) Modernist painters were producing art that was radical.
(d) Great artists of different genres were working together.

52

Some of you have asked me if it is true that our brain cells, or neurons, stop growing and developing in adulthood. Well, no, it's not true. Our neurons do continue to grow and change into adulthood. A recent study found that dendrites, which transmit electrical signals among neurons and play an essential role in neuronal function, are still physically malleable in adults. So, it is a myth that adult brain cells are largely static. They can indeed continue to change and develop in response to new experiences.

Q: What is the main idea of the lecture?
(a) Adult brain cells grow just as fast as children's do.
(b) Dendrites play an important part in brain development.
(c) It is a common misperception that adults have rigid minds.
(d) Despite views to the contrary brain cells develop even in adulthood.

53

Welcome to Ahren Airlines' automated customer response menu. If you would like to check flight arrival times, please press one. If you are calling about domestic reservations, please press two. If you are calling about international flight reservations, please press three. For other information, please stay on the line and a friendly Ahren's agent will be with you shortly. Thank you for calling Ahren Airlines.

Q: What should a person do to reserve a flight to another country?
(a) Press one.
(b) Press two.
(c) Press three.
(d) Remain on the line.

54

Welcome aboard our Trailways bus to Philadelphia, Pittsburgh, New Castle and Erie. We will arrive in Philadelphia at 2:45 this afternoon. There will be a ten-minute rest stop at that time. Later, we will have a thirty-minute stop for dinner in Pittsburgh at 6:45, for those of you who are continuing on to New Castle and Erie. We should arrive in New Castle at around 8:45 and in Erie at 11 pm.

Q: Which is correct according to the announcement?
(a) The bus will stop for ten minutes in Philadelphia.
(b) There will be a half hour stop for dinner in Erie.
(c) The last stop on the bus route is New Castle.
(d) The bus gets to Pittsburgh before 6 pm.

55

I mentioned earlier that bats have evolved a unique ability to navigate and hunt in the dark. They do this by sending out ultrasonic sounds produced in their larynx, or voice box, as they fly through the night. These sound vibrations strike objects—such as trees, walls or insects they can eat—and send back echoes. By interpreting the returning echoes, bats can know what is ahead of them, whether an obstacle or food.

Q: Which is correct about bats according to the lecture?
(a) They paralyze their prey with ultrasonic sounds.
(b) They use ultrasonic sounds to hunt during the day.
(c) They identify their prey through ultrasonic sounds.
(d) They emit ultrasonic sounds through their foreheads.

56

And now for international news. The United Nations mission in East Timor is set to reduce its 1,700 strong peacekeeping force because of concerns over costs and possible social problems that might arise with its continued military presence. UN representatives in East Timor said last week that a reduced force is in keeping with the improved security situation.

Q: Which is correct according to the news report?
(a) People in East Timor welcomed the UN's presence.
(b) East Timor is promising to improve the security situation.
(c) The UN will reduce the number of peacekeepers in East Timor.
(d) Social problems were created in East Timor by UN peacekeepers.

57

In today's lecture, I'll speak further on French colonialism and how, from the onset of the 16th century, a great part of France's military efforts was focused on securing its overseas possessions and settling dissent with the natives of its colonies. This French colonialism was brought to an end in the late 1950s with the failure to bring Algerian nationalists under control. However, many former French colonies, up to this day, still expect France to provide military assistance occasionally.

Q: Which is correct according to the lecture?
(a) France began securing overseas possessions in the 15th century.
(b) French colonies sometimes rebelled against French authorities.
(c) France waged a military campaign in Algeria in the early 1950s.
(d) French colonies were ruled by military troops comprising natives.

58

Simon Ambinbola, a singer who became a legend in South Africa, has passed away at age 61. Ambinbola was the rugged-voiced lead vocalist for the 1970s group the African Queens, the first band to make Zulu music globally popular. Juluka Music Company announced Ambinbola's death Friday morning, stating he had been fighting diabetes for several years.

Q: What can be inferred about Ambinbola?
(a) His music company will cease to exist.
(b) His style of music is no longer popular.
(c) His songs were against racism in Africa.
(d) His band introduced Zulu music to the world.

59

I'm an atheist philosopher with an interest in evolutionary biology and all things related to evolution. So, you probably expect my new book to be an extended exercise in debunking religious belief. That is certainly true of my books, I admit, but you can never accuse me of taking a disrespectful approach. What I always try to do is engage religious readers in a rational discussion, not turn them away before they can assess my arguments.

Q: What can be inferred about the speaker from the speech?
(a) He has a reputation for being against religion.
(b) He will stop writing about religion in his books.
(c) He implicitly accepts the need for religious belief.
(d) He has separate degrees in religion and philosophy.

60

As you know, Egyptian pictographic writing began simply as a way to represent concrete objects—often for the purpose of trade. Today I want to discuss a more sophisticated type of pictography the Egyptians developed. This involved juxtapositions of existing pictographs to represent intangible things, such as their idea of a human soul. For instance, to represent the soul, their convention was to draw an eagle over a man's head.

Q: What can be inferred from the lecture?
(a) Pictographs sometimes confused ancient Egyptians.
(b) Pictography is an inherently inflexible kind of writing.
(c) Egyptian writing has changed very little since ancient times.
(d) Egyptian pictographic writing depicted more than just concrete objects.

Listening Comprehension

1 (b)	**2** (b)	**3** (c)	**4** (d)	**5** (a)	**6** (b)	**7** (d)	**8** (d)	**9** (d)	**10** (a)
11 (d)	**12** (b)	**13** (d)	**14** (b)	**15** (b)	**16** (c)	**17** (d)	**18** (a)	**19** (a)	**20** (a)
21 (c)	**22** (d)	**23** (d)	**24** (b)	**25** (c)	**26** (b)	**27** (a)	**28** (b)	**29** (a)	**30** (c)
31 (d)	**32** (a)	**33** (a)	**34** (d)	**35** (c)	**36** (d)	**37** (c)	**38** (d)	**39** (d)	**40** (b)
41 (a)	**42** (d)	**43** (b)	**44** (a)	**45** (a)	**46** (d)	**47** (c)	**48** (a)	**49** (b)	**50** (a)
51 (c)	**52** (c)	**53** (c)	**54** (b)	**55** (c)	**56** (d)	**57** (b)	**58** (d)	**59** (d)	**60** (c)

Grammar

1 (d)	**2** (a)	**3** (a)	**4** (b)	**5** (a)	**6** (d)	**7** (b)	**8** (c)	**9** (d)	**10** (a)
11 (c)	**12** (a)	**13** (d)	**14** (a)	**15** (b)	**16** (b)	**17** (c)	**18** (d)	**19** (d)	**20** (b)
21 (b)	**22** (b)	**23** (c)	**24** (d)	**25** (b)	**26** (c)	**27** (b)	**28** (c)	**29** (d)	**30** (b)
31 (b)	**32** (d)	**33** (c)	**34** (a)	**35** (c)	**36** (c)	**37** (b)	**38** (c)	**39** (d)	**40** (b)
41 (a)	**42** (c)	**43** (d)	**44** (c)	**45** (c)	**46** (d)	**47** (b)	**48** (d)	**49** (d)	**50** (d)

Vocabulary

1 (a)	**2** (a)	**3** (a)	**4** (b)	**5** (d)	**6** (c)	**7** (b)	**8** (b)	**9** (c)	**10** (d)
11 (b)	**12** (c)	**13** (a)	**14** (a)	**15** (c)	**16** (d)	**17** (c)	**18** (d)	**19** (c)	**20** (d)
21 (b)	**22** (d)	**23** (b)	**24** (a)	**25** (a)	**26** (b)	**27** (a)	**28** (d)	**29** (a)	**30** (d)
31 (c)	**32** (a)	**33** (b)	**34** (b)	**35** (c)	**36** (b)	**37** (a)	**38** (d)	**39** (c)	**40** (a)
41 (c)	**42** (b)	**43** (a)	**44** (a)	**45** (d)	**46** (c)	**47** (c)	**48** (b)	**49** (a)	**50** (a)

Reading Comprehension

1 (b)	**2** (a)	**3** (a)	**4** (b)	**5** (d)	**6** (d)	**7** (d)	**8** (b)	**9** (c)	**10** (c)
11 (d)	**12** (b)	**13** (c)	**14** (d)	**15** (a)	**16** (b)	**17** (c)	**18** (d)	**19** (a)	**20** (c)
21 (c)	**22** (c)	**23** (a)	**24** (c)	**25** (c)	**26** (c)	**27** (d)	**28** (b)	**29** (b)	**30** (c)
31 (b)	**32** (d)	**33** (d)	**34** (b)	**35** (b)	**36** (c)	**37** (c)	**38** (b)	**39** (b)	**40** (a)

Answer Keys

Listening Comprehension

1	(a)	**2**	(c)	**3**	(b)	**4**	(b)	**5**	(a)	**6**	(b)	**7**	(b)	**8**	(a)	**9**	(d)	**10**	(b)
11	(a)	**12**	(b)	**13**	(c)	**14**	(d)	**15**	(c)	**16**	(a)	**17**	(a)	**18**	(c)	**19**	(b)	**20**	(d)
21	(c)	**22**	(b)	**23**	(b)	**24**	(b)	**25**	(a)	**26**	(d)	**27**	(b)	**28**	(b)	**29**	(c)	**30**	(a)
31	(c)	**32**	(b)	**33**	(d)	**34**	(a)	**35**	(d)	**36**	(a)	**37**	(a)	**38**	(d)	**39**	(d)	**40**	(c)
41	(c)	**42**	(d)	**43**	(b)	**44**	(c)	**45**	(b)	**46**	(d)	**47**	(a)	**48**	(a)	**49**	(b)	**50**	(d)
51	(c)	**52**	(b)	**53**	(c)	**54**	(d)	**55**	(d)	**56**	(b)	**57**	(d)	**58**	(d)	**59**	(d)	**60**	(d)

Grammar

1	(b)	**2**	(a)	**3**	(d)	**4**	(c)	**5**	(b)	**6**	(d)	**7**	(a)	**8**	(c)	**9**	(a)	**10**	(a)
11	(a)	**12**	(c)	**13**	(d)	**14**	(d)	**15**	(c)	**16**	(d)	**17**	(c)	**18**	(a)	**19**	(a)	**20**	(b)
21	(d)	**22**	(a)	**23**	(c)	**24**	(c)	**25**	(c)	**26**	(a)	**27**	(b)	**28**	(b)	**29**	(b)	**30**	(c)
31	(b)	**32**	(c)	**33**	(c)	**34**	(d)	**35**	(d)	**36**	(b)	**37**	(b)	**38**	(d)	**39**	(d)	**40**	(a)
41	(b)	**42**	(b)	**43**	(a)	**44**	(a)	**45**	(c)	**46**	(c)	**47**	(b)	**48**	(c)	**49**	(d)	**50**	(c)

Vocabulary

1	(c)	**2**	(b)	**3**	(d)	**4**	(c)	**5**	(b)	**6**	(b)	**7**	(d)	**8**	(c)	**9**	(a)	**10**	(d)
11	(a)	**12**	(d)	**13**	(c)	**14**	(a)	**15**	(d)	**16**	(c)	**17**	(d)	**18**	(b)	**19**	(d)	**20**	(c)
21	(c)	**22**	(d)	**23**	(a)	**24**	(c)	**25**	(b)	**26**	(b)	**27**	(c)	**28**	(b)	**29**	(d)	**30**	(b)
31	(b)	**32**	(c)	**33**	(b)	**34**	(b)	**35**	(d)	**36**	(c)	**37**	(a)	**38**	(b)	**39**	(a)	**40**	(b)
41	(d)	**42**	(a)	**43**	(a)	**44**	(a)	**45**	(d)	**46**	(b)	**47**	(b)	**48**	(c)	**49**	(a)	**50**	(b)

Reading Comprehension

1	(b)	**2**	(a)	**3**	(c)	**4**	(c)	**5**	(c)	**6**	(b)	**7**	(b)	**8**	(a)	**9**	(a)	**10**	(b)
11	(b)	**12**	(b)	**13**	(c)	**14**	(c)	**15**	(b)	**16**	(a)	**17**	(b)	**18**	(d)	**19**	(a)	**20**	(c)
21	(a)	**22**	(d)	**23**	(d)	**24**	(a)	**25**	(c)	**26**	(d)	**27**	(c)	**28**	(c)	**29**	(d)	**30**	(c)
31	(b)	**32**	(d)	**33**	(b)	**34**	(a)	**35**	(b)	**36**	(b)	**37**	(c)	**38**	(b)	**39**	(b)	**40**	(d)

Answer Keys

Listening Comprehension

1 (b)	2 (c)	3 (a)	4 (c)	5 (b)	6 (a)	7 (a)	8 (c)	9 (c)	10 (b)
11 (d)	12 (d)	13 (c)	14 (b)	15 (a)	16 (c)	17 (b)	18 (c)	19 (d)	20 (a)
21 (a)	22 (d)	23 (b)	24 (b)	25 (d)	26 (d)	27 (b)	28 (b)	29 (d)	30 (d)
31 (a)	32 (a)	33 (a)	34 (b)	35 (a)	36 (b)	37 (c)	38 (a)	39 (b)	40 (b)
41 (d)	42 (c)	43 (c)	44 (a)	45 (d)	46 (a)	47 (a)	48 (c)	49 (d)	50 (d)
51 (d)	52 (b)	53 (c)	54 (c)	55 (c)	56 (b)	57 (d)	58 (c)	59 (c)	60 (b)

Grammar

1 (c)	2 (b)	3 (a)	4 (b)	5 (c)	6 (d)	7 (a)	8 (b)	9 (c)	10 (b)
11 (d)	12 (b)	13 (c)	14 (d)	15 (b)	16 (b)	17 (d)	18 (c)	19 (d)	20 (c)
21 (c)	22 (d)	23 (a)	24 (c)	25 (c)	26 (c)	27 (d)	28 (b)	29 (c)	30 (b)
31 (d)	32 (c)	33 (d)	34 (d)	35 (d)	36 (c)	37 (d)	38 (a)	39 (d)	40 (b)
41 (b)	42 (c)	43 (b)	44 (b)	45 (a)	46 (c)	47 (c)	48 (c)	49 (c)	50 (b)

Vocabulary

1 (b)	2 (b)	3 (c)	4 (d)	5 (b)	6 (a)	7 (c)	8 (c)	9 (a)	10 (a)
11 (d)	12 (b)	13 (a)	14 (b)	15 (b)	16 (d)	17 (a)	18 (b)	19 (b)	20 (b)
21 (d)	22 (c)	23 (d)	24 (b)	25 (a)	26 (a)	27 (a)	28 (d)	29 (c)	30 (b)
31 (b)	32 (b)	33 (a)	34 (b)	35 (a)	36 (c)	37 (d)	38 (a)	39 (a)	40 (b)
41 (d)	42 (d)	43 (d)	44 (b)	45 (a)	46 (a)	47 (b)	48 (c)	49 (a)	50 (b)

Reading Comprehension

1 (c)	2 (d)	3 (b)	4 (d)	5 (a)	6 (b)	7 (b)	8 (d)	9 (d)	10 (d)
11 (c)	12 (c)	13 (a)	14 (d)	15 (b)	16 (b)	17 (a)	18 (a)	19 (c)	20 (c)
21 (a)	22 (d)	23 (c)	24 (a)	25 (b)	26 (d)	27 (a)	28 (c)	29 (c)	30 (a)
31 (d)	32 (c)	33 (c)	34 (c)	35 (b)	36 (a)	37 (a)	38 (c)	39 (a)	40 (a)

Answer Keys

Listening Comprehension

1 (a)	2 (c)	3 (a)	4 (d)	5 (d)	6 (b)	7 (c)	8 (c)	9 (a)	10 (c)
11 (c)	12 (d)	13 (d)	14 (b)	15 (d)	16 (b)	17 (b)	18 (c)	19 (b)	20 (b)
21 (d)	22 (a)	23 (b)	24 (a)	25 (a)	26 (d)	27 (a)	28 (a)	29 (d)	30 (d)
31 (a)	32 (d)	33 (c)	34 (d)	35 (a)	36 (d)	37 (d)	38 (a)	39 (c)	40 (b)
41 (c)	42 (d)	43 (d)	44 (a)	45 (d)	46 (a)	47 (c)	48 (d)	49 (c)	50 (d)
51 (d)	52 (d)	53 (b)	54 (d)	55 (a)	56 (a)	57 (b)	58 (d)	59 (c)	60 (a)

Grammar

1 (c)	2 (d)	3 (a)	4 (a)	5 (d)	6 (a)	7 (a)	8 (d)	9 (b)	10 (c)
11 (a)	12 (b)	13 (d)	14 (b)	15 (a)	16 (d)	17 (a)	18 (b)	19 (b)	20 (b)
21 (d)	22 (a)	23 (d)	24 (c)	25 (b)	26 (d)	27 (c)	28 (b)	29 (b)	30 (a)
31 (c)	32 (d)	33 (c)	34 (d)	35 (b)	36 (a)	37 (b)	38 (c)	39 (c)	40 (d)
41 (c)	42 (c)	43 (b)	44 (d)	45 (b)	46 (d)	47 (b)	48 (a)	49 (a)	50 (c)

Vocabulary

1 (a)	2 (b)	3 (c)	4 (b)	5 (b)	6 (a)	7 (d)	8 (b)	9 (a)	10 (b)
11 (b)	12 (d)	13 (b)	14 (c)	15 (a)	16 (a)	17 (c)	18 (d)	19 (a)	20 (d)
21 (a)	22 (a)	23 (a)	24 (c)	25 (c)	26 (a)	27 (d)	28 (b)	29 (b)	30 (b)
31 (c)	32 (c)	33 (d)	34 (b)	35 (d)	36 (d)	37 (a)	38 (d)	39 (c)	40 (c)
41 (b)	42 (b)	43 (d)	44 (b)	45 (a)	46 (d)	47 (c)	48 (a)	49 (d)	50 (c)

Reading Comprehension

1 (a)	2 (b)	3 (c)	4 (d)	5 (d)	6 (b)	7 (a)	8 (a)	9 (d)	10 (a)
11 (c)	12 (b)	13 (a)	14 (b)	15 (b)	16 (d)	17 (c)	18 (d)	19 (d)	20 (b)
21 (b)	22 (a)	23 (b)	24 (d)	25 (c)	26 (d)	27 (a)	28 (b)	29 (d)	30 (b)
31 (b)	32 (d)	33 (c)	34 (a)	35 (b)	36 (a)	37 (c)	38 (d)	39 (c)	40 (c)

Answer Keys

Listening Comprehension

1 (c)	**2** (b)	**3** (c)	**4** (a)	**5** (b)	**6** (d)	**7** (a)	**8** (c)	**9** (a)	**10** (b)
11 (d)	**12** (a)	**13** (d)	**14** (a)	**15** (b)	**16** (d)	**17** (c)	**18** (b)	**19** (b)	**20** (d)
21 (a)	**22** (b)	**23** (c)	**24** (a)	**25** (b)	**26** (a)	**27** (d)	**28** (c)	**29** (b)	**30** (d)
31 (c)	**32** (b)	**33** (b)	**34** (c)	**35** (b)	**36** (b)	**37** (c)	**38** (c)	**39** (d)	**40** (b)
41 (b)	**42** (d)	**43** (c)	**44** (a)	**45** (a)	**46** (d)	**47** (d)	**48** (b)	**49** (a)	**50** (d)
51 (a)	**52** (a)	**53** (c)	**54** (d)	**55** (d)	**56** (b)	**57** (b)	**58** (a)	**59** (d)	**60** (c)

Grammar

1 (d)	**2** (b)	**3** (b)	**4** (d)	**5** (d)	**6** (d)	**7** (b)	**8** (c)	**9** (c)	**10** (a)
11 (d)	**12** (b)	**13** (c)	**14** (c)	**15** (b)	**16** (c)	**17** (b)	**18** (d)	**19** (d)	**20** (b)
21 (d)	**22** (b)	**23** (b)	**24** (c)	**25** (b)	**26** (d)	**27** (c)	**28** (c)	**29** (d)	**30** (c)
31 (a)	**32** (c)	**33** (b)	**34** (b)	**35** (c)	**36** (c)	**37** (d)	**38** (a)	**39** (b)	**40** (c)
41 (d)	**42** (b)	**43** (b)	**44** (d)	**45** (d)	**46** (d)	**47** (c)	**48** (c)	**49** (a)	**50** (b)

Vocabulary

1 (b)	**2** (a)	**3** (a)	**4** (c)	**5** (b)	**6** (a)	**7** (b)	**8** (d)	**9** (c)	**10** (d)
11 (c)	**12** (c)	**13** (d)	**14** (c)	**15** (b)	**16** (d)	**17** (b)	**18** (a)	**19** (c)	**20** (a)
21 (a)	**22** (b)	**23** (d)	**24** (b)	**25** (c)	**26** (c)	**27** (a)	**28** (d)	**29** (d)	**30** (b)
31 (b)	**32** (b)	**33** (d)	**34** (c)	**35** (c)	**36** (b)	**37** (d)	**38** (b)	**39** (a)	**40** (a)
41 (a)	**42** (c)	**43** (b)	**44** (a)	**45** (b)	**46** (c)	**47** (d)	**48** (d)	**49** (c)	**50** (b)

Reading Comprehension

1 (a)	**2** (b)	**3** (c)	**4** (a)	**5** (b)	**6** (b)	**7** (a)	**8** (a)	**9** (d)	**10** (c)
11 (c)	**12** (b)	**13** (d)	**14** (a)	**15** (b)	**16** (d)	**17** (b)	**18** (d)	**19** (d)	**20** (c)
21 (c)	**22** (a)	**23** (c)	**24** (c)	**25** (b)	**26** (c)	**27** (c)	**28** (b)	**29** (d)	**30** (d)
31 (c)	**32** (c)	**33** (c)	**34** (a)	**35** (b)	**36** (d)	**37** (a)	**38** (b)	**39** (a)	**40** (d)

Answer Keys

Listening Comprehension

1 (b)	2 (c)	3 (a)	4 (a)	5 (b)	6 (a)	7 (a)	8 (a)	9 (c)	10 (d)
11 (b)	12 (a)	13 (b)	14 (b)	15 (d)	16 (c)	17 (b)	18 (a)	19 (d)	20 (b)
21 (c)	22 (a)	23 (a)	24 (c)	25 (c)	26 (d)	27 (a)	28 (c)	29 (d)	30 (d)
31 (a)	32 (c)	33 (d)	34 (b)	35 (b)	36 (b)	37 (b)	38 (a)	39 (d)	40 (d)
41 (b)	42 (d)	43 (a)	44 (c)	45 (b)	46 (a)	47 (c)	48 (c)	49 (d)	50 (c)
51 (a)	52 (d)	53 (c)	54 (a)	55 (c)	56 (c)	57 (b)	58 (d)	59 (a)	60 (d)

Grammar

1 (a)	2 (a)	3 (d)	4 (d)	5 (c)	6 (d)	7 (a)	8 (c)	9 (b)	10 (a)
11 (d)	12 (d)	13 (c)	14 (d)	15 (b)	16 (d)	17 (a)	18 (c)	19 (a)	20 (c)
21 (c)	22 (c)	23 (d)	24 (c)	25 (a)	26 (d)	27 (c)	28 (b)	29 (c)	30 (c)
31 (c)	32 (c)	33 (d)	34 (b)	35 (b)	36 (b)	37 (d)	38 (c)	39 (b)	40 (d)
41 (c)	42 (c)	43 (b)	44 (d)	45 (a)	46 (d)	47 (d)	48 (a)	49 (c)	50 (b)

Vocabulary

1 (c)	2 (b)	3 (d)	4 (b)	5 (d)	6 (c)	7 (b)	8 (b)	9 (d)	10 (d)
11 (d)	12 (c)	13 (d)	14 (a)	15 (b)	16 (a)	17 (b)	18 (c)	19 (c)	20 (c)
21 (c)	22 (d)	23 (d)	24 (b)	25 (b)	26 (a)	27 (a)	28 (b)	29 (c)	30 (b)
31 (a)	32 (a)	33 (a)	34 (b)	35 (d)	36 (b)	37 (a)	38 (c)	39 (b)	40 (b)
41 (a)	42 (b)	43 (c)	44 (a)	45 (b)	46 (a)	47 (b)	48 (c)	49 (a)	50 (a)

Reading Comprehension

1 (a)	2 (d)	3 (c)	4 (b)	5 (a)	6 (b)	7 (d)	8 (c)	9 (d)	10 (d)
11 (c)	12 (d)	13 (a)	14 (a)	15 (c)	16 (c)	17 (a)	18 (b)	19 (a)	20 (b)
21 (c)	22 (c)	23 (a)	24 (b)	25 (d)	26 (d)	27 (a)	28 (d)	29 (c)	30 (d)
31 (b)	32 (c)	33 (a)	34 (d)	35 (b)	36 (a)	37 (a)	38 (a)	39 (c)	40 (b)

i-TEPS 미리보기

국내 최초 통합 영어능력 평가
integrated-TEPS

⇒ 의사소통에 필요한 듣기, 말하기, 읽기, 쓰기 능력을 통합하여 평가한다.

듣기, 말하기, 읽기, 쓰기 능력은 서로 밀접한 관계를 가진 요소로 듣기, 읽기 능력 혹은 말하기, 쓰기 능력만을 단순히 측정해서는 정확한 영어능력을 평가하기 어렵다. *i*-TEPS는 유기적인 연관성을 지닌 이 네 가지 의사소통 능력을 통합적으로 측정하여 수험자의 영어능력을 정확하게 평가한다.

⇒ 변별력과 신뢰도가 있는 시험이다.

i-TEPS는 국내 최고 권위의 영어능력 평가로 듣기, 읽기 분야에서 탁월한 변별력을 인정받은 TEPS와 국내 최초 CBT 방식의 영어 말하기 · 쓰기 시험인 TEPS-Speaking & Writing의 성공 노하우를 바탕으로 개발되었다. 실전 영어능력을 보다 정밀하게 측정할 수 있도록 세분화된 채점 요소를 적용하고 있으며, 출제자와 채점자를 어학 분야의 최고 전문가들로 선정하여 높은 신뢰도와 탁월한 변별력을 지니고 있다.

⇒ 실전 영어능력을 측정한다.

간단한 대화를 할 수 있는 능력부터 도표를 보고 발표하는 분석력과 구성력까지, 접하는 상황에 따라 필요한 영어능력도 다양하다. *i*-TEPS는 유학이나 비즈니스 등 특정한 분야에서의 영어 활용 능력을 집중적으로 평가하는 타 시험과는 달리, 비즈니스 상황을 포함한 다양한 영어 사용 환경을 재현하여 실질적으로 활용 가능한 영어능력을 평가한다.

⇒ 경제성과 효율성을 갖춘 시험이다.

i-TEPS는 타 통합 영어능력 평가시험에 비해 응시료가 저렴하다. 한 번의 시험으로 듣기, 말하기, 읽기, 쓰기 능력을 종합적으로 평가하여 각각의 영역을 별도로 평가해야 하는 타 시험과 비교해도 응시료 부담이 적다. *i*-TEPS는 최소의 시간과 비용으로 수험자의 영어능력을 정확히 측정하는 높은 효율성을 갖춘 시험이다.

i-TEPS 영역별 유형 및 설명

i-TEPS는 기존의 TEPS와 TEPS-Speaking & Writing 시험을 토대로 듣기, 말하기, 읽기, 쓰기 능력을 종합적으로 측정하는 통합형 시험으로 개발되었다. Listening, Grammar & Vocabulary, Reading, Speaking, Writing의 5개 영역에 걸쳐 약 3시간 동안 진행되며, 총 143문항, 400점 만점으로 구성되어 있다.

영역		문제유형	문항수	시간		총점
Listening	Part 1	짧은 대화를 듣고 이어질 대화로 가장 적절한 답 고르기	15	35분		80점
	Part 2	긴 대화를 듣고 질문에 가장 적절한 답 고르기	15			
	Part 3	담화를 듣고 질문에 가장 적절한 답 고르기	10			
Grammar & Vocabulary	Part 1	대화문의 빈칸에 가장 적절한 답 고르기	15	20분		20점
	Part 2	단문의 빈칸에 가장 적절한 답 고르기	15			
	Part 3	대화문의 빈칸에 가장 적절한 어휘 고르기	15			20점
	Part 4	단문의 빈칸에 가장 적절한 어휘 고르기	15			
Reading	Part 1	지문을 읽고 빈칸에 가장 적절한 답 고르기	10	40분		80점
	Part 2	지문을 읽고 질문에 가장 적절한 답 고르기 (1지문 1문항)	19			
	Part 3	지문을 읽고 질문에 가장 적절한 답 고르기 (1지문 2문항)	6			
Speaking	Part 1	간단한 질문에 대답하기	1(3)		답변 10초	100점
	Part 2	소리내어 읽기	1	준비 30초	답변 45초	
	Part 3	일상 대화 상황에서 질문에 답하기	1(5)	준비 15초	답변 10초	
	Part 4	그림 보고 연결하여 이야기하기	1	준비 60초	답변 60초	
	Part 5	도표 보고 발표하기	1	준비 120초	답변 90초	
Writing	Part 1	받아쓰기	1	10분		100점
	Part 2	이메일 쓰기	1	15분		
	Part 3	의견 쓰기	1	30분		
계						400점

TEPS 등급표

등급	점수	영역	능력검정기준(Description)
1⁺급 Level 1⁺	901~990	전반	외국인으로서 최상급 수준의 의사소통 능력 교양 있는 원어민에 버금가는 정도로 의사소통이 가능하고 전문분야 업무에 대처할 수 있음. (Native Level of Communicative Competence)
1급 Level 1	801~900	전반	외국인으로서 거의 최상급 수준의 의사소통 능력 단기간 집중 교육을 받으면 대부분의 의사소통이 가능하고 전문분야 업무에 별 무리 없이 대처할 수 있음. (Near-Native Level of Communicative Competence)
2⁺급 Level 2⁺	701~800	전반	외국인으로서 상급 수준의 의사소통 능력 단기간 집중 교육을 받으면 일반분야 업무를 큰 어려움 없이 수행할 수 있음. (Advanced Level of Communicative Competence)
2급 Level 2	601~700	전반	외국인으로서 중상급 수준의 의사소통 능력 중장기간 집중 교육을 받으면 일반분야 업무를 큰 어려움 없이 수행할 수 있음. (High Intermediate Level of Communicative Competence)
3⁺급 Level 3⁺	501~600	전반	외국인으로서 중급 수준의 의사소통 능력 중장기간 집중 교육을 받으면 한정된 분야의 업무를 큰 어려움 없이 수행할 수 있음. (Mid Intermediate Level of Communicative Competence)
3급 Level 3	401~500	전반	외국인으로서 중하급 수준의 의사소통 능력 중장기간 집중 교육을 받으면 한정된 분야의 업무를 다소 미흡하지만 큰 지장 없이 수행할 수 있음. (Low Intermediate Level of Communicative Competence)
4⁺급 Level 4	201~400	전반	외국인으로서 하급 수준의 의사소통 능력 장기간의 집중 교육을 받으면 한정된 분야의 업무를 대체로 어렵게 수행할 수 있음. (Novice Level of Communicative Competence)
5⁺급 Level 5	10~200	전반	외국인으로서 최하급 수준의 의사소통 능력 단편적인 지식만을 갖추고 있어 의사소통이 거의 불가능함. (Near-Zero Level of Communicative Competence)

Memo

TEPS

Test of English Proficiency
developed by
Seoul National University

TEPS

Test of English Proficiency
developed by
Seoul National University

수험번호
Registration No.

성 명
Name
한글
한자

문 제 지 번 호
Test Booklet No.

감독관확인란

청 해 Listening Comprehension	문 법 Grammar	어 휘 Vocabulary	독 해 Reading Comprehension

주 민 등 록 번 호
National ID No.

고사실란
Room No.

수 험 번 호
Registration No.

비밀번호
Password

좌석번호
Seat No.

서 약	본인은 필기구 및 기재오류와 답안지 훼손으로 인한 책임을 지고, 부정행위 처리규정을 준수할 것을 서약합니다.

답안작성시 유의사항

1. 답안 작성은 반드시 **컴퓨터용 싸인펜**을 사용해야 합니다.

2. 답안을 정정할 경우 수정테이프(수정액 불가)를 사용해야 합니다.

3. 본 답안지는 컴퓨터로 처리되므로 훼손해서는 안되며, 답안지 하단의
타이밍마크(|||)를 찢거나, 낙서 등으로 인한 훼손시 불이익이 발생할 수 있습니다.

4. 답안은 문항당 정답을 1개만 골라 ● 와 같이 정확히 기재해야 하며, 필기구 오류나 본인의 부주의로
잘못 표기한 경우에는 당 관리위원회의 OMR판독기의 판독결과에 따르며, 그 결과는 본인이 책임집니다.

Good ● Bad ◑ ⊙ ◐ ✕ ✓

5. 감독관의 확인이 없는 답안지는 무효처리됩니다.

TEPS

Test of English Proficiency
developed by
Seoul National University

성	영문	
명	서명	

응시일자 : 20   년   월   일

<부정행위 및 규정위반 처리규정>

1. 모든 부정행위 및 규정위반 적발 및 이에 대한 조치는 TEPS관리위원회의 처리규정에 따라 이루어집니다.

2. 부정행위 및 규정위반 행위는 현장 적발 뿐만 아니라 사후에도 적발될 수 있으며 모두 동일한 조치가 취해집니다.

3. 부정행위 적발 시 당해 성적은 무효화되며 사안에 따라 최대 5년까지 TEPS관리위원회에서 주관하는 모든 시험의 응시자격이 제한됩니다.

4. 문제지 이외에 메모를 하는 행위와 시험 문제의 일부 또는 전부를 유출하거나 공개하는 경우 부정행위로 처리됩니다.

5. 각 파트별 시간을 준수하지 않거나, 시험 종료 후 답안 작성을 계속할 경우 규정위반으로 처리됩니다.

성 명 (성·이름순으로 기재)

EX H O N G   G I L   D O N G

(마킹란: A B C D E F G H I J K L M N O P Q R S T U V W X Y Z)

단 체 구 분

학생	일반
○	○

질 문 란

1. 귀하의 TEPS 응시목적은?
  - (a) 입사지원   (b) 인사정책
  - (c) 개인실력측정   (d) 입시
  - (e) 국가고시 지원   (f) 기타

2. 귀하의 영어권 체류 경험은?
  - (a) 없다   (b) 6개월 미만
  - (c) 6개월 이상 1년 미만   (d) 1년 이상 3년 미만
  - (e) 3년 이상 5년 미만   (f) 5년 이상

3. 귀하께서 응시하고 계신 고사장에 대한 만족도는?
  - (a) 0점   (b) 1점
  - (c) 2점   (d) 3점
  - (e) 4점   (f) 5점

4. 최근 2년내 TEPS 응시횟수는?
  - (a) 없다   (b) 1회
  - (c) 2회   (d) 3회
  - (e) 4회   (f) 5회 이상

학 력

학력	재학 / 졸업
초 등 학 교	○
중 학 교	○
고 등 학 교	○
전 문 대 학	○
대 학 교	○
대 학 원	○

전 공

전공	
인 문 학	○
사회과학·법학	○
경제학·경영학	○
자 연 과 학	○
의학·약학·간호학	○
공 학	○
교 육 학	○
음악·미술·체육	○
기 타	○

직 업

직업	
공 무 원	○
고시준비	○
교 사	○
군 인	○
의 료 인	○
자 영 업	○
학 생	○
회 사 원	○
무 직	○
기 타	○

직 종

직종	
고 위 임 직 원	○
전문직(과학.공학)	○
전 문 직 (교육)	○
전문직(법률.회계.금융)	○
기 술 직	○
영 업	○
홍 보	○
총 무	○
인 사	○
경 리	○
기 획	○
구 매	○

직 책

(직종 - 가운데 열)

무 역	○
외 환	○
자 금	○
공 무	○
업 무	○
품 질 관 리	○
전 산	○
행 정 직	○
생 산 관 리	○
서 비 스	○
기 타	○

직 책

직책	
임 원	○
부 장	○
차 장	○
과 장	○
대 리	○
계 장	○
사 원	○
인 턴	○
기 타	○

앞면(Side1)

TEPS

Test of English Proficiency
developed by
Seoul National University

수험번호
Registration No.

성명
Name
한글
한자

문 제 지 번 호
Test Booklet No.

감독관확인란

청 해
Listening Comprehension

문 법
Grammar

어 휘
Vocabulary

독 해
Reading Comprehension

주 민 등 록 번 호
National ID No.

고사실란
Room No.

수 험 번 호
Registration No.

비밀번호
Password

좌석번호
Seat No.

서 약

본인은 필기구 및 기재오류와 답안지 훼손으로 인한 책임을 지고, 부정행위 처리규정을 준수할 것을 서약합니다.

답안작성시
유 의 사 항

1. 답안 작성은 반드시 **컴퓨터용 싸인펜**을 사용해야 합니다.

2. 답안을 정정할 경우 수정테이프(수정액 불가)를 사용해야 합니다.

3. 본 답안지는 컴퓨터로 처리되므로 훼손해서는 안되며, 답안지 하단의
타이밍마크(ⅠⅠⅠ)를 찢거나, 낙서 등으로 인한 훼손시 불이익이 발생할 수 있습니다.

4. 답안은 문항당 정답을 1개만 골라 ● 와 같이 정확히 기재해야 하며, 필기구 오류나 본인의 부주의로
잘못 표기한 경우에는 당 관리위원회의 OMR판독기의 판독결과에 따르며, 그 결과는 본인이 책임집니다.

Good ●   Bad ◐ ◑ ● Ⓧ Ⓥ

5. 감독관의 확인이 없는 답안지는 무효처리됩니다.

TEPS
Test of English Proficiency
developed by
Seoul National University

성	영문	
명	서명	

응시일자 : 20   년   월   일

<부정행위 및 규정위반 처리규정>

1. 모든 부정행위 및 규정위반 적발 및 이에 대한 조치는 TEPS관리위원회의 처리규정에 따라 이루어집니다.

2. 부정행위 및 규정위반 행위는 현장 적발 뿐만 아니라 사후에도 적발될 수 있으며 모두 동일한 조치가 취해집니다.

3. 부정행위 적발 시 당해 성적은 무효화되며 사안에 따라 최대 5년까지 TEPS관리위원회에서 주관하는 모든 시험의 응시자격이 제한됩니다.

4. 문제지 이외에 메모를 하는 행위와 시험 문제의 일부 또는 전부를 유출하거나 공개하는 경우 부정행위로 처리됩니다.

5. 각 파트별 시간을 준수하지 않거나, 시험 종료 후 답안 작성을 계속할 경우 규정위반으로 처리됩니다.

성   명 (성·이름순으로 기재)

EX HONG GIL DONG

A B C D E F G H I J K L M N O P Q R S T U V W X Y Z

단체구분

학생	일반
○	○

질문란

1. 귀하의 TEPS 응시목적은?
   - ⓐ 입사지원
   - ⓑ 인사정책
   - ⓒ 개인실력측정
   - ⓓ 입시
   - ⓔ 국가고시 지원
   - ⓕ 기타

2. 귀하의 영어권 체류 경험은?
   - ⓐ 없다
   - ⓑ 6개월 미만
   - ⓒ 6개월 이상 1년 미만
   - ⓓ 1년 이상 3년 미만
   - ⓔ 3년 이상 5년 미만
   - ⓕ 5년 이상

3. 귀하께서 응시하고 계신 고사장에 대한 만족도는?
   - ⓐ 0점
   - ⓑ 1점
   - ⓒ 2점
   - ⓓ 3점
   - ⓔ 4점
   - ⓕ 5점

4. 최근 2년내 TEPS 응시횟수는?
   - ⓐ 없다
   - ⓑ 1회
   - ⓒ 2회
   - ⓓ 3회
   - ⓔ 4회
   - ⓕ 5회 이상

학력 / 전공 / 직업

학력	재학	졸업	전공		직업	
초등학교	○	○	인 문 학	○	공 무 원	○
중 학 교	○	○	사회과학·법학	○	고시준비	○
고등학교	○	○	경제학·경영학	○	교 사	○
전문대학	○	○	자 연 과 학	○	군 인	○
대 학 교	○	○	의학·약학·간호학	○	의 료 인	○
대 학 원	○	○	공 학	○	자 영 업	○
			교 육 학	○	학 생	○
			음악·미술·체육	○	회 사 원	○
			기 타	○	무 직	○
					기 타	○

직종 / 직책

직종				직책	
고 위 임 직 원	○	무 역	○	임 원	○
전문직(과학.공학)	○	외 환	○	부 장	○
전 문 직 (교육)	○	자 금	○	차 장	○
전문직(법률.회계.금융)	○	공 무	○	과 장	○
기 술 직	○	업 무	○	대 리	○
영 업	○	품 질 관 리	○	계 장	○
홍 보	○	전 산	○	사 원	○
총 무	○	행 정 직	○	인 턴	○
인 사	○	생 산 관 리	○	기 타	○
경 리	○	서 비 스	○		
기 획	○	기 타	○		
구 매	○				

뒷면(Side2)

TEPS

Test of English Proficiency
developed by
Seoul National University

성 영문
명 서명

응시일자 : 20   년   월   일

<부정행위 및 규정위반 처리규정>

1. 모든 부정행위 및 규정위반 적발
   및 이에 대한 조치는 TEPS관리위원
   회의 처리규정에 따라 이루어집니다.

2. 부정행위 및 규정위반 행위는 현장
   적발 뿐만 아니라 사후에도 적발될
   수 있으며 모두 동일한 조치가 취해
   집니다.

3. 부정행위 적발 시 당해 성적은 무효
   화되며 사안에 따라 최대 5년까지
   TEPS관리위원회에서 주관하는
   모든 시험의 응시자격이 제한됩니다.

4. 문제지 이외에 메모를 하는 행위와
   시험 문제의 일부 또는 전부를 유출
   하거나 공개하는 경우 부정행위로
   처리됩니다.

5. 각 파트별 시간을 준수하지 않거나,
   시험 종료 후 답안 작성을 계속할
   경우 규정위반으로 처리됩니다.

성   명 (성·이름순으로 기재)

EX HONG GIL DONG

(답안 마킹란: A B C D E F G H I J K L M N O P Q R S T U V W X Y Z)

단 체 구 분

학생	일반
◯	◯

질 문 란

1. 귀하의 TEPS 응시목적은?
   a 입사지원   b 인사정책
   c 개인실력측정 d 입시
   e 국가고시 지원 f 기타

2. 귀하의 영어권 체류 경험은?
   a 없다   b 6개월 미만
   c 6개월 이상 1년 미만   d 1년 이상 3년 미만
   e 3년 이상 5년 미만   f 5년 이상

3. 귀하께서 응시하고 계신 고사장에
   대한 만족도는?
   a 0점   b 1점
   c 2점   d 3점
   e 4점   f 5점

4. 최근 2년내 TEPS 응시횟수는?
   a 없다   b 1회
   c 2회   d 3회
   e 4회   f 5회 이상

학 력

	재학	졸업
초 등 학 교	◯	◯
중 학 교	◯	◯
고 등 학 교	◯	◯
전 문 대 학	◯	◯
대 학 교	◯	◯
대 학 원	◯	◯

전 공

인 문 학 ◯
사회과학·법학 ◯
경제학·경영학 ◯
자 연 과 학 ◯
의학·약학·간호학 ◯
공 학 ◯
교 육 학 ◯
음악·미술·체육 ◯
기 타 ◯

직 업

공 무 원 ◯
고시준비 ◯
교 사 ◯
군 인 ◯
의 료 인 ◯
자 영 업 ◯
학 생 ◯
회 사 원 ◯
무 직 ◯
기 타 ◯

직 종

고 위 임 직 원 ◯
전문직(과학.공학) ◯
전 문 직 (교육) ◯
전문직(법률.회계.금융) ◯
기 술 직 ◯
영 업 ◯
홍 보 ◯
총 무 ◯
인 사 ◯
경 리 ◯
기 획 ◯
구 매 ◯
무 역 ◯
외 환 ◯
자 금 ◯
공 무 ◯
업 무 ◯
품 질 관 리 ◯
전 산 ◯
행 정 직 ◯
생 산 관 리 ◯
서 비 스 ◯
기 타 ◯

직 책

임 원 ◯
부 장 ◯
차 장 ◯
과 장 ◯
대 리 ◯
계 장 ◯
사 원 ◯
인 턴 ◯
기 타 ◯

TEPS

Test of English Proficiency
developed by
Seoul National University

수험번호
Registration No.

성명
Name
한글
영문
한자

문제지번호
Test Booklet No.

감독관확인란

주민등록번호
National ID No.

고사실번호
Room No.

청해
Listening Comprehension

문법
Grammar

어휘
Vocabulary

독해
Reading Comprehension

수험번호
Registration No.

비밀번호
Password

좌석번호
Seat No.

서약

본인은 필기구 및 기재오류와 답안지 훼손으로 인한 책임을 지고, 부정행위 처리규정을 준수할 것을 서약합니다.

답안작성시
유의사항

1. 답안 작성은 반드시 컴퓨터용 싸인펜을 사용해야 합니다.
2. 답안을 정정할 경우 수정테이프(수정액 불가)를 사용해야 합니다.
3. 본 답안지는 컴퓨터로 처리되므로 훼손해서는 안되며, 답안지 하단의
   타이밍마크(∥∥)를 찢거나, 낙서 등으로 인한 훼손시 불이익을 받을 수 있습니다.
4. 답안은 문항당 정답을 1개만 골라 위 같이 정확히 기재해야 하며, 필기구 오류나 본인의 부주의로
   잘못 표기한 경우에는 답 관리위원회의 OMR판독기의 판독결과에 따르며, 그 결과는 본인이 책임집니다.

Good ● Bad ◑ ◐ ⊗ ⊘

5. 감독관의 확인이 없는 답안지는 무효처리됩니다.

TEPS

Test of English Proficiency
developed by
Seoul National University

성	영문	
명	서명	

응시일자 : 20   년   월   일

<부정행위 및 규정위반 처리규정>

1. 모든 부정행위 및 규정위반 적발 및 이에 대한 조치는 TEPS관리위원회의 처리규정에 따라 이루어집니다.

2. 부정행위 및 규정위반 행위는 현장 적발 뿐만 아니라 사후에도 적발될 수 있으며 모두 동일한 조치가 취해집니다.

3. 부정행위 적발 시 당해 성적은 무효화되며 사안에 따라 최대 5년까지 TEPS관리위원회에서 주관하는 모든 시험의 응시자격이 제한됩니다.

4. 문제지 이외에 메모를 하는 행위와 시험 문제의 일부 또는 전부를 유출하거나 공개하는 경우 부정행위로 처리됩니다.

5. 각 파트별 시간을 준수하지 않거나, 시험 종료 후 답안 작성을 계속할 경우 규정위반으로 처리됩니다.

성   명 (성·이름순으로 기재)

EX HONG GIL DONG

A B C D E F G H I J K L M N O P Q R S T U V W X Y Z

단체구분

학생	일반
○	○

질 문 란

1. 귀하의 TEPS 응시목적은?

   (a) 입사지원   (b) 인사정책
   (c) 개인실력측정   (d) 입시
   (e) 국가고시 지원   (f) 기타

2. 귀하의 영어권 체류 경험은?

   (a) 없다   (b) 6개월 미만
   (c) 6개월 이상 1년 미만   (d) 1년 이상 3년 미만
   (e) 3년 이상 5년 미만   (f) 5년 이상

3. 귀하께서 응시하고 계신 고사장에 대한 만족도는?

   (a) 0점   (b) 1점
   (c) 2점   (d) 3점
   (e) 4점   (f) 5점

4. 최근 2년내 TEPS 응시횟수는?

   (a) 없다   (b) 1회
   (c) 2회   (d) 3회
   (e) 4회   (f) 5회 이상

학 력

	재학	졸업
초등학교		○
중 학 교		○
고등학교		○
전 문 대 학		○
대 학 교		○
대 학 원		○

전 공

- 인 문 학 ○
- 사회과학·법학 ○
- 경제학·경영학 ○
- 자 연 과 학 ○
- 의학·약학·간호학 ○
- 공 학 ○
- 교 육 학 ○
- 음악·미술·체육 ○
- 기 타 ○

직 업

- 공 무 원 ○
- 고시준비 ○
- 교 사 ○
- 군 인 ○
- 의 료 인 ○
- 자 영 업 ○
- 학 생 ○
- 회 사 원 ○
- 무 직 ○
- 기 타 ○

직 종

- 고 위 임 직 원 ○
- 전문직(과학.공학) ○
- 전 문 직 (교육) ○
- 전문직(법률.회계.금융) ○
- 기 술 직 ○
- 영 업 ○
- 홍 보 ○
- 총 무 ○
- 인 사 ○
- 경 리 ○
- 기 획 ○
- 구 매 ○

직 책

- 무 역 ○
- 외 환 ○
- 자 금 ○
- 공 무 ○
- 업 무 ○
- 품 질 관 리 ○
- 전 산 ○
- 행 정 직 ○
- 생 산 관 리 ○
- 서 비 스 ○
- 기 타 ○
- 임 원 ○
- 부 장 ○
- 차 장 ○
- 과 장 ○
- 대 리 ○
- 계 장 ○
- 사 원 ○
- 인 턴 ○
- 기 타 ○

앞면(Side1)

TEPS

Test of English Proficiency
developed by
Seoul National University

수험번호
Registration No.

성명
Name
한글
한자

문제지번호
Test Booklet No.

감독관확인란

| 청 해 | 문 법 | 어 휘 | 독 해 | 주 민 등 록 번 호 | 고사실란 |
| Listening Comprehension | Grammar | Vocabulary | Reading Comprehension | National ID No. | Room No. |

수험번호
Registration No.

비밀번호
Password

좌석번호
Seat No.

서 약   본인은 필기구 및 기재오류와 답안지 훼손으로 인한 책임을 지고, 부정행위 처리규정을 준수할 것을 서약합니다.

답안작성시
유의사항

1. 답안 작성은 반드시 **컴퓨터용 싸인펜**을 사용해야 합니다.

2. 답안을 정정할 경우 수정테이프(수정액 불가)를 사용해야 합니다.

3. 본 답안지는 컴퓨터로 처리되므로 훼손해서는 안되며, 답안지 하단의
   타이밍마크(|||)를 찢거나, 낙서 등으로 인한 훼손시 불이익이 발생할 수 있습니다.

4. 답안은 문항당 정답을 1개만 골라 ● 와 같이 정확히 기재해야 하며, 필기구 오류나 본인의 부주의로
   잘못 표기한 경우에는 당 관리위원회의 OMR판독기의 판독결과에 따르며, 그 결과는 본인이 책임집니다.

   Good ●   Bad ◖ ◔ ◗ ✗ ✓

5. 감독관의 확인이 없는 답안지는 무효처리됩니다.

뒷면(Side2)

TEPS

Test of English Proficiency
developed by
Seoul National University

성명	영문	
	서명	

응시일자 : 20 년 월 일

<부정행위 및 규정위반 처리규정>

1. 모든 부정행위 및 규정위반 적발 및 이에 대한 조치는 TEPS관리위원회의 처리규정에 따라 이루어집니다.
2. 부정행위 및 규정위반 행위는 현장 적발 뿐만 아니라 사후에도 적발될 수 있으며 모두 동일한 조치가 취해집니다.
3. 부정행위 적발 시 당해 성적은 무효화되며 사안에 따라 최대 5년까지 TEPS관리위원회에서 주관하는 모든 시험의 응시자격이 제한됩니다.
4. 문제지 이외에 메모를 하는 행위와 시험 문제의 일부 또는 전부를 유출하거나 공개하는 경우 부정행위로 처리됩니다.
5. 각 파트별 시간을 준수하지 않거나, 시험 종료 후 답안 작성을 계속할 경우 규정위반으로 처리됩니다.

성 명 (성 · 이름순으로 기재)

EX H O N G G I L D O N G

A B C D E F G H I J K L M N O P Q R S T U V W X Y Z

단 체 구 분

학생	일반
( )	( )

질 문 란

1. 귀하의 TEPS 응시목적은?
   - ⓐ 입사지원 ⓑ 인사정책
   - ⓒ 개인실력측정 ⓓ 입시
   - ⓔ 국가고시 지원 ⓕ 기타

2. 귀하의 영어권 체류 경험은?
   - ⓐ 없다 ⓑ 6개월 미만
   - ⓒ 6개월 이상 1년 미만 ⓓ 1년 이상 3년 미만
   - ⓔ 3년 이상 5년 미만 ⓕ 5년 이상

3. 귀하께서 응시하고 계신 고사장에 대한 만족도는?
   - ⓐ 0점 ⓑ 1점
   - ⓒ 2점 ⓓ 3점
   - ⓔ 4점 ⓕ 5점

4. 최근 2년내 TEPS 응시횟수는?
   - ⓐ 없다 ⓑ 1회
   - ⓒ 2회 ⓓ 3회
   - ⓔ 4회 ⓕ 5회 이상

학력	재학	졸업	전공	직업
초등학교	( )	( )	인문학 ( )	공무원 ( )
중학교	( )	( )	사회과학 · 법학 ( )	고시준비 ( )
고등학교	( )	( )	경제학 · 경영학 ( )	교사 ( )
전문대학	( )	( )	자연과학 ( )	군인 ( )
대학교	( )	( )	의학 · 약학 · 간호학 ( )	의료인 ( )
대학원	( )	( )	공학 ( )	자영업 ( )
			교육학 ( )	학생 ( )
			음악 · 미술 · 체육 ( )	회사원 ( )
			기타 ( )	무직 ( )
				기타 ( )

직종		직책
고위임직원 ( )	무역 ( )	임원 ( )
전문직(과학,공학) ( )	외환 ( )	부장 ( )
전문직(교육) ( )	자금 ( )	차장 ( )
전문직(법률,회계,금융) ( )	공무 ( )	과장 ( )
기술직 ( )	업무 ( )	대리 ( )
영업 ( )	품질관리 ( )	계장 ( )
홍보 ( )	전산 ( )	사원 ( )
총무 ( )	행정직 ( )	인턴 ( )
인사 ( )	생산관리 ( )	기타 ( )
경리 ( )	서비스 ( )	
기획 ( )	기타 ( )	
구매 ( )		

TEPS

Test of English Proficiency
developed by
Seoul National University

수험번호 Registration No.

문제지번호 Test Booklet No.

감독관확인란

성명 Name — 한글 / 한자

청해 Listening Comprehension

문법 Grammar

어휘 Vocabulary

독해 Reading Comprehension

주민등록번호 National ID No.

고사실란 Room No.

수험번호 Registration No.

비밀번호 Password

좌석번호 Seat No.

서 약	본인은 필기구 및 기재오류와 답안지 훼손으로 인한 책임을 지고, 부정행위 처리규정을 준수할 것을 서약합니다.

답안작성시 유의사항

1. 답안 작성은 반드시 **컴퓨터용 싸인펜**을 사용해야 합니다.

2. 답안을 정정할 경우 수정테이프(수정액 불가)를 사용해야 합니다.

3. 본 답안지는 컴퓨터로 처리되므로 훼손해서는 안되며, 답안지 하단의 타이밍마크(|||)를 찢거나, 낙서 등으로 인한 훼손시 불이익이 발생할 수 있습니다.

4. 답안은 문항당 정답을 1개만 골라 ● 와 같이 정확히 기재해야 하며, 필기구 오류나 본인의 부주의로 잘못 표기한 경우에는 당 관리위원회의 OMR판독기의 판독결과에 따르며, 그 결과는 본인이 책임집니다.

Good ● Bad 〰〰〰〰〰

5. 감독관의 확인이 없는 답안지는 무효처리됩니다.

TEPS

Test of English Proficiency
developed by
Seoul National University

성 영문

명 서명

응시일자 : 20   년   월   일

〈부정행위 및 규정위반 처리규정〉

1. 모든 부정행위 및 규정위반 적발 및 이에 대한 조치는 TEPS관리위원회의 처리규정에 따라 이루어집니다.

2. 부정행위 및 규정위반 행위는 현장 적발 뿐만 아니라 사후에도 적발될 수 있으며 모두 동일한 조치가 취해집니다.

3. 부정행위 적발 시 당해 성적은 무효화되며 사안에 따라 최대 5년까지 TEPS관리위원회에서 주관하는 모든 시험의 응시자격이 제한됩니다.

4. 문제지 이외에 메모를 하는 행위와 시험 문제의 일부 또는 전부를 유출하거나 공개하는 경우 부정행위로 처리됩니다.

5. 각 파트별 시간을 준수하지 않거나, 시험 종료 후 답안 작성을 계속할 경우 규정위반으로 처리됩니다.

성   명 (성·이름순으로 기재)

EX HONG GIL DONG

(A B C D E F G H I J K L M N O P Q R S T U V W X Y Z 표기란)

단체구분

학생	일반
○	○

질문란

1. 귀하의 TEPS 응시목적은?
   - ⓐ 입사지원
   - ⓑ 인사정책
   - ⓒ 개인실력측정
   - ⓓ 입시
   - ⓔ 국가고시 지원
   - ⓕ 기타

2. 귀하의 영어권 체류 경험은?
   - ⓐ 없다
   - ⓑ 6개월 미만
   - ⓒ 6개월 이상 1년 미만
   - ⓓ 1년 이상 3년 미만
   - ⓔ 3년 이상 5년 미만
   - ⓕ 5년 이상

3. 귀하께서 응시하고 계신 고사장에 대한 만족도는?
   - ⓐ 0점
   - ⓑ 1점
   - ⓒ 2점
   - ⓓ 3점
   - ⓔ 4점
   - ⓕ 5점

4. 최근 2년내 TEPS 응시횟수는?
   - ⓐ 없다
   - ⓑ 1회
   - ⓒ 2회
   - ⓓ 3회
   - ⓔ 4회
   - ⓕ 5회 이상

학력

학력	재학	졸업
초등학교	○	○
중학교	○	○
고등학교	○	○
전문대학	○	○
대학교	○	○
대학원	○	○

전공

- 인문학 ○
- 사회과학·법학 ○
- 경제학·경영학 ○
- 자연과학 ○
- 의학·약학·간호학 ○
- 공학 ○
- 교육학 ○
- 음악·미술·체육 ○
- 기타 ○

직업

- 공무원 ○
- 고시준비 ○
- 교사 ○
- 군인 ○
- 의료인 ○
- 자영업 ○
- 학생 ○
- 회사원 ○
- 무직 ○
- 기타 ○

직종

- 고위임직원 ○
- 전문직(과학·공학) ○
- 전문직(교육) ○
- 전문직(법률·회계·금융) ○
- 기술직 ○
- 영업 ○
- 홍보 ○
- 총무 ○
- 인사 ○
- 경리 ○
- 기획 ○
- 구매 ○
- 무역 ○
- 외환 ○
- 자금 ○
- 공무 ○
- 업무 ○
- 품질관리 ○
- 전산 ○
- 행정직 ○
- 생산관리 ○
- 서비스 ○
- 기타 ○

직책

- 임원 ○
- 부장 ○
- 차장 ○
- 과장 ○
- 대리 ○
- 계장 ○
- 사원 ○
- 인턴 ○
- 기타 ○

TEPS

Test of English Proficiency
developed by
Seoul National University

수험번호 Registration No.		문 제 지 번 호 Test Booklet No.	감독관확인란
성 명 Name	한글 / 한자		

청 해 — Listening Comprehension

문 법 — Grammar

어 휘 — Vocabulary

독 해 — Reading Comprehension

주 민 등 록 번 호 — National ID No.

고사실란 — Room No.

수 험 번 호 — Registration No.

비밀번호 — Password

좌석번호 — Seat No.

서 약	본인은 필기구 및 기재오류와 답안지 훼손으로 인한 책임을 지고, 부정행위 처리규정을 준수할 것을 서약합니다.

답안작성시 유의사항

1. 답안 작성은 반드시 **컴퓨터용 싸인펜**을 사용해야 합니다.
2. 답안을 정정할 경우 수정테이프(수정액 불가)를 사용해야 합니다.
3. 본 답안지는 컴퓨터로 처리되므로 훼손해서는 안되며, 답안지 하단의 타이밍마크(ⅠⅠⅠ)를 찢거나, 낙서 등으로 인한 훼손시 불이익이 발생할 수 있습니다.
4. 답안은 문항당 정답을 1개만 골라 ●와 같이 정확히 기재해야 하며, 필기구 오류나 본인의 부주의로 잘못 표기한 경우에는 당 관리위원회의 OMR판독기의 판독결과에 따르며, 그 결과는 본인이 책임집니다.
   - Good ● Bad ◖ · ◗ Ⓧ Ⓥ
5. 감독관의 확인이 없는 답안지는 무효처리됩니다.

TEPS

Test of English Proficiency
developed by
Seoul National University

성	영문	
명	서명	

응시일자 : 20   년   월   일

성   명 (성·이름순으로 기재)

EX HONG GIL DONG

〈부정행위 및 규정위반 처리규정〉

1. 모든 부정행위 및 규정위반 적발 및 이에 대한 조치는 TEPS관리위원회의 처리규정에 따라 이루어집니다.

2. 부정행위 및 규정위반 행위는 현장 적발 뿐만 아니라 사후에도 적발될 수 있으며 모두 동일한 조치가 취해집니다.

3. 부정행위 적발 시 당해 성적은 무효화되며 사안에 따라 최대 5년까지 TEPS관리위원회에서 주관하는 모든 시험의 응시자격이 제한됩니다.

4. 문제지 이외에 메모를 하는 행위와 시험 문제의 일부 또는 전부를 유출하거나 공개하는 경우 부정행위로 처리됩니다.

5. 각 파트별 시간을 준수하지 않거나, 시험 종료 후 답안 작성을 계속할 경우 규정위반으로 처리됩니다.

단 체 구 분

학생	일반
〇	〇

질 문 란

1. 귀하의 TEPS 응시목적은?
   - (a) 입사지원
   - (b) 인사정책
   - (c) 개인실력측정
   - (d) 입시
   - (e) 국가고시 지원
   - (f) 기타

2. 귀하의 영어권 체류 경험은?
   - (a) 없다
   - (b) 6개월 미만
   - (c) 6개월 이상 1년 미만
   - (d) 1년 이상 3년 미만
   - (e) 3년 이상 5년 미만
   - (f) 5년 이상

3. 귀하께서 응시하고 계신 고사장에 대한 만족도는?
   - (a) 0점
   - (b) 1점
   - (c) 2점
   - (d) 3점
   - (e) 4점
   - (f) 5점

4. 최근 2년내 TEPS 응시횟수는?
   - (a) 없다
   - (b) 1회
   - (c) 2회
   - (d) 3회
   - (e) 4회
   - (f) 5회 이상

학 력

학력	재학	졸업
초 등 학 교	〇	〇
중 학 교	〇	〇
고 등 학 교	〇	〇
전 문 대 학	〇	〇
대 학 교	〇	〇
대 학 원	〇	〇

전 공

- 인 문 학 〇
- 사회과학 · 법학 〇
- 경제학 · 경영학 〇
- 자 연 과 학 〇
- 의학 · 약학 · 간호학 〇
- 공 학 〇
- 교 육 학 〇
- 음악 · 미술 · 체육 〇
- 기 타 〇

직 업

- 공 무 원 〇
- 고 시 준 비 〇
- 교 사 〇
- 군 인 〇
- 의 료 인 〇
- 자 영 업 〇
- 학 생 〇
- 회 사 원 〇
- 무 직 〇
- 기 타 〇

직 종

- 고 위 임 직 원 〇
- 전문직(과학.공학) 〇
- 전 문 직(교육) 〇
- 전문직(법률.회계.금융) 〇
- 기 술 직 〇
- 영 업 〇
- 홍 보 〇
- 총 무 〇
- 인 사 〇
- 경 리 〇
- 기 획 〇
- 구 매 〇
- 무 역 〇
- 외 환 〇
- 자 금 〇
- 공 무 〇
- 업 무 〇
- 품 질 관 리 〇
- 전 산 〇
- 행 정 직 〇
- 생 산 관 리 〇
- 서 비 스 〇
- 기 타 〇

직 책

- 임 원 〇
- 부 장 〇
- 차 장 〇
- 과 장 〇
- 대 리 〇
- 계 장 〇
- 사 원 〇
- 인 턴 〇
- 기 타 〇

TEPS

Test of English Proficiency
developed by
Seoul National University

성 영문
명 서명

응시일자 : 20　년　월　일

〈부정행위 및 규정위반 처리규정〉

1. 모든 부정행위 및 규정위반 적발 및 이에 대한 조치는 TEPS관리위원회의 처리규정에 따라 이루어집니다.

2. 부정행위 및 규정위반 행위는 현장 적발 뿐만 아니라 사후에도 적발될 수 있으며 모두 동일한 조치가 취해집니다.

3. 부정행위 적발 시 당해 성적은 무효화되며 사안에 따라 최대 5년까지 TEPS관리위원회에서 주관하는 모든 시험의 응시자격이 제한됩니다.

4. 문제지 이외에 메모를 하는 행위와 시험 문제의 일부 또는 전부를 유출하거나 공개하는 경우 부정행위로 처리됩니다.

5. 각 파트별 시간을 준수하지 않거나, 시험 종료 후 답안 작성을 계속할 경우 규정위반으로 처리됩니다.

성　명 (성·이름순으로 기재)

EX HONG GIL DONG

(A B C D E F G H I J K L M N O P Q R S T U V W X Y Z 마킹란)

단체구분

학생	일반
◯	◯

질문란

1. 귀하의 TEPS 응시목적은?

　ⓐ 입사지원　　ⓑ 인사정책
　ⓒ 개인실력측정　ⓓ 입시
　ⓔ 국가고시 지원　ⓕ 기타

2. 귀하의 영어권 체류 경험은?

　ⓐ 없다　　　　　ⓑ 6개월 미만
　ⓒ 6개월 이상 1년 미만　ⓓ 1년 이상 3년 미만
　ⓔ 3년 이상 5년 미만　ⓕ 5년 이상

3. 귀하께서 응시하고 계신 고사장에 대한 만족도는?

　ⓐ 0점　　　　ⓑ 1점
　ⓒ 2점　　　　ⓓ 3점
　ⓔ 4점　　　　ⓕ 5점

4. 최근 2년내 TEPS 응시횟수는?

　ⓐ 없다　　　　ⓑ 1회
　ⓒ 2회　　　　ⓓ 3회
　ⓔ 4회　　　　ⓕ 5회 이상

학력 / 전공 / 직업

학력			전공	직업
	재학	졸업		
초등학교	◯	◯	인문학 ◯	공무원 ◯
중학교	◯	◯	사회과학·법학 ◯	고시준비 ◯
고등학교	◯	◯	경제학·경영학 ◯	교사 ◯
전문대학	◯	◯	자연과학 ◯	군인 ◯
대학교	◯	◯	의학·약학·간호학 ◯	의료인 ◯
대학원	◯	◯	공학 ◯	자영업 ◯
			교육학 ◯	학생 ◯
			음악·미술·체육 ◯	회사원 ◯
			기타 ◯	무직 ◯
				기타 ◯

직종 / 직책

직종		직책	
고위임직원 ◯	무역 ◯	임원 ◯	
전문직(과학·공학) ◯	외환 ◯	부장 ◯	
전문직 (교육) ◯	자금 ◯	차장 ◯	
전문직(법률·회계·금융) ◯	공무 ◯	과장 ◯	
기술직 ◯	업무 ◯	대리 ◯	
영업 ◯	품질관리 ◯	계장 ◯	
홍보 ◯	전산 ◯	사원 ◯	
총무 ◯	행정직 ◯	인턴 ◯	
인사 ◯	생산관리 ◯	기타 ◯	
경리 ◯	서비스 ◯		
기획 ◯	기타 ◯		
구매 ◯			

● 넥서스 수준별 TEPS 맞춤 학습 프로그램

서울대 기출문제

서울대 텝스 관리위원회 최신기출 1000 | 서울대학교 TEPS관리위원회 문제 제공 · 양준희 해설 | 628쪽 | 28,000원
서울대 텝스 관리위원회 최신기출 1200 / SEASON 2~3 문제집 | 서울대학교 TEPS관리위원회 문제 제공 | 352쪽 | 19,500원
서울대 텝스 관리위원회 최신기출 1200 / SEASON 2~3 해설집 | 서울대학교 TEPS관리위원회 문제 제공 · 넥서스 TEPS연구소 해설 | 472쪽 | 25,000원
서울대 텝스 관리위원회 최신기출 Listening | 서울대학교 TEPS관리위원회 문제 제공 · 넥서스 TEPS연구소 해설 | 320쪽 | 19,800원
서울대 텝스 관리위원회 최신기출 Reading | 서울대학교 TEPS관리위원회 문제 제공 · 넥서스 TEPS연구소 해설 | 568쪽 | 24,800원

기출 · 독해

실전 모의고사

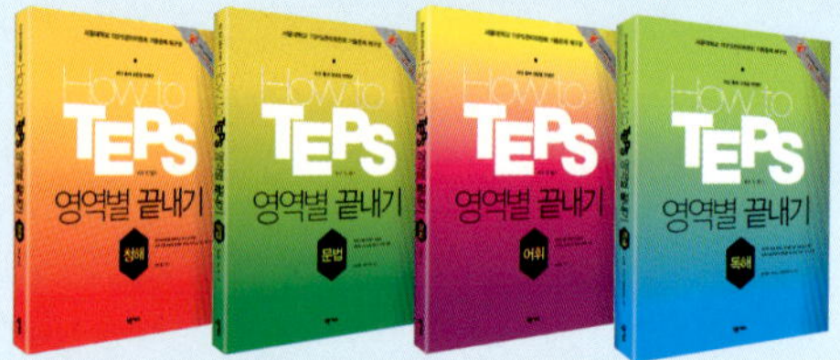

How to TEPS 영역별 끝내기 청해 | 테리 홍 지음 | 424쪽 | 19,800원
How to TEPS 영역별 끝내기 문법 | 장보금 · 써니 박 지음 | 260쪽 | 13,500원
How to TEPS 영역별 끝내기 어휘 | 양준희 지음 | 240쪽 | 13,500원
How to TEPS 영역별 끝내기 독해 | 김무룡 · 넥서스 TEPS연구소 지음 | 504쪽 | 25,000원

How to TEPS 시험 직전 리얼 청해 | 넥서스 TEPS연구소 지음 | 296쪽 | 19,500원
How to TEPS 시험 직전 리얼 문법 | 장보금 · 써니 박 지음 | 260쪽 | 14,000원
How to TEPS 시험 직전 리얼 어휘 | 양준희 지음 | 252쪽 | 14,000원
How to TEPS 시험 직전 리얼 독해 | 넥서스 TEPS연구소 지음 | 504쪽 | 25,000원

실전 · 어휘

초급 (400~500점) / 중급 (600~700점)

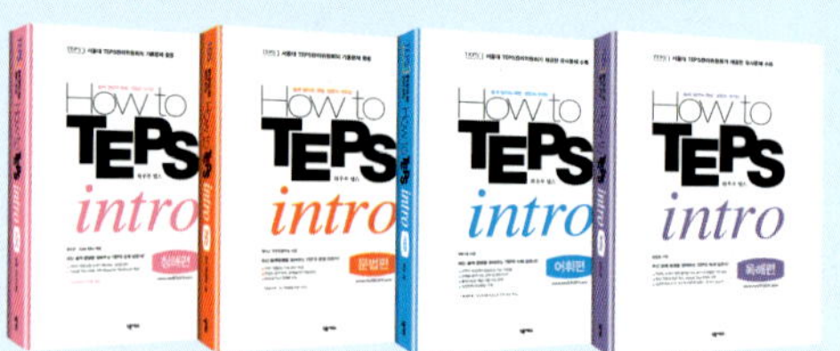

How to TEPS intro 청해편 | 강소영 · Jane Kim 지음 | 444쪽 | 22,000원
How to TEPS intro 문법편 | 넥서스 TEPS연구소 지음 | 424쪽 | 19,000원
How to TEPS intro 어휘편 | 에릭 김 지음 | 368쪽 | 15,000원
How to TEPS intro 독해편 | 한정림 지음 | 392쪽 | 19,500원

How to TEPS 실전 600 어휘편 · 청해편 · 문법편 · 독해편 | 서울대학교 TEPS관리위원회 문제 제공(어휘), 이기현(청해), 장보금 · 써니 박(문법), 황수경 · 넥서스 TEPS연구소(독해) 지음 | 어휘: 15,000원, 청해: 19,800원, 문법: 17,500원, 독해: 19,000원
How to TEPS 실전 700 청해편 · 문법편 · 독해편 | 강소영 · 넥서스 TEPS연구소(청해), 이신영 · 넥서스 TEPS연구소(문법), 오정우 · 넥서스 TEPS연구소(독해) 지음 | 청해: 16,000원, 문법: 15,000원, 독해: 19,000원

영역별

How to 텝스 뉴스타터 | 넥서스 TEPS연구소 지음 | 584쪽 | 25,900원
How to 텝스 초급용 모의고사 10회 | 넥서스 TEPS연구소 지음 | 296쪽 | 15,000원
How to 텝스 베이직 리스닝 | 고명희 · 넥서스 TEPS연구소 지음 | 320쪽 | 18,500원
How to 텝스 베이직 리딩 | 박미영 · 넥서스 TEPS연구소 지음 | 368쪽 | 19,500원

종합서

서울대 텝스 관리위원회 최신기출 스피킹·라이팅 | 서울대학교 TEPS관리위원회 문제 제공 · 유경하 해설 | 340쪽 | 28,000원
서울대 텝스 관리위원회 최신기출 *i-TEPS* | 서울대학교 TEPS관리위원회 문제 제공 · 넥서스 TEPS연구소 해설 | 296쪽 | 19,800원

독해 · 청해 · 문법

How to 텝스 독해 기본편 | 양준희 · 넥서스 TEPS연구소 지음 | 312쪽 | 17,500원
How to 텝스 독해 중급편 | 장우리 지음 | 360쪽 | 17,500원
How to 텝스 독해 고난도편 | 넥서스 TEPS연구소 지음 | 324쪽 | 17,500원
How to 텝스 청해 중급편 | 양준희 지음 | 276쪽 | 18,500원
How to 텝스 문법 고난도편 | 테스 김 · 넥서스 TEPS연구소 지음 | 160쪽 | 12,500원

텝스 기출모의 1200 | 넥서스 TEPS연구소 지음 | 456쪽 | 18,500원
How to TEPS 실전력 500 · 600 · 700 · 800 · 900 | 넥서스 TEPS연구소 지음 | 308쪽 | 실전력 500~800: 16,500원, 실전력 900: 18,000원
서울대 텝스 관리위원회 속성 실전테스트 | 서울대학교 TEPS관리위원회 문제 제공 | 164쪽 | 9,800원
텝스 기출모의 5회분 | 김학수 · 넥서스 TEPS연구소 지음 | 364쪽 | 14,500원

어휘

서울대 최신 TEPS VOCA | 넥서스 TEPS연구소 · 문덕 지음 | 544쪽 | 15,000원
How to TEPS VOCA | 김무룡 · 넥서스 TEPS연구소 지음 | 320쪽 | 12,800원
How to TEPS 넥서스 텝스 보카 | 이기헌 지음 | 536쪽 | 15,000원
How to 텝스 어휘 기본편 | 고명희 · 넥서스 TEPS연구소 지음 | 304쪽 | 15,500원
How to 텝스 어휘 고난도편 | 김무룡 · 넥서스 TEPS연구소 지음 | 296쪽 | 17,000원

How to TEPS 시크릿 청해편 · 독해편 | 유니스 정(청해), 정성수(독해) 지음 | 청해: 22,500원, 독해: 14,500원
텝스, 어려운 파트만 콕콕 찍어 점수 따기(청해 PART 4 · 문법 PART 3,4) | 이성희 · 전종삼 지음 | 176쪽 | 13,000원

고급 (800점 이상)

How to TEPS 실전 800 어휘편 · 청해편 · 문법편 · 독해편 | 넥서스 TEPS연구소 (어휘, 청해, 독해), 테스 김(문법) 지음 | 어휘: 12,800원, 청해: 19,000원, 문법: 16,000원, 독해: 19,000원
How to TEPS 실전 900 청해편 · 문법편 · 독해편 | 김철용(청해), 이용재(문법), 김철용(독해) 지음 | 청해: 17,000원, 문법: 16,500원, 독해: 17,500원

How to TEPS L/C | 이성희 지음 | 400쪽 | 19,800원
How to TEPS R/C | 이정은 · 넥서스 TEPS연구소 지음 | 396쪽 | 19,800원

How to TEPS Expert L | 박영주 지음 | 340쪽 | 21,000원
How to TEPS Expert GVR | 박영주 지음 | 520쪽 | 28,000원
How to TEPS Expert 고난도 실전 모의고사 | 넥서스 TEPS연구소 지음 | 388쪽 | 21,500원